The Simplest Book for Learning

TallyPrime

Training Guide

Asok K Nadhani

कान्ता नाढ़ाणी

bpb

www.bpbonline.com

FIRST EDITION 2021
Reprinted 2022

ISBN: 978-93-90684-22-9

Distributors:

BPB PUBLICATIONS
20, Ansari Road, Darya Ganj
New Delhi-110002
Ph: 23254990/23254991

DECCAN AGENCIES
4-3-329, Bank Street,
Hyderabad-500195
Ph: 24756967/24756400

MICRO MEDIA
Shop No. 5, Mahendra Chambers,
150 DN Rd. Next to Capital Cinema,
V.T. (C.S.T.) Station, MUMBAI-400 001
Ph: 22078296/22078297

BPB BOOK CENTRE
376 Old Lajpat Rai Market,
Delhi-110006
Ph: 23861747

Published by Manish Jain for BPB Publications, 20 Ansari Road, Darya Ganj, New Delhi-110002 and Printed at Akash Press, Delhi.

www.bpbonline.com

Preface

This book is complete rewrite exploring the all new Tally Prime. In this small book, we have tried to cover all important features, covering all the four areas, viz, **Financial Accounting, Invoicing & Inventory, Tax Accounting & Payroll Accounting**. I hope learning the skills covered in the book will enable anyone to perform complete Accounting work with Tally in Business Organisation.

The operational steps are clearly explained with screen shots of each component with proper data. Blank spaces of full screen shots have been trimmed off (without removing relevant info) to fit hundreds of screen shots, even in this small book. All Configuration screens, showing important options of using Tally Prime efficiently as per user needs are incorporated for complete understanding of each operational features.

Practical Work Assignments

Accounting work cannot be learned without practical work. Simple project assignments, covering various typical practical aspects, normally encountered in business process, are placed at the end. Readers should work out these assignments to get thorough knowledge of maintaining Accounts with Tally Prime. You may visit the website **dvidya.com/tallyprime** and play videos of practical assignments described in this book for easier learning. You may also read Blogs, e-books and play Videos in the website **dvidya.com**, accessing FREE learning resources for Tally Prime Business Accounting Software

आसानी से समझने के लिए खास बातें संक्षेप में हिंदी में भी लिखे हैं। हर Chapter के अंत में Hindi में सारांश दिए हैं, उसे जरूर पढ़ें। इस छोटी सी किताब से Tally Prime में Financial Accounting, Invoicing & Inventory, Tax Accounting और Payroll Accounting के सभी महत्वपूर्ण पहलू को सरल तरीके से समझाया है। Tally के बड़े screenshot के खाली हिस्से को काटकर, सभी Part और Configuration option को एक साथ दिखाया है ताकि पूरा process समझ में आए।

अंत में दिए गए Practical Project work जरूर पूरा करे। Phone या Computer से **dvidya.com/tallyprime** website में Project work का पूरा video, audio और blog देखे। घर बैठे FREE में Tally सीखे।

March 2021

Contents at Glance

Table of Contents

PART 1

Basic Financial Accounting

In this part, we explain the entire process of Accounting with Tally Prime, from Creation of Company, Accounts Masters, Accounts Vouchers, Viewing & Printing of various Books of Accounts, to getting Final Accounts Statements (Profit & Loss Statement & Balance Sheet). Finally, the steps of Data Maintenance & various administrative tasks are also explained.

इस भाग में, Company creation से Final Accounts बनाने तक का पूरा चक्र (cycle), जैसे, Accounts Masters, Accounts Vouchers की entry, विभिन्न Accounts Reports तैयारी की प्रक्रिया, Final Accounts तैयार करना, समझाया गया है। अंत में, डेटा रखरखाव (Data Maintenance) और Tally के विभिन्न प्रशासनिक कार्य (administrative task) को भी समझाया गया है।

Company Creation explains the process of creation of a Company in Tally Prime to enter data and manage accounts of an accounting entity.

डेटा entry करने के लिए Tally Prime में एकाउंटिंग इकाई (accounting entity) के निर्माण की प्रक्रिया को समझाया गया है।

Gateway of Tally explains various components and tasks to work with Tally PRIME.

Tally Prime से काम करने के लिए Tally के सारे कार्य का वर्णन किया गया है।

Accounts Masters Discusses about the Reserved Accounts Masters auto created by Tally Prime & about Creation of Accounts Groups & Accounts Ledgers.

स्वतः बनाए गए आरक्षित खातों (Reserved Accounts Masters) और नए Masters के निर्माण समझाया गया है।

Accounts Vouchers explains the rules and steps of creation of various types of Accounts Vouchers, recording complete details of transactions.

विभिन्न प्रकार के Voucher Entry के नियम, लेनदेन (transaction) के पूर्ण विवरण record करना समझाया गया है।

Reports explains immediate display of reports on screen & seamlessly drill down & trace back through allied & subordinate areas, throughout the system, and printing of reports & vouchers.

स्क्रीन पर तत्काल Reports प्रदर्शन की व्याख्या, पूरे सिस्टम में drill down (अंदर के details देखना) & trace back (अंदर level से वापस ऊपर level आना), Report और Voucher Printing का तरीका समझाया गया है।

Cash Bank Book explains Display & Printing of Cash / Bank Books, the primary Books of Accounts, showing details of daily transactions through Cash & Bank Accounts.

Cash और Bank बैंक खातों के माध्यम से दैनिक लेनदेन का विवरण record करना और Cash Bank Book Printing का तरीका समझाया गया है।

Journal Book: Explains the Display & Printing of Journal Books, including Sales & Purchase, Debit Note & Credit Note registers.

बिक्री (Sale), खरीद (Purchase) और Journal Register प्रदर्शन (Display), और Printing के तरीके को समझाया गया है।

Ledger Book shows Display & Printing of Ledger Accounts

लेजर अकाउंट (Ledger Account) के Display और Printing के तरीके को भी समझाया गया है।

Trial Balance shows Display & Printing of Trial Balance

Trial Balance प्रदर्शन (Display) और Printing का तरीका समझाया गया है।

Profit & Loss Statement shows Closing Stock value entry, printing of Profit & Loss Statement. Closing Stock value entry करने का तरीका, Profit / Loss समायोजन (appropriation) voucher, Profit & Loss Statement प्रदर्शन (Display) और Printing का तरीका समझाया गया है।

Balance Sheet shows Display & Printing of Balance Sheet

Final Accounts का अंतिम Report, Balance Sheet का प्रदर्शन (Display) और Printing का तरीका समझाया गया है।

Accounts Receivables & Payables explains tracking of Bill wise details of Open Accounts, Age Analysis, printing of Outstanding Reminder letters, etc

प्राप्य (Receivables) और देय (payables) के Bill details, आयु विश्लेषण (Age Analysis), Report का प्रदर्शन (Display) और Printing का तरीका समझाया गया है।

Banking explains various Banking Job like Cheque details entry in Voucher, Cheque Printing, Bank Reconciliation etc.

Bank वाउचर (Voucher), चेक (Cheque) prinitng, Bank Reconciliation आदि Report का प्रदर्शन (Display) और Printing का तरीका समझाया गया है।

Tally Administration shows important chores of Back Up, Restore, Re-writing etc,

Accounts Data रखाव (Back Up), पुनर्स्थापन (Restore), पुनर्लिखन (Re-writing) इत्यादि महत्वपूर्ण काम के तरीके को समझाया गया है।

Company Creation 01-01

01 Company in Tally Prime

The Term *Company* in Tally Prime means an Accounting Entity, for which a separate set of Accounting Records are maintained (referred as *Tally Company*). So, a *Tally Company* may be created for Personal Accounts, Business Organization of any form (Proprietorship, Partnership, Company), Association, Trust or any entity for which a separate set of accounts are maintained.

Tally PRIME में *Company* शब्द का अर्थ है कोई Accounting Entity (इकाई) जिसके लिए अलग Account Books maintain किया जाता है। इसलिए, Tally PRIME में किसी भी तरह का बिजनेस, जैसे Proprietorship, Partnership, Company, Association, Trust, Personal Accounts, Business Organization of any form (Proprietorship, Partnership, Company), Association, Trust, का Accounts maintain किया जाता है, और इन सभी Accounts को Tally में Company कहते हैं।

When separate set of Accounting Records of a Company (called *Business Entity*) are maintained for its various branches, warehouses, Sales / Purchase depots, collection centres etc, each of these separate *Accounting entities* will be called a *Company*, even if they are legally same Company or Organisation. Separate Tally Companies will be created for each of such accounting entity.

जब एक कंपनी, अपने व्यापार इकाई के विभिंन शाखाओं (Branch), बिक्री/खरीद (Sales / Purchase Office) संग्रह केंद्रों (Collection Centre), का Accounts को अलग Books Maintain करते है, तो हर एकाउंट्स को Tally में अलग-अलग कंपनी कहा जाएगा, भले ही ये कानूनी रूप से एक ही कंपनी या संगठन का हो। ऐसी प्रत्येक Accounts के लिए पृथक टैली कंपनियां बनाई जाएंगी।

So, for one legal Company, say *ABC Company*, several *Companies* may be created, if separate accounts are maintained for its different Branches, Warehouses, Factories etc, such as:

- ABC Company (HO)
- ABC Company (Patna)

एक Organisation, जैसे ABC Company के अलग units लिए, अगर अलग Accounts maintain करने के लिए, अलग Tally Company बनाई जाएगी, जैसे-

- ABC Company (HO)
- ABC Company (Patna)

ऐसे ही, प्रत्येक वित्तीय वर्ष (Financial Year) के लिए अलग-अलग Accounts Maintain करने के लिए, अलग Tally Company बनायीं जाएगी।

- ABC Company (HO) 20-21
- ABC Company (Patna) 20-21

02 Data Migration from Tally ERP 9 to Tally Prime

The old Tally ERP 9 data cannot be opened directly by Tally Prime. The steps of Opening Old Tally ERP 9 data and migration to Tally Prime are now explained.

Tally ERP9 का डाटा Tally Prime में Open कर Data माइग्रेट (Migrate) कर Tally Prime में इस तरह काम करे

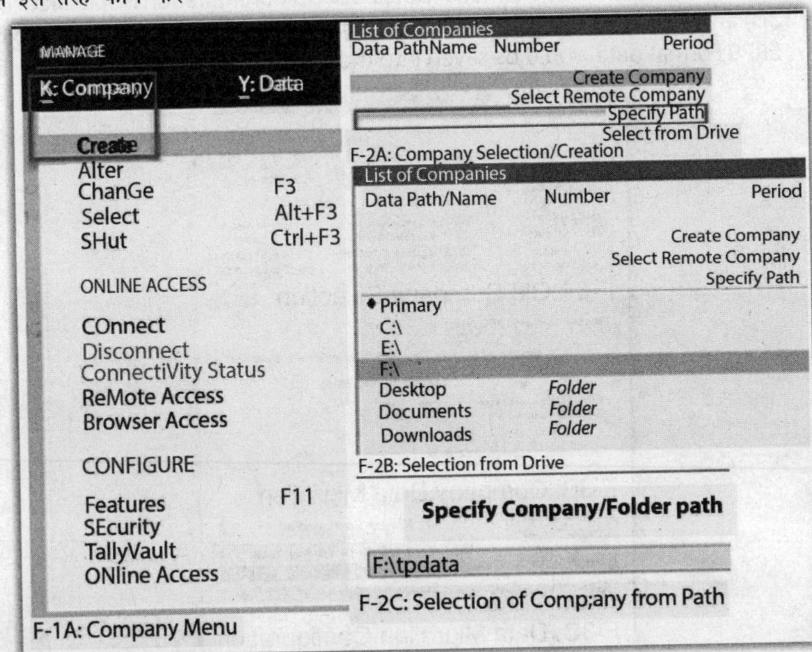

F-1A: Company Menu

F-2A: Company Selection/Creation

F-2B: Selection from Drive

F-2C: Selection of Comp;any from Path

Old Company Selection: At Top Main Menu Bar, at *K:Company* Menu (F-1A), select *'Select'* option to get Company Creation / Selection option list (F-2A). Now select *Specify Path* (if the Company Data Path is known) and enter the Data path (F-2C), or select 'Select from Drive' (Company Data Path is not known) and select the Data Path (F-2B). All the existing Companies in the selected Data Path would be displayed (F-3A). Now select the desired Company from the list of Companies.

Top Main Menu Bar में K:Company select करे। कंपनी मेनू मिलेगा (1A). कंपनी मेनू में Select ऑप्शन क्लिक करने से कंपनी सिलेक्शन/क्रिएशन ऑप्शन लिस्ट मिलेगा (2A)। अगर

कंपनी Data Path Name मालूम है तो Specify Path ऑप्शन Select करे (2A) और Data Path एंट्री करे (2C)। नहीं तो *Select from Drive* से Data Folder select करे।

Old Company Data Migration : On selection of old ERP 9 data Company from list (F-3A), (indicated by *Migration Required*), Data Migration screen will appear (F-3B).

- **Data Path Up path Configuration:** You may optionally click *C:Configure* button (F-3B) to set up Data Migration Configuration. To keep Data Back Up of the Company before Migration, set *Yes* at Back Up of the Company before Migration (F-3C) and enter *Back Up Destination Path* (F-3D/3E).
- **Data Migration:** Click *R:Migrate* Button (F-3B). The ERP 9 format Data will be converted to Prime Format. If Data Back Up Configuration is specified (F-3D) and *Back Up Company data before Migration* is set to Yes (F-3B), then old ERP9 Format data would be saved into the specified Back Up Path (F-3F).

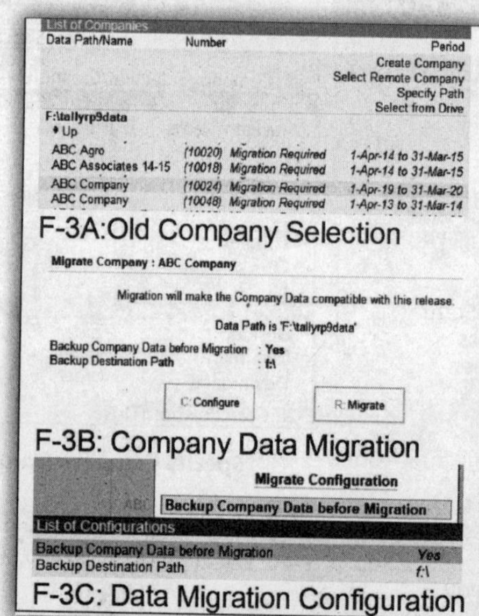

F-3A:Old Company Selection

F-3B: Company Data Migration

F-3C: Data Migration Configuration

Data Folder की Company की list मिलेगी (F-3A)। अब पुरानी Company के Data को Tally ERP9 से Tally Prime में migrate करना होगा। जिस Company का data migrate करना है, list से उस Company को select करे (F-3A)।

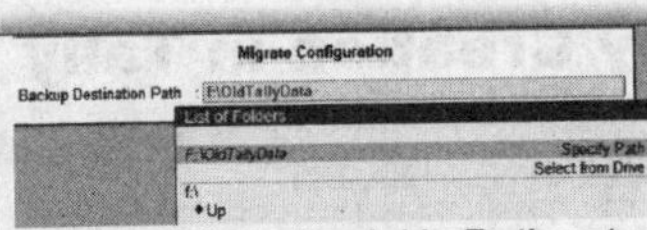

F-3D:Old Data Back Up Path set up

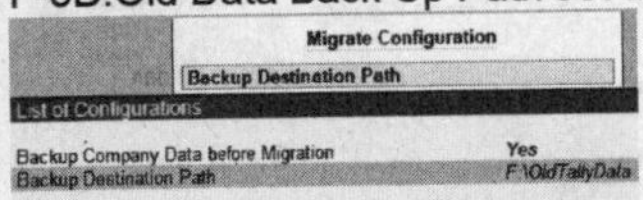

F-3E:Old Data Back Up Folder set up

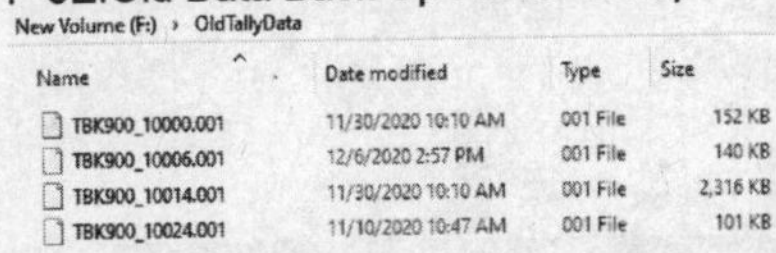

F-3F: Old Data Back Up files

अब आपको Company Data Migration screen मिलेगा (F-3B)। Back Up Data Configuration करने के लिए Configure Button click कर (F-3B) Back Up Data folder set करे। (F-3C) Migration करने पर सारे Old Data वही Back Up होंगे। अब selected Company का Tally ERP 9 का पुराना Data उस folder में Back Up हो जायेंगे, ताकि जरूरत होने पर आप वहाँ से Restore कर सके।

इस तरह Migrate Button (F-3B) select कर Company के Old ERP का Data Tally Prime में migrate करे। Old tally data Back Up folder में copy होता है। Current Tally ERP data Tally Prime के structure में convert (बदल) हो जाता है।

Data Folder में जिन Company के data migrate नहीं हुए है, उन Company के आगे 'Migration Required' show करेगा (F-4A)। Migrated Company को आप Tally Prime में सीधा Open कर सकते है (लेकिन Tally ERP9 में ओपन नहीं कर सकते)। Tally ERP से entry किये हुए सभी data Tally Prime में मिलेंगे।

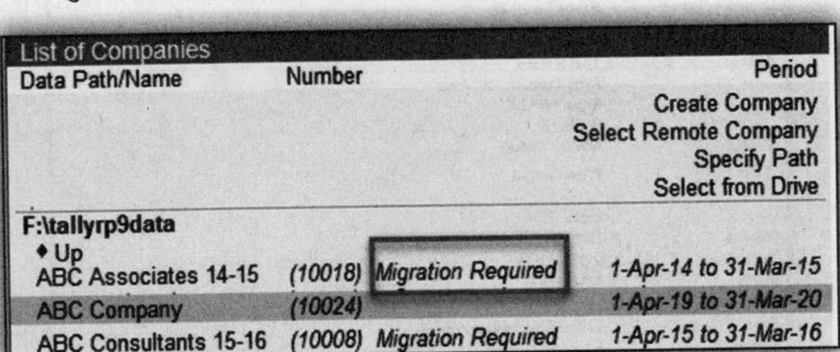

F-4A: List of Companies in Data Path

03 New Company Creation in Tally Prime

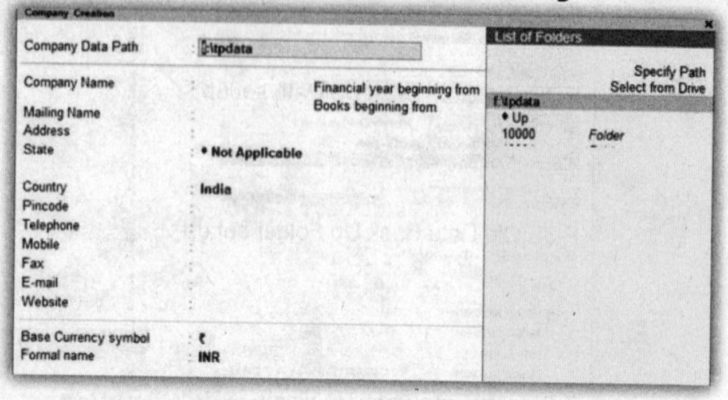

5A:Selection of Data Folder for Company Creation

Company Creation: To create New Company, select Create at Company Menu (F-1A) to get Company Creation screen (F-5A).

नयी Company create करने के लिए, Company Menu (F-1A) में Create select करें। आपको Company Creation screen मिलेगा (F-5A)।

Path Specification: Now select 'Select from Drive' or 'Specify Path' (F-2A) from the top options and specify Data path, as explained earlier. At Company Creation screen, specify as follows:

अब top options से 'Select from Drive' या 'Specify Path' (F-2A) select कर *Company Data Path* set करे (जैसे पहले बताया गया है)।

अब Company Creation स्क्रीन में इस तरह एंट्री करे:

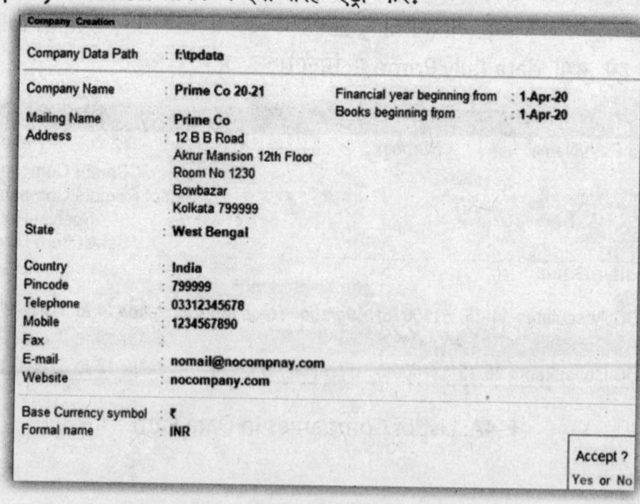

5B:Company Creation screen

Quick Entry

For Quick Start, at *Company Creation* Screen (F-5B), you may just enter only the following basic Info about the Company

जल्दी शुरू करने के लिए, कंपनी निर्माण (Company Creation) स्क्रीन पर (F-5B), कंपनी के बारे में केवल निम्नलिखित बुनियादी जानकारी (basic Information) entry कर सकते है।

- **Name:** Enter Name of the Enterprise at the *Name* field. The Company is identified and selected by this Name (called *Tally Company Name*). To identify the Company for each Year, you may add the FY after the Company name (like ABC Company HO 20-21). So, in the next year, when you create separate Company for 21-22, you may name it like ABC Company HO 21-22, to identify Accounts of the respective year from the *Company Name.*

  Name पर Tally Company Name entry करें। Company Name के अंत में Financial Year / Branch Name (जैसे ABC Co 20-21, ABC Co (Patna Br) 20-21) भी जोडें, ताकि आप सही पहचान सकें।

- **Mailing Name:** The Company Name is carried in the next field Mailing Name. At Mailing name, keep only the Company Legal name (which would be printed in Invoice, Receipt etc), deleting the additional portion of name (like HO 17-18 etc).

  मेलिंग नाम पर, केवल कंपनी कानूनी नाम रखें (जो Cheque, Invoice, Receipt आदि में मुद्रित किया जाएगा), नाम के अतिरिक्त भाग (जैसे HO, 20-21 आदि) को हटाए।

- **Financial year from:** Normally you should enter Beginning Date of financial year (like 1-4-2020), to maintain accounts for full financial year. Tally initially creates Accounting period of 1 year from Financial Year from date.

  आम तौर पर, पूर्ण वित्तीय वर्ष के खाते तैयार रखने के करने Financial year की शुरुआत की तारीख (जैसे 1-4-2020) दर्ज करना चाहिए। टैली शुरू में Financial year से 1 वर्ष की तिथि तक पूर्ण वित्तीय वर्ष बनाता है।

Other Info: You may enter other details in respective field now, or may enter later when needed, through Company Alteration option (explained next)

बाकि Data भी अभी entry करे या Company Alteration option से बाद में भी Entry कर सकते हैं।

Saving the Company: After entering the particulars, to save the entered Company, either press *Ctrl+A* or click *Yes* at *'Accept Yes No'* button at the bottom right. After Saving, a Tally Company gets created and shown in the list of *Selected Companies*, at the left side of GoT (Gateway of Tally). This way, you may create multiple Tally Companies and maintain separate accounting records for each of them.

Entry करने के बाद, Company Save करने के लिए, Ctrl+A press करे, या नीचे दाहिने (Right) side में *Accept Yes No'* में *Yes* Click करे। Entry किया गया Particulars Company profile में save होगा। Save करने के बाद एक Tally company create होती है और उसका नाम Gateway of Tally (GoT) screen के left side में display होता है। इस तरह कई अलग अलग Tally Company create कर सकते हैं।

04 Company Selection

To work with the desired Company from many Companies created, at Gateway of Tally (GoT), at *K:Company Menu*(F-6A*), type Alt+F3* (Select 'Specify Path' or 'Select from Drive' option, as explained earlier to select from another folder). Then select the Company from the list of Companies.

Company select करने के लिए, Gateway of Tally (GoT), में K :Company Menu से *Alt+F3 type* कर (दूसरे folder से select करने के लिए Specify Path' या 'Select from Drive' option से) Company Select करे।

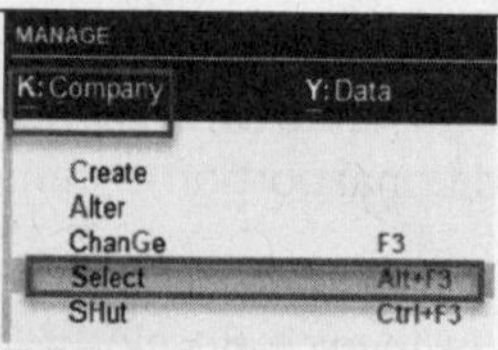

F-6A: Selection From Company menu

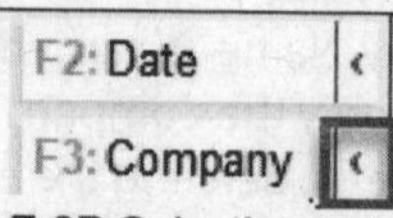

F-6B:Selection From Right Button Bar

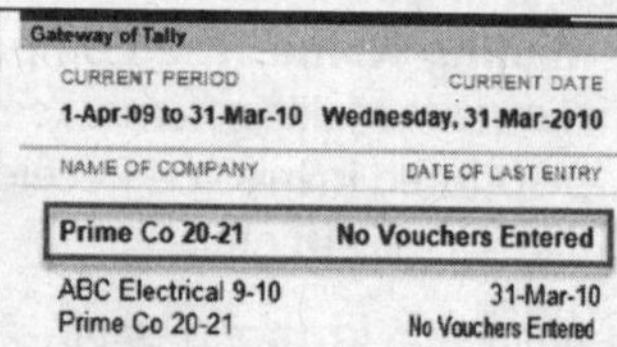

F-6C:Selected Company List at GoT

This way, you may select multiple Companies from any Data path. The name of the last selected Company appears in Bold at the top line, at the left side of Gateway of Tally. This becomes the Active Company to work with (F-7A).

इस तरह कई Company एक साथ selected रख सकते है। सबसे बाद में Select की हुई Company का नाम (Active Company) सबसे ऊपर दिखेगा (F-7A)।

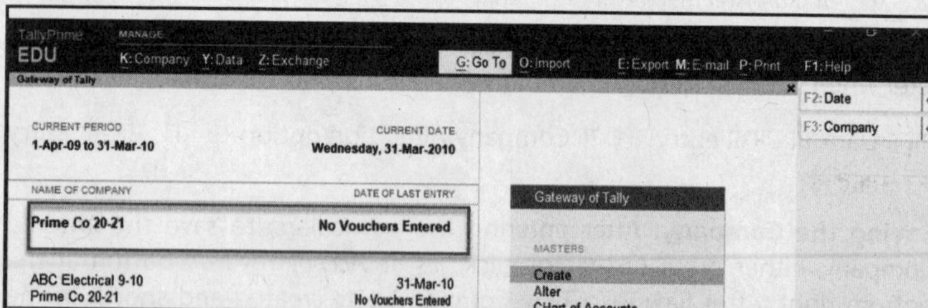

F-7A: Gateway of Tally with Active and Selected Companies List

Switching between selected Companies: Click on any company shown at Selected Company List at the left panel of GoT (F-7A) to make it as Active Company (which will appear at the top in Bold). Now work with the currently Active Company.

GoT screen के left panel में selected company (F-7A) से कोई भी company पर click कर उसे Active करे और उसमें काम करे।

05 Company Profile Modification (Company Alteration)

To Alter (modify) any data of Company Profile, or to enter unfilled data, at Company Menu (F-1A), select *Alter*, select Path Name and then select the Company to be altered from the list of Companies. Now modify any data or enter unfilled data in same way as Company Creation (F-5B). Press Ctl+A to save. After voucher entry, you should not change *Financial Year From* date. The data may get damaged.

Company data Alter करने के लिए, या (अपूर्ण विवरण, जैसे Mailing Name, Address, Contact Details), fill up करने के लिए, Company Menu (F-1A) में *Alter* select करे, Data Path select करे, और Company Select करे। अब कोई भी data change या fill up करे। Save करने के लिए Ctl+A press करे (F-5B) । Voucher entry के बाद, *Financial Year From Date* change न करे, इससे Data Damage हो सकता है।

06 Company Deletion

Company Deletion is to be carried out through Company Alteration Option. At Company Alteration screen, as explained, press *Alt+D* to Delete the Company.

You get a confirmation screen (Delete ? Yes / No). Click *Yes* (or type Y) to *Proceed to Delete* the Company data (click *No* if you do not want to Delete). After you type Y at *Delete ? Yes / No* option, you get another prompt *'Are You Sure ?'*. Click Yes (or type Y) to Delete the Company (to finally Delete the Company), else Type N, if you do not want to Delete.

On Deletion of the Company, the particulars entered at the Company Creation screen and all data recorded subsequently, also get wiped out. Be careful!. You will no more get trace of Deleted Company in Tally System, any more!

Company Data Deletion के लिए Tally में कोई प्रत्यक्ष Option नहीं है, (इस मामले में लोग अक्सर Confuse हो जाते है)। Company Alteration screen में, जैसे पहले समझाया गया है, Alt + D press करें; कंपनी डेटा को हटाने के लिए (Delete Yes / No) पर Yes क्लिक करें, फिर Are you sure Yes / No option पर Yes क्लिक करें। Company Data पूरी तरह से Delete हो जाएगी. सावधान रहे!। कंपनी Deletion के बाद Company का Data वापस नहीं पा सकते। हटाई गई कंपनी (Deleted Company) का कोई भी पता (Trace) नहीं मिलेगा।

07 Shutting of Company

To *Shut* a Company, at Gateway, at *K :Company Menu* (F-6A) select *'Shut'* option (or press Ctrl+F3) or click the small left arrow sign (<) against the F3:Company button from the right side Button Bar and select F3:Shut Company). Then select the Data Path from 'Specify Path' or 'Select from Drive' option, as explained earlier. Then select the Company to Shut from the list of Companies.

The company will be *Shut* and no more appear in the list of selected companies. To work with that Company next time, *Select* the Company again.

कोई कंपनी को बंद (Shut) करने के लिए, K :Company Menu (F-6A) से 'Shut' option select करे (या Ctrl+F3 press करे)। जिस Company को Shut करनी है, उसे List से select करे. वह कंपनी बंद होगी। Selected Company की list में और दिखाई नहीं देगी। अगली बार उसं कंपनी के साथ काम करने के लिए कंपनी को फिर से Select करे।

08 Company Features set up

At GoT, K:Company Menu (F-1A), select Features (or press F11), select the Company from the list. (F-4A). Set Yes at *Maintain Accounts* (F-8A).

GoT screen के K:Company Menu (F-1A) से Features click करे (या F11press करे). Company Features screen (F-4A) में *Maintain Accounts* में Yes set करे (F-8A)।

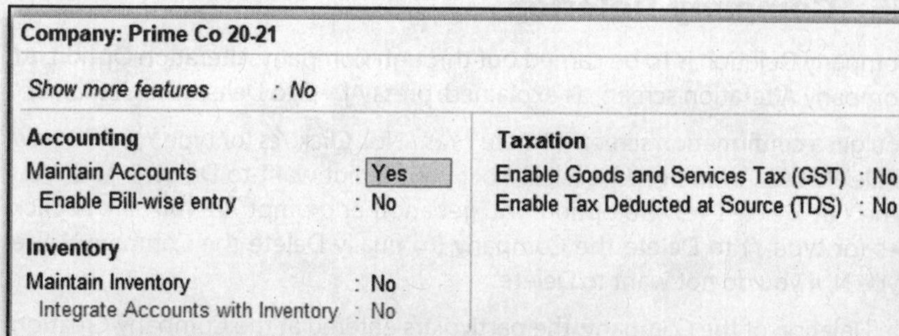

F-8A: Company Features set up

09 Company Creation - Key Points

- Tally ERP 9 का पुराना data (Tally Prime में ऐसी Company में Migration Required दिखेगा) Tally Prime से select करते ही Migration screen मिलेगा (F-3B). Data Migrate करते ही पुराना ERP Data Old Data Folder में copy हो जायेगा (F-3F) और working Directory में Tally Prime के Format में data change हो जायेगा। Tally Prime में migrated data को फिर और Tally ERP में नहीं open कर सकते।

पुराना Data Tally ERP 9 से ही Open कर पाएंगे; इसलिए, Tally ERP 9 software भी computer में install रखे. एक साथ Tally ERP 9 और Tally Prime software दोनों ही अलग रख सकते है। वैसे ही, Tally ERP 9 का data और Tally Prime का data भी अलग folder में रख सकते है.

- Tally में चाहे जितनी Company create कर सकते है। कोई भी Company अपने योजना (plan) अनुसार Directory में create करे, एक Data Directory में हर company का serial number Tally से allot होता है। अगर कई Data Directory में Company create करे तो एक serial number के कई Company create हो सकती है।
- विभिन्न कंपनी के डेटा विभिन्न Data Path में अपने अनुसार संगठित (Organise) कर सकते हैं। Company Creation के पहले plan कर Data path set करे। बाद में, एक Path से दूसरे Path में Data move कर Company Data फिर से संगठित (reorganize) करना मुश्किल होगा। Company Alter screen में Company data Path नहीं रहता. Company Create करने के बाद Company data Path change नहीं कर सकते।
- Company data Path में अगर नए folder नाम एंट्री करते है, जो बना हुआ नहीं है, तो Tally एक message देगा, उस पर Yes type करे, नया folder create हो जायेगा और उस data path में नयी company का data store होगा।
- तुरंत और सरल रूप से काम करने के लिए सिर्फ 3 अनिवार्य data (1. Company Data Path. 2. Company Name, 3.Financial Year Beginning From) ही Company Creation के समय entry करे और Company Save करे (F-5B)। बाकि सभी data बाद में company Alteration option से entry कर सकते है।

Gateway of Tally 01-02

01 Gateway of Tally (GoT)

On creation of the first Company, Gateway of Tally (GoT) Screen appears (F-1A). The Gateway of Tally is the main entry point from where any part of the Tally can be accessed to perform any task.

कंपनी Create करने के बाद, GoT screen दिखाई देती है (F-1A). GoT स्क्रीन (screen) में, Main Menu / Top Menu Bar से कोई भी काम select कर सकते है। तब GoT के जगह, उस काम का स्क्रीन मिलेगा।

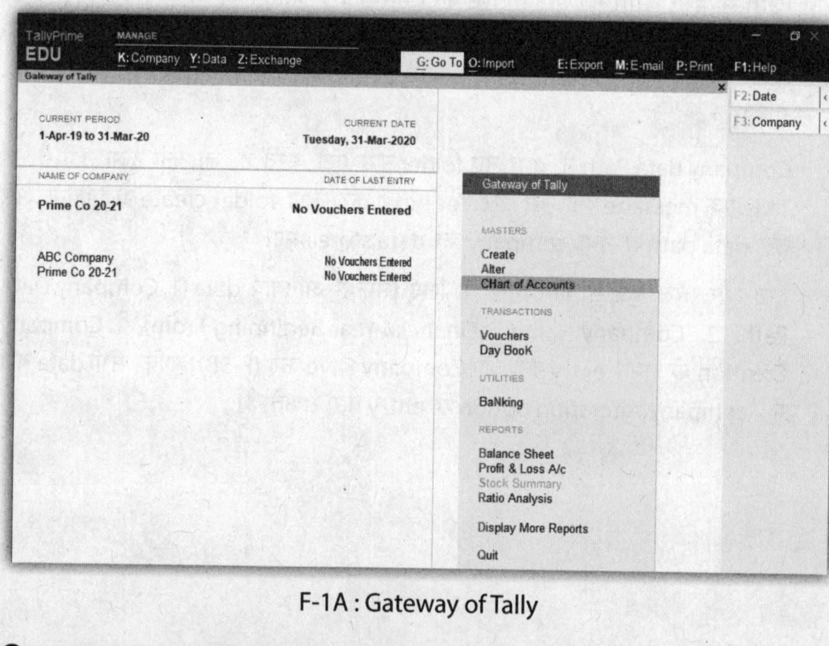

F-1A : Gateway of Tally

Components of Gateway of Tally

The Gateway of Tally (GoT) screen (F-1A) may be divided in following main sections:

- **Horizontal Button Bar:** Contains various Buttons to perform allied tasks (F-1B) :
    - **License**: At the first option, the License type (e.g EDU, Gold etc) is shown.
    - **K:Company**: For Creation, selection, connecting Company etc, and to set up Company (F-2A) Features.

- **Y:Data:** For Company Data management tasks, like Back Up, Restore, Split etc. To set default Data path (F-2B).
- **Z:Exchage:** Data Synchronisation and its Configuration (F-2C).
- **G:Go To:** To select and search Reports (F-2D).
- **O:Import:** For Data Import and its configuration (F-2E)
- **E:Export:** For Data Export and its configuration (F-2F)
- **M:E-mail:** For Reports e-mailing, e-mail set up and configuration (F-2G)
- **P:Print:** For Reports Printing & Printing Configuration (F-2H)
- **F1:Help:** To access On-line Help (F-2I)

– **Main Area:** Tally Main (F-1A) area (below the Horizontal Bar) is divided into two parts.

- **Current Status:** Left Part is about the *Current status* (Current Period, Current Date, currently Active & Selected Companies (F-1A / F-3A to F-3C)
- **Tally Menu:** Right part shows the current *Tally Menu.*

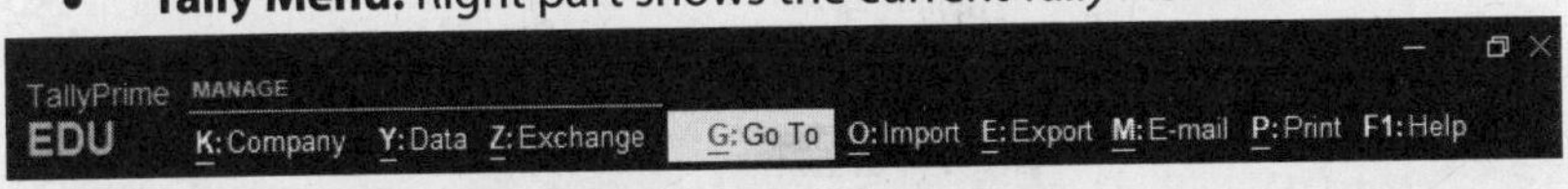

F-1B: Horizontal Top Bar

Tally Calculator: Click Ctrl+N. At Calculator panel, type an arithmetic expression using +,-,/, * operators and ( ) parenthesis only. Press Ctrl+N again to hide the Calculator panel.

गेटवे ऑफ टैली (GoT) स्क्रीन (F-1A) को निम्नलिखित मुख्य वर्गों में विभाजित किया जा सकता है:

– **Horizontal Top Bar:** सबसे उपर Bar में विभिन्न कार्य करने के लिए विभिन्न बटन शामिल हैं (F-1B):

- **License:** बाई ओर सबसे पहले लाइसेंस Type (जैसे EDU, Gold आदि) दिखता है।
- **K:Company:** Company Creation, selection वगैरह और Company Features set up करने के लिए (F-2A)।
- **Y: Data: Company** Data Manage जैसे बैकअप, रिस्टोर, स्प्लिट आदि, और Data Path set करने के लिए (F-2B)।
- **Z: Exchange:** Data Synchronisation और उसका Configuration करने के लिए (F-2C)।
- **G: Go To:** रिपोर्ट्स चुनने और खोजने के लिए (F-2D)।
- **O: Import:** Data Import और उसके Configuration के लिए (F-2E)।
- **E: Export :** Data Export और उसके Configuration के लिए (F-2F)।
- **M: E-mail:** रिपोर्ट ई-मेलिंग के लिए, ई-मेल set up और उसके Configuration के लिए (F-2G)।

- **P: Print:** रिपोर्ट Printing और Configuration के लिए (F-2H)
- **F1: Help:** Help के लिए (F-2I)

– **Main Area:** Menu Bar के नीचे टैली मुख्य क्षेत्र को दो भागों में विभाजित है (F-1A)

- **Current Status:** बायीं ओर वर्तमान स्थिति (Current Period, Current Date, Selected Companies) दिखता है। (F-1A/ F-3A to F-3C)
- **GoT Menu:** दाई ओर GoT Main Menu दिखता है।

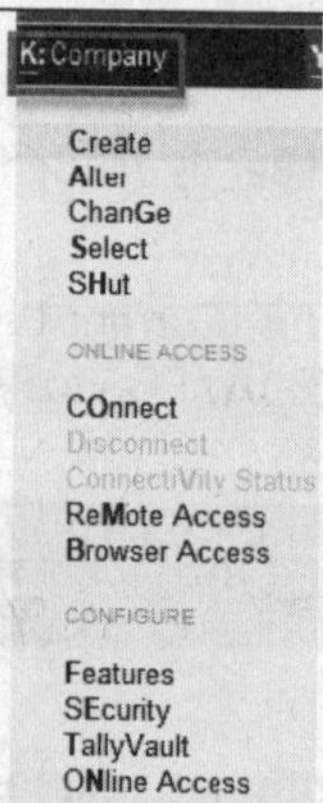

F-2A:Company Menu

F-2B:Data menu

F-2C:Exchange Menu

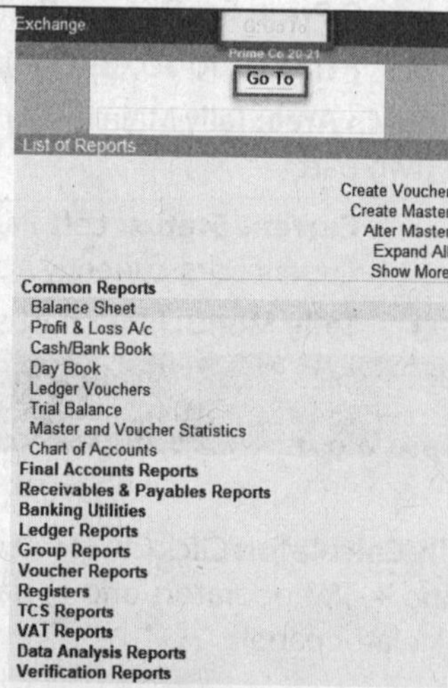

F-2D:Go To Menu

F-2E:Import Menu

F-2F:Export Menu

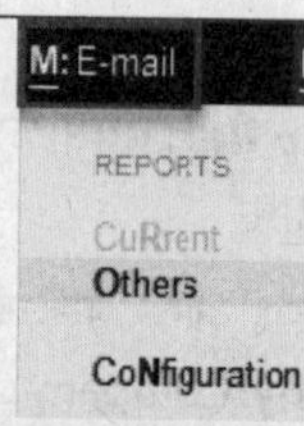

F-2G:E-Mail Menu

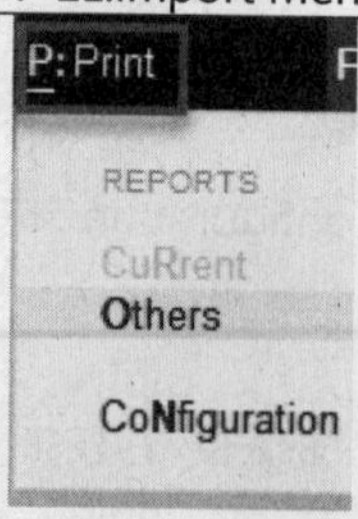

F-2H:Print Menu

F-2I: Help menu

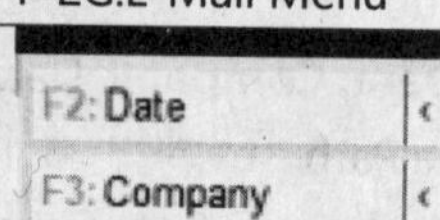

F-2J: Button Bar

02 Current Period & Date Setting

During working, set the Date and Period as follows:

- **Current Date setting:** Press F2 key and enter the Current Date for voucher entry Date (F-3A).
- **Current Period setting:** Press Alt+F2 key to get the Change Period screen. Enter the *From* & *To* Date set the Current Period (F-3B)

Current Date & Current Period as set are displayed at the top left of Gateway of Tally (F-1A).

Current Date	Change Period
1-5-2020	From : 1-5-2020 To : 31-5-2021
F-3A: Current Date set up	F-3A: Current Date set up

काम करने के दौरान, **Current Date** और **Current Period** निम्न प्रकार से set करें:

- **Current Date**: F2:Date बटन दबाएं और Voucher Date entry के लिए Current Date set करें (F-3A)।
- **Current Period**: Alt+F2 key दबाएं और From और To Date entry करें (F-3B)।

03 Tally Calculator

To make arithmetical calculation while working with Tally, type Ctrl+N. The Calculator line will appear (F-4A). Type arithmetic expression using + (addition), - (Subtraction), * Multiplication), / (Division). To group the operators, use parenthesis ( ) pair. Typing wrong expression would produce error message. Use up / Dn arrow keys to move to any line, copy / paste formula / results.

Calculator ✕

```
11>  (12+3)/5 +9
12   12
13>  (12+3)/5 +9*4
14   39
15>
```

F-4A: Tally Calculator

Ctrl+N type कर Tally calculator में Calculation का formula type कर <enter> press करे। Next line में Calculation का result दिखेगा। Calculator हटाने (Hide) के लिए फिर Ctrl+N type करे (या Calculator panel में X पर click करें)।

04 Closing & Exiting Tally

To exit from Tally, at GoT (F-1A), *select Quit* or press <Esc> key or click on rightmost upper Cross (x) button (F-5A). A confirmation screen 'Quit Yes or No' appears (F-5B). Click *Yes (*Press *Y)* to exit from Tally, else press *N* to continue to work with Tally.

F-5A: Close Button to exit from Tally

F-5B: Confirmation

टैली से निकलने के लिए, GoT पर (F-1A), Quit select करें, या <Esc> key दबाएं, या दाई ओर सबसे ऊपरी Close क्रॉस (x) बटन पर क्लिक करें (F-5A)। एक Confirmation screen Yes or No या दिखाई देगा (F-5B)। टैली से बाहर निकलने के लिए Yes क्लिक करें, अन्यथा टैली के काम जारी रखने के लिए No क्लिक करें।

05 Gateway of Tally- Key Points

- **GoT:** गेटवे ऑफ टैली (GoT), टैली में काम शुरू करने का मुख्य द्वार है।
- **Current Period & Current Date:** Current Period & Date GoT में ऊपरी बाईं ओर दिखता है। Current Period और Date के नीचे सभी Selected Company के नाम दिखते हैं।
- **Company Selection :** कई Company एक साथ selected रख सकते हैं, लेकिन सिर्फ currently काम करनेवाले Company ही selected रखे। बाकी कंपनी Shut करे. Company Select कर उसके अनुसार Current Period set करे, नहीं तो Data सही रूप से दिखाई नहीं देखा।
- **Top Horizontal Menu:** हर स्क्रीन में हर समय शीर्ष (Top Horizontal) Menu दिखाई देगा।
- **Exit Tally:** Tally से exit करते ही सभी selected company के साथ Tally भी close हो जाएँगी।
- **Tally Calculator:** कोई भी जगह से Ctl+N press करने से last लाइन के Calculator पैनल में calculation formula type करे (F-4A)। Calculated result display होगा। Calculator Panel में पहले का calculation भी दिखता है. Up / Dn Arrow key से पहले का calculation line में move कर उसे Copy (Ctrl+C) / Paste (Ctrl+V) कर सकते हैं।

Account Masters 01-03

01 Account Masters

After Company Creation, the Account Masters are to be created first and organised as desired. To maintain Basic Accounting System, create the following Masters.

Company Creation के बाद सबसे पहले अपने तरीके से Accounts Masters organise कर Masters create करना है। Basic Accounting System के लिए सबसे पहले निम्नलिखित Accounts Masters create करे।

- **Account Groups:** Account Groups are just convenient & systematic grouping of *Ledger Accounts* of similar nature. Account Group helps to present summarised Accounting Reports in systematic manner. The Account Group may be organised in multiple Levels to get accounting figures and report for each such sub level Groups.

  Account Group एक ही प्रकार के Ledger Account के organisation है। Accounting Reports को Systematically orgasnised तरीके से प्रस्तुत करने के लिए Ledger Accounts को Accounts Group में organise किया जाता है।

- **Account Ledgers:** Account Ledgers are entities representing similar transactions. For example, Travelling Expenses Ledger contains all transactions (vouchers) related to Travelling Expenses. The transactions of a Ledger account are summed up (Debit & Credit) and balanced (net Debit / Credit).

  Account Ledger एक Account से सम्बंधित सभी लेनेदन का record है। जैसे कि, Travelling Expenses के Ledger में Datewise Travelling Expenses के सारे Transaction रहेंगे।

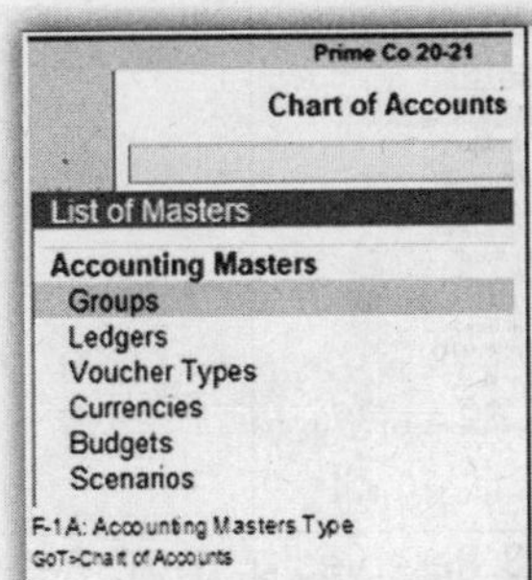

F-1A: Accounting Masters Type
GoT>Chart of Accounts

Select GoT>Chart of Accounts to get the Accounts Masters Types List (F-1A)।

Accounts Master Type List के लिए *GoT>Chart of Accounts* select करे (F-1A)।

02 Reserved Accounts Masters

During Company creation, Tally automatically creates 28 Reserved Account Groups and 2 Reserved Ledger Accounts. Select *GoT>Chart of Accounts>Group* to display list of all Account Groups.

Company creation के समय, Tally automatically 28 Reserved Account Groups और 2 Reserved Ledger Accounts create करता है। Primary Account Group के alphabetical list display करने के लिए GoT>Chart of Accounts>Group select करे।

- **Reserved Groups:** Tally creates 15 Primary Groups and 13 Sub-Groups (known as Reserved Groups) for each Company (F-2A).
- **Reserved Ledger Accounts:** Tally also auto creates 2 Reserved Ledger accounts (Cash and Profit & Loss Account : F-1A). So, do not create any new ledger for these Ledger Accounts. All other Ledger Accounts are to be created.

Cash और Profit Loss Ledger Account create ना करे, क्योंकि Tally इसे अपने आप Create कर लेते हैं (F-2D)।

Chart of Accounts List of Groups Branch / Divisions Capital Account Reserves & Surplus Current Assets Bank Accounts Cash-in-Hand Deposits (Asset) Loans & Advances (Asset) Stock-in-Hand Sundry Debtors Current Liabilities Duties & Taxes Provisions Sundry Creditors Direct Expenses Direct Incomes Fixed Assets Indirect Expenses Indirect Incomes Investments Loans (Liability) Bank OD A/c Secured Loans Unsecured Loans Misc. Expenses (ASSET) Purchase Accounts Sales Accounts Suspense A/c 28 Group(s)	**Reserved Groups (Liabilities)** Chart of Accounts List of Groups Capital Account Reserves & Surplus Current Liabilities Duties & Taxes Provisions Sundry Creditors Loans (Liability) Bank OD A/c Secured Loans Unsecured Loans Suspense A/c **Reserved Groups (Assets)** Chart of Accounts List of Groups Branch / Divisions Current Assets Bank Accounts Cash-in-Hand Deposits (Asset) Loans & Advances (Asset) Stock-in-Hand Sundry Debtors Fixed Assets Investments Misc. Expenses (ASSET)	**List of Reserved Groups (Expenses & Income)** **Expenses** Direct Expenses Indirect Expenses Purchase Accounts **Income** Direct Incomes Indirect Incomes Sales Accounts	Chart of Accounts List of Ledgers Assets Current Assets Bank Accounts Cash-in-Hand Cash ← Reserved Ledger Deposits (Asset) Loans & Advances (Asset) Stock-in-Hand Sundry Debtors Fixed Assets Investments Misc. Expenses (ASSET) Liabilities Branch / Divisions Capital Account Reserves & Surplus Current Liabilities Duties & Taxes Provisions Sundry Creditors Loans (Liability) Bank OD A/c Secured Loans Unsecured Loans Suspense A/c Profit & Loss A/c ← Reserved Ledger Expenses Direct Expenses Indirect Expenses Purchase Accounts 28 Group(s) and 2 Ledger(s)
F-2A : Alphabetical list of Reserved Account Groups GoT>Chart of Accounts>Groups	F-2B: Reserved Accounts Groups (Liabilities & Assets)	F-2C: Reserved Accounts Groups (Income & Expenses)	F-2D:Reserved Ledger Accounts

The Reserved Groups appear in Alphabetical order and the subordinate groups appear below the respective Reserved Group in hierarchical order. Reserved Account Group appear in Bold, subordinate Account Group appear in Normal Font and Ledger Accounts appear in Italics (F-2A to F-2D).

Reserved Account Group Bold में दिखते हैं, Created Group Normal Font में दिखते है, Ledger Accounts Italic Font में दिखते हैं (F-2A to F-2D)।

03 Reserved Accounts Characteristics

To organise the Financial statements easily and correctly, Tally creates Reserved Groups for each Type of Accounts. We now explain Reserved Account Groups and nature of Accounts of each such Account Group.

Reserved Account Groups of Liabilities: The Groups of Liabilities of Balance Sheet are shown below:

Capital: It represents Capital and Reserves & Surplus of the Company.

- **Capital Account:** Represents Owners Capital. These may be placed under Capital Group. Common example are Share (or Equity) Capital, Partners' Capital Accounts, Proprietors Capital Account. Members Capital A/c etc. Separate Ledgers may be created for Equity Capital, Preference Capital A/c etc.
- **Reserves & Surplus**: Represents Reserve Accounts like General Reserve, Capital Reserve, Investment Allowance Reserve, Share Premium Account etc.

Loans (Liabilities): Represents all loans taken (Borrowings) by Company. Tally further divides this Groups into following 3 reserved sub-groups for better organisation

– **Bank OD Accounts**: While Current Bank A/c should be placed under Current Assets (explained later), Bank Overdraft and Cash/Credit Accounts availed under Hypothecation, Bill Discounting etc. operated on a day-to-day basis should be placed under this group.

– **Secured Loans**: Debentures, Borrowings like Term Loans (Medium/Long term), Secured Loans taken from Banks, Financial Institutes etc. against security (like mortgage/ hypothecation, pledge etc) should be placed under this group.

– **Unsecured Loans**: Borrowings from outside Parties, Directors, Friends and Relatives (without any collateral security), Deposits etc, should be placed under this group.

Current Liabilities : This Group normally constitutes a large number of Ledger Accounts and Sub Groups and is subdivided into following 3 sub-groups:

- **Duties and Taxes**: This sub-group is for all Indirect taxes normally charged on Goods & Services, like GST etc.
- **Provisions**: It is a place for all sorts of Provisions (like Provision for Bad Debts etc). However, Depreciation Provided should go under Fixed Assets (explained later).
- **Sundry Creditors**: Ledger accounts of all Trade Creditors / Suppliers
- **Current Liabilities**: It may contain all other liability accounts (not placed in any the above 3 groups), like Liabilities for Expenses, Employees contribution for ESI/PF, TDS realized etc.

Suspense Account: This may contain temporary Accounts containing transactions whose nature are not yet finally known.

Account Groups of Assets

Fixed Assets: All Fixed Assets used for business over long period, like Immovable Properties (Land, Building), Rights (Patents, Trade Rights), Plant & Machinery, Vehicle etc, should be placed under this Group.

Investments: All Ledger Accounts related to Investments in Shares, Bonds, Govt. Securities and Investment in other companies.

Current Assets: It constitutes 6 Reserved Sub Groups: Stock-in-hand, Deposits (Assets), Loans & Advances (Assets), Cash-in-hand, Bank Accounts, Sundry Debtors.

- **Stock-in-hand**: Ledger Accounts for Stock should be placed under this group.
- **Deposits (Assets)**: Deposits made by the Company like Fixed Deposits, Security Deposits, Deposits with Electricity, Telephone dept, Deposits in other companies, Rental Deposits accounts etc. should be placed under this Group.
- **Loans and Advances (Assets)**: All Loans & Advances of non-trading nature given, like Advances against Salary, Loans to Employees, Advances to Fixed Assets Suppliers etc.
- **Sundry Debtors**: All the Trade Customer Ledger Accounts.
- **Cash-in-Hand**: It contains all types of Cash Accounts. Tally auto creates a Cash Ledger Account (Cash-in-Hand) under this group.
- **Bank Accounts**: All Bank Accounts like Current Accounts, Savings Accounts etc, should be placed here.

Misc. Expenses (Asset): For Limited Companies, Preliminary, Pre-operative and similar expenses (to the extent not written off to Profit & Loss A/cs) should fall here.

Account Groups of Profit & Loss Account

- **Sales:** All sorts of Trade Sales (Goods as well Services). Sale of Fixed Assets should not be included in Sale.
- **Direct Income:** Accounts for direct Income other than those placed under Sales.
- **Indirect Income:** All Incomes other than placed under the above two groups (like Rent, Interest, Commission, Dividend Income etc).
- **Purchase:** All trade Purchases. Purchase of Fixed Assets should not be included in Purchase.
- **Direct Expenses:** Accounts of Direct Expenses (like Carriage Inwards, Wages etc) considered for computing Gross Profit/Loss.
- **Indirect Expenses:** All expenses considered for computation of Net Profit/ Loss only not included in the above Groups should be placed here.

सही तरह Accounts organise करने के लिए, Accounts के nature के rule के अनुसार Tally में Reserved Accounts के group अपने आप create होता है। एक Reserved Group के अंतर्गत सभी Ledger Accounts में उसके rules लागू होते हैं; इसलिए, नए Account Group और नए ledger Accounts उपर्युक्त Accounts Group के nature के अनुसार सही Account Group में set कर create करें।

04 Account Masters Creation

Create new Account Group or Account Ledger (in addition to the Reserved Groups or Ledgers auto-created by Tally on creation of a Company), as required. Select *Gateway of Tally > Create* to get Master Type list (F-1A).

नए Account Master, जैसे Account Group और Ledger Account create करने के लिए *Gateway of Tally > Create* select करे और Master Type list पाए (F-1A).

Account Group

For a small company (or individual accounts), the Tally created Reserved account groups (F-2A to F-2C) may be adequate, and you may not need to create new Account Groups. However, for better organization of larger number of accounts, new Account Groups need to be created. The Reserved Groups bear their own characteristics. The Ledger Accounts placed under these Groups inherit the properties of the respective Reserve Group.

Tally पहले से Reserved Account Group create कर लेते हैं (F-2A to F-2C), लेकिन अपने अनुसार Chart of Accounts संगठित (Organsie) करने के लिए नए Accounts Group बना सकते हैं।

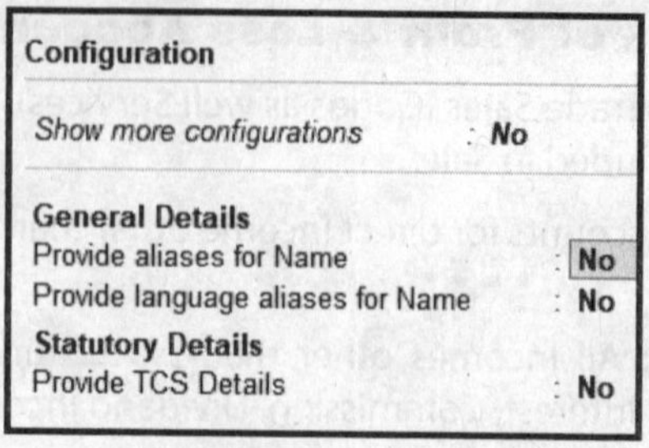

F-3A: Account Group Configuration set up

Account Group Creation: Select *GoT>Create>Group* (F-1A). At *Account Groups* creation screen (F-3A), enter as follows :

- **Account Group Name:** At *Name*, enter unique Account Group Name.
- **Parent Group**: At *Under*, select the Parent Group from List of Groups. The new Group would be placed under the selected Parent Group.

At other options, select No / Not Applicable. This way you can create a new Account Group under a Reserved Group or new created Group. This way create new Groups one by one (One Group at a time)

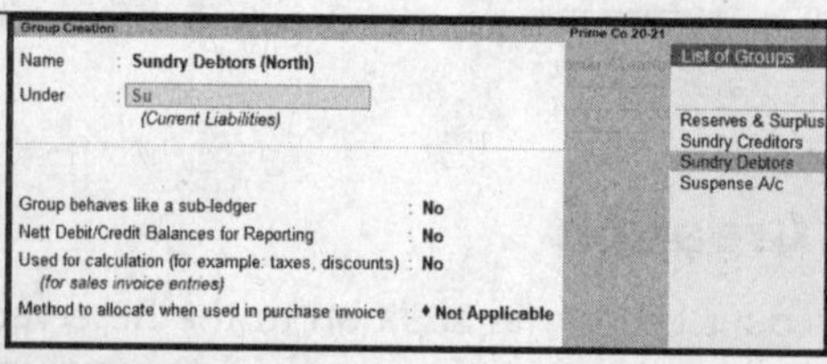

F-3B: Account Group Creation

GoT>Create>Groups

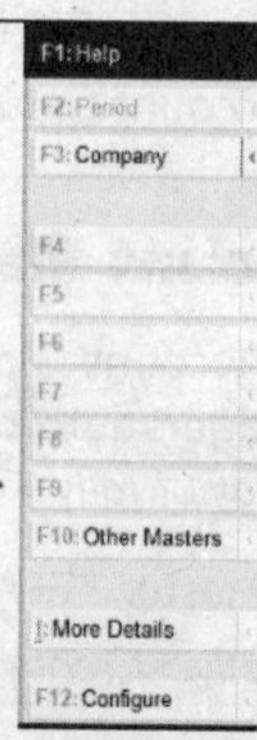

F-3C:Buttons at Account Group & Ledger Creation screen

Account Groups creation (F-3A) के लिए *GoT>Create>Group* select करे (F-1A). *Account Group Creation* Screen (F-3A), में Name field में Group Name enter करे और *Under* field में Parent (मूल) Group Name select करे।

Account Ledger

Select *GoT>Create>Ledger* (F-1A). At *Account Ledger* creation screen (F-4B), click *F12:Configure*, set the Configuration option (F-4A), and enter as follows (F-4B) :

- **Account Ledger Name: At** *Name*, **e**nter the unique Name of the Ledger. This name will be printed in all internal records (like Ledger, Trial Balance etc) and will be available in drop down list for selection of Ledger.
- **Parent Group: At** *Under*, **s**elect the Parent Group of the Ledger from *List of Groups.*

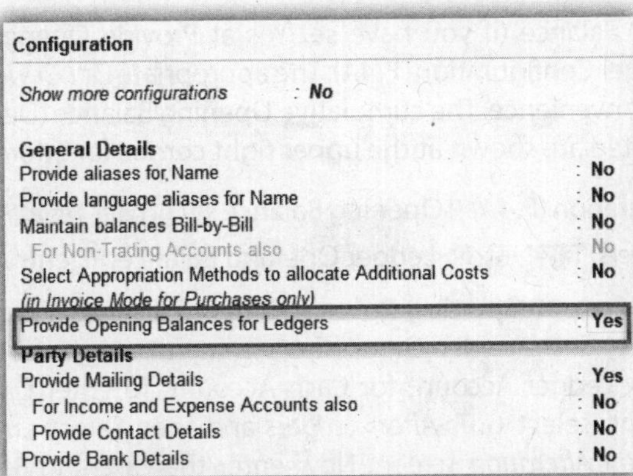

F-4A: Account Ledger Configuration

Account Ledger Creation Screen (F-4B), के लिए *GoT>Create>Ledger* select करे (F-1A). *Name* field में Ledger Name enter करे और *Under* field में Parent (मूल) Group Name select करे।

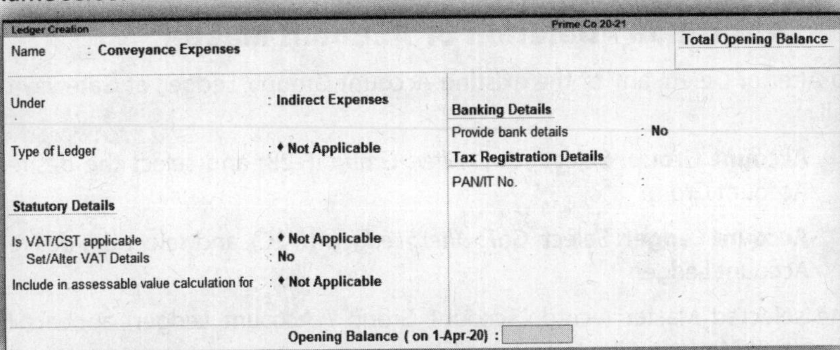

F-4B: Account Ledger Creation

GoT>Create>Ledger

Creation of new Parent Group

During Account Group or Ledger Account entry (F-3B/ F-4B), if you find that the parent group is not existing, press *Alt+C* at *'Under'* field to get *Account Group Creation (Secondary)* screen (like F-3B). Create the parent Account Group and select the parent group at *Under* field in Group Entry (F-3B) / Ledger Entry (F-4B) as usual.

Group या Ledger Creation के समय गैर-मौजूदा (Non-existing) Account Group create करने के लिए Under field में Alt+C press कर Parent Group भी उसी समय create कर सकते हैं।

Ledger Opening Balance Entry

Enter Opening Balance (if you have set Yes at Provide Opening Balance for Ledgers at Ledger Configuration- F-4A). The appropriate Dr / Cr would be carried as default for convenience. The cumulative Opening Balance (Debit & Credit) of all ledgers created are shown at the upper right corner, for information.

Ledger Configuration (F-4A) में Opening Balance set up (*set Yes* at *Provide Opening Balance for Ledgers)* किया हो तो Ledger Opening Balance भी entry कर सकते हैं।

Cash Ledger Account Opening Balance Entry: Tally auto creates a reserved Ledger Account *Cash* (under Group Cash-in-hand). So, you do not need to create any new Ledger Account for Cash Account. To enter *Opening Balance* of Cash Account, select *GoT>Alter>Ledgers* and then select *Cash* Account to get *Cash Account Alteration* screen. Now enter the Opening Balance of Cash Account at Opening Balance field, as explained.

Cash Ledger Account automatic Create होता है। इसलिए, Cash Account का Opening Balance के लिए *GoT>Alter>Ledgers* से Cash Ledger Account Alteration कर Cash Account का Opening Balance entry करें।

05 Alteration / Deletion of Account Master

To Alter or Delete any of the existing Account Group / Ledger, at Gateway of Tally :

- **Account Group:** Select *GoT>Alter>Group* (F-2B) and select the desired Account Group
- **Account Ledger:** Select *GoT>Alter>Ledger*>(F-2C), and select the desired Account Ledger

The selected Master record (Account Group / Account Ledger) appears in Alteration Mode (similar to creation screen).

- **Alteration:** Now you may alter data of any field of the master record (Group or Ledger). Press *Alt+A* to save the changes made.
- **Deletion:** To Delete the Master Record, Press Alt+D and press Y at '*Delete? Yes or No.*' to confirm Deletion.

Reserved Group Name and other properties can be altered, but its Parent Group cannot be Altered

Restriction on Deletion of Master: An Account Master (Group or Ledger) cannot be deleted in following cases:

- **Deletion of Account Group:** An Account Group can not be Deleted, if there is any child ledger of the Group. The Tally created Reserved Group also cannot be deleted.
- **Deletion of Account Ledger:** An Account Ledger can not be Deleted if it is transacted in a Voucher. The Tally created Reserved Ledger Accounts (Cash and P& L A/c) also cannot be deleted.

Account Group / Ledger Alteration के लिए, *GoT>Alter>Group*, या *GoT>Alter>Ledger* select कर Alter या Delete करनेवाले Account Group या Ledger Account select करे। Alter करने के लिए field में data change करे. Delete करने के लिए Alt+D press करे। Reserved Group या Reserved Ledger Account Delete नहीं कर सकते. Voucher में entry किया हुआ Ledger Account भी Delete नहीं कर सकते।

06 Some Common Ledger Accounts Creation

Some important Ledger Accounts creation screen with the Parent Account Group (Under) and other info are shown for guidance and understanding (F-5A to 5H). To set the Ledger Account Configuration, click *F12:Configure* button at the right side Button Bar of Ledger creation screen and set the options as desired. To keep the things simple, set Yes at *Provide Opening Balance* in Ledger Accounts and set *No* at all other options (F-5A).

कुछ important Ledger Account creation, उसके Configuration और Parent group, example के तौर पर दिखा रहे हैं (F-5A to 5H)।

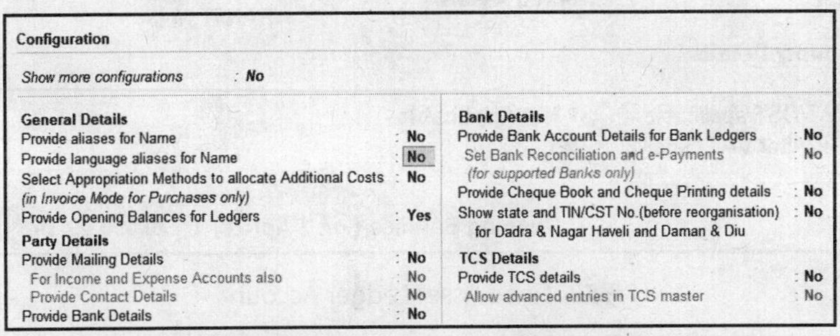

Configuration

Show more configurations : **No**

General Details		Bank Details	
Provide aliases for Name	: No	Provide Bank Account Details for Bank Ledgers	: No
Provide language aliases for Name	: No	Set Bank Reconciliation and e-Payments *(for supported Banks only)*	: No
Select Appropriation Methods to allocate Additional Costs *(in Invoice Mode for Purchases only)*	: No	Provide Cheque Book and Cheque Printing details	: No
Provide Opening Balances for Ledgers	: Yes	Show state and TIN/CST No.(before reorganisation) for Dadra & Nagar Haveli and Daman & Diu	: No
Party Details		**TCS Details**	
Provide Mailing Details	: No	Provide TCS details	: No
For Income and Expense Accounts also	: No	Allow advanced entries in TCS master	: No
Provide Contact Details	: No		
Provide Bank Details	: No		

F-5A: Ledger Account Configuration

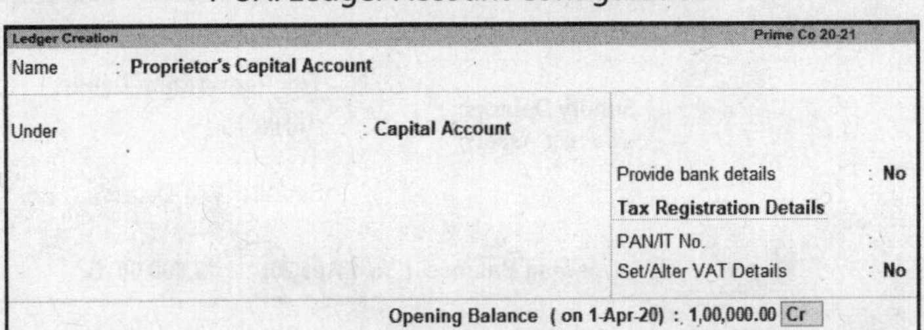

Ledger Creation Prime Co 20-21

Name : **Proprietor's Capital Account**

Under : **Capital Account**

Provide bank details : **No**

Tax Registration Details

PAN/IT No. :

Set/Alter VAT Details : **No**

Opening Balance (on 1-Apr-20) : 1,00,000.00 Cr

F-5B: Proprietor's Capital Account

Ledger Creation — Prime Co 20-21

Name : **HDFC Bank**

Under : **Bank Accounts** *(Current Assets)*

Opening Balance (on 1-Apr-20) :20,000.00 Dr

F-5C: Bank Current Account

Ledger Creation — Prime Co 20-21

Name : **A B C Supplier**

Under : **Sundry Creditors** *(Current Liabilities)*

Tax Registration Details

PAN/IT No. :

Set/Alter VAT Details : **No**

Opening Balance (on 1-Apr-20) : 12,000.00 Cr

F-5D: Supplier Ledger Account

Ledger Creation — Prime Co 20-21

Name : **Furniture**

Under : **Fixed Assets**

Statutory Details

Is VAT/CST applicable : ♦ **Not Applicable**

Set/Alter VAT Details : **No**

Tax Registration Details

PAN/IT No.

Opening Balance (on 1-Apr-20) : 20,000.00 Dr

F-5E : Fixed Asset Ledger Account

Ledger Creation — Prime Co 20-21

Name : **ABC Traders**

Under : **Sundry Debtors** *(Current Assets)*

Tax Registration Details

PAN/IT No. :

Set/Alter VAT Details : **No**

Opening Balance (on 1-Apr-20) : 12,000.00 Dr

F-5F: Customer Ledger Account

Ledger Creation		Prime Co 20-21
Name	: **Sales**	
Under	: **Sales Accounts**	**Tax Registration Details** PAN/IT No.
Type of Ledger	: ♦ **Not Applicable**	
Statutory Details		
Is VAT/CST applicable	: ♦ **Not Applicable**	
Set/Alter VAT Details	: **No**	
Include in assessable value calculation for	: ♦ **Not Applicable**	
Opening Balance (on 1-Apr-20) :		

F-5G: Sales Ledger Account

Ledger Creation		Prime Co 20-21
Name	: **Purchase**	
Under	: **Purchase Accounts**	**Tax Registration Details** PAN/IT No.
Type of Ledger	: ♦ **Not Applicable**	
Statutory Details		
Is VAT/CST applicable	: ♦ **Applicable**	
Set/Alter VAT Details	: **No**	
Opening Balance (on 1-Apr-20) :		

F-5H: Purchase Ledger Account

07 Account Master - Key Points

- हर company के लिए 28 Reserved Group और 2 Reserved Ledger Account auto create होते है। हर Reserved Group के अपने चरित्र (characteristics) होते हैं। नए Account Group एक Reserved Group या नया created Account Group के under ही create कर सकते हैं। कोई भी Group के नीचे के सारे Account Group और Ledger Account के चरित्र (nature) एक जैसे होंगे।
- हर Account Group / Ledger Account कोई एक Account Group के नीचे रहेगा।
- *GoT>Chart of Accounts>Group* में Primary Group, alphabetical order के अनुसार hierarchical structure में Account Group list होते हैं, Accounting structure के अनुसार नहीं होते।
- नए Account Group या Ledger Account create करते वक्त, उसी entry screen से नया parent (मूल) Account Group भी एक साथ create कर सकते है।

- छोटे और सरल Accounts के लिए, नए Account group create न कर Tally created Reserved Group के नीचे ही सारे Ledger Account create कर सकते हैं। लेकिन Accounts के बेहतरीन ढांचा के लिए, जरूरत अनुसार, नए Account Group create करे।
- Ledger creation के समय Ledger Opening Balance भी entry करे। Ledger creation के बाद भी Ledger Alteration से Ledger Opening Balance entry कर सकते है। Cash Ledger Account Reserved Ledger Account है, जो Company creation के समय ही create हो जाता है, इसलिए Cash Ledger Account के Opening Balance Ledger Alteration से entry करे।
- Chart of Accounts में सिर्फ Account Name, Alias Name show होते है। Master में entry किए गए Opening Balance और सभी info के Master List data checking के लिए, सही तरह से chart of Accounts organise करने के लिए, reference के लिए, user को बहुत ही जरूरत होती है। लेकिन Tally से ऐसी Master list print नहीं कर सकते।
- Data Deletion भी Data Alteration से ही करे।

Accounts Vouchers 01-04

01 Accounts Vouchers

Voucher is a complete & comprehensive record of all important details related to the transaction.

Voucher Types: Academically, all types of transactions (Cash or Non Cash) may be entered in *Journal Voucher* and recorded in Journal Book. However, for better control and division of accounting tasks to various persons, Transactions are classified into several Voucher Types. Accordingly, different types of vouchers are used to record as per nature of transactions. In this chapter, we will discuss various types of Vouchers available in Tally Prime system.

सारे Business Transaction Voucher में record किए जाते है। काम की सुविधा के लिए और Accounts अच्छी तरह organise करने के लिए, Tally में कई तरह के Voucher उपयोग किए जाते हैं।

02 Voucher Entry

Select *GoT>Vouchers* (F-1A) to get Voucher entry screen. At the rightmost part, you get Buttons (F4 to F9) for each Accounts Voucher Type (F-1B). Click the respective button (or type the Function Key) and enter data in Voucher Entry Screen.

Voucher entry के लिए *GoT> Vouchers* select करे (F-1A)। Voucher Type के अनुसार (F4 से F9) Button click / press कर (F-1B) Voucher Entry screen में Voucher data entry करे।

At Voucher entry screen, click H:Change Mode Button (or type Ctrl+H) and select *Double Entry* to enter in Double Entry Mode (Ledger Amount in Dr / Cr column). Single Entry Mode will be explained later. In Double entry mode, Voucher would be saved when total debits are equal to total credits of the voucher.

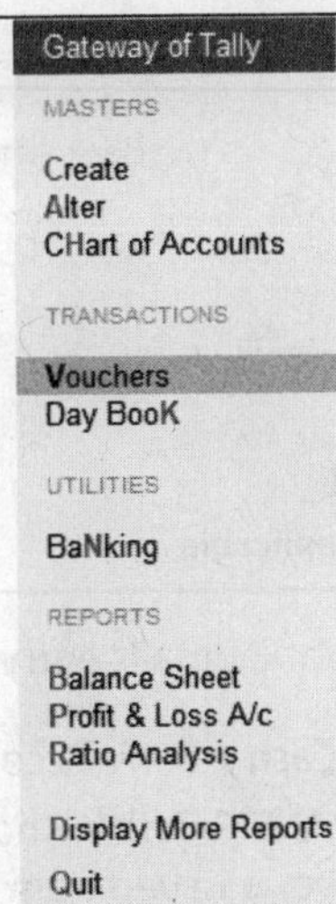

F-1A: GoT Main Menu

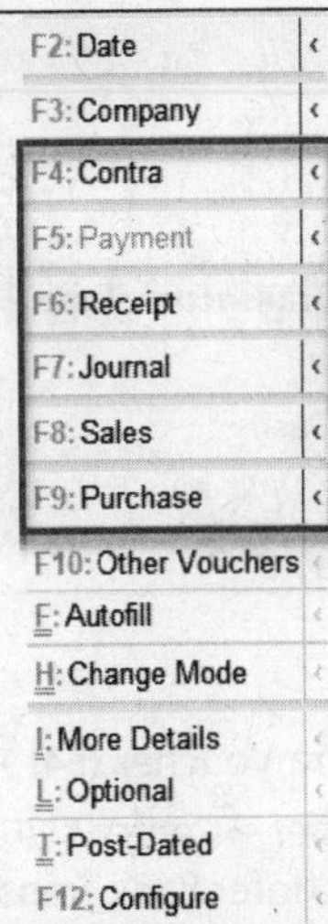

F-1B: Accounts Voucher entry Buttons

हम यहाँ Double entry mode समझायेंगे. इसमें Debit और Credit column में Amount entry होता है। हर Voucher में Debit और Credit का Total बराबर होना चाहिए।

Contra Voucher: Contra Voucher (click *F4:Contra*) is used to record transfer of fund from one Cash / Bank / Bank OCC to another Cash / Bank / Bank OCC a/c (like Cash Withdrawal from Bank, Cash Deposit to bank, Transfer from one Bank Account to another, Transfer between Main Cash and Petty Cash and Petty Cash). So, in contra voucher, you can transact only Cash / Bank / Bank OCC a/c ledgers.

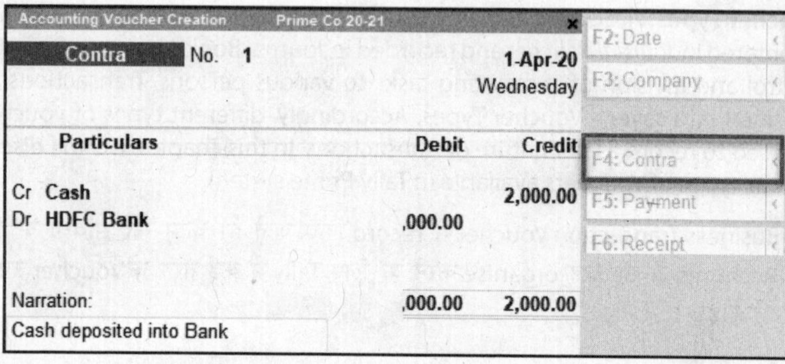

F-2A : Contra Voucher

The first entry is always Credit (Cash / Bank Account from where money is taken out). From 2nd entry onwards you may Credit or Debit Cash / Bank Ledger Account (where money is deposited into) under Cash, Bank Accounts and Bank OCC group only.

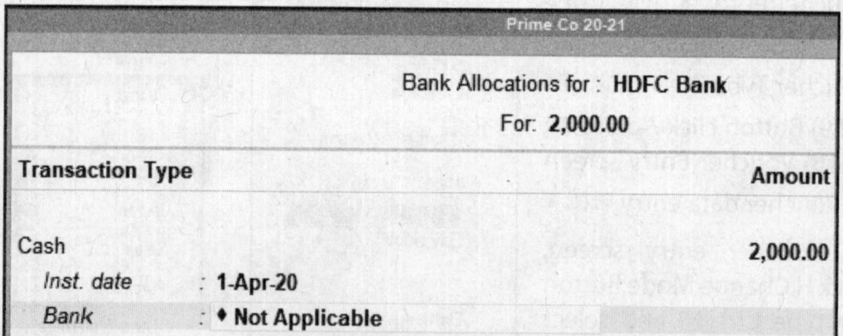

F-2B: Bank details entry in Voucher

Contra Voucher (F4) में एक Cash / Bank Account से दूसरे Cash Bank Account में transfer की entry होती है। (F-2A), जैसे Cash Withdrawal from Bank, Cash Deposit to Bank, Inter Bank Transfer, Cheque issued from one Bank Account and deposited into another बगैरह। इसलिए Contra Voucher में सिर्फ Cash/ Bank Account ही entry होता है।

Payment Voucher: Payment Voucher is used for any sort of outgo of money (from Bank Account or Cash Account). In Payment voucher (click *F5: Payment)*, Ledger Account paid to is Debited and a Cash / Bank / Bank OCC A/c from where money is taken out, is Credited (F-3A).

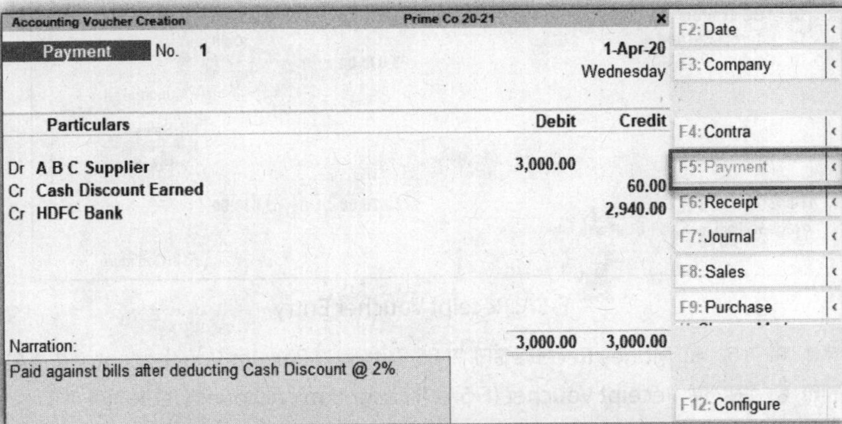

F-3A Payment Voucher

The first entry is always Debit (other than Cash / Bank/ Bank OCC a/c) and second entry onwards you may specify Debit or Credit. The Cash / Bank / Bank OCC A/c must be Credited.

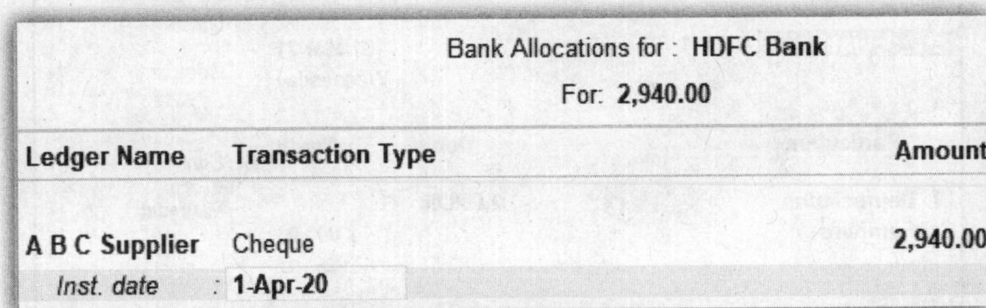

F-4A: Bank details screen

कोई भी तरह के payment के लिए F5 type या Click कर Payment Voucher entry होता है। इसलिए Payment Voucher में Cash/ Bank Account Credit होता है (F-3A)।

Receipt Voucher: Receipt Voucher is used for any sort of inflow of money (in Bank Account or Cash Account). In Receipt Voucher (click *F6: Receipt*), ledger account received from is Credited, and Cash / Bank/ Bank OCC A/c, where money is going to, is Debited (F-5A). The first entry is always Credit (other than Cash / Bank Account), and second entry onwards you may specify Debit or Credit. The Cash / Bank / Bank OCC A/c must be Debited.

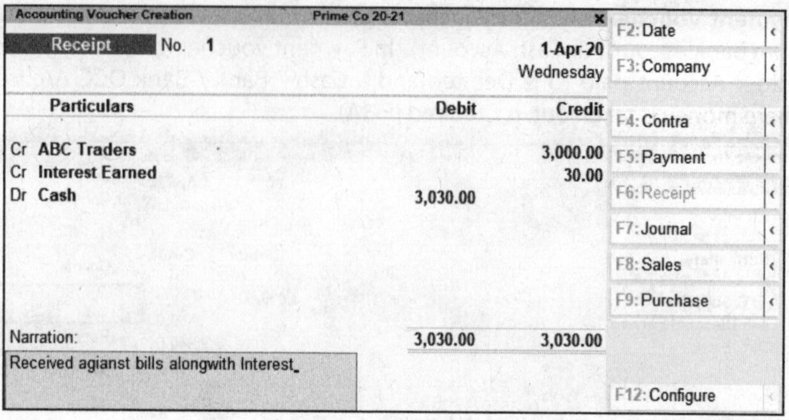

F-5A: Receipt Voucher Entry

कोई भी तरह का Money Receive होने से F6 Button से Receipt Voucher entry (F-5A) होता है। इसलिए Receipt Voucher (F-5A) में Cash/ Bank Account Debit होता है।

Journal Voucher: Journal Voucher is used for all non cash transaction (other than Receipt, Payment & Contra). Click *F7:*Journal (or type F7). The first entry is Debit (F-6A). Any Ledger Account (other than under Cash, Bank or Bank OCC) may be Debited or Credited.

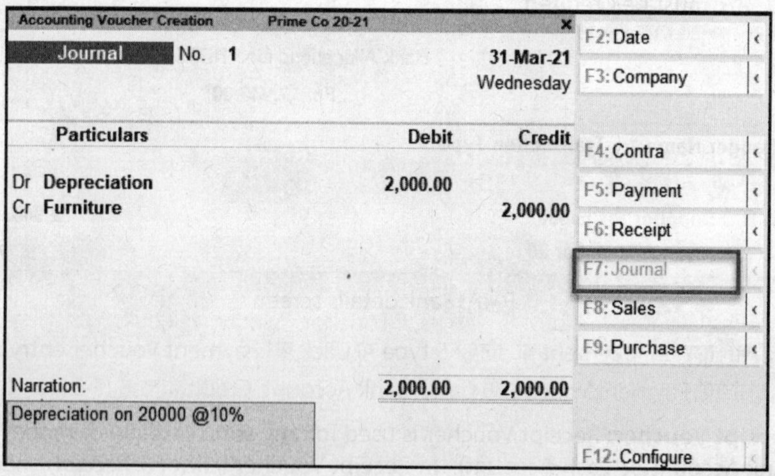

F-6A: Journal Voucher Entry

Payment, Receipt और Contra Voucher में entry के अलावा हर तरह के entry Journal Voucher में होते है। F7 Button click कर Journal Voucher entry करे (F-6A)।

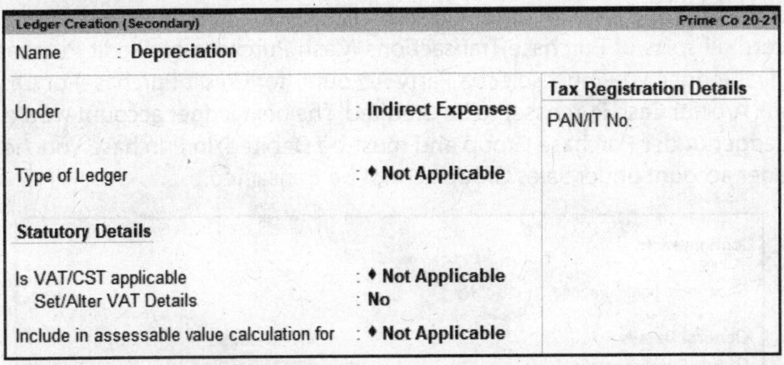

F-6B: New Ledger Account from Voucher entry

Sales Voucher: Sales Voucher (Click *F8: Sales*): is created (F-7B) to record all sorts of Sales Transactions (Cash Sales or Credit Sales). At first ledger, select a Party Account (for Credit Sales) or Cash / Bank A/c (for Cash Sales), to be Debited. The next ledger account would be a Ledger under Sales Group and must be Credited. In Sales Voucher, a ledger account under Purchase Group cannot be transacted.

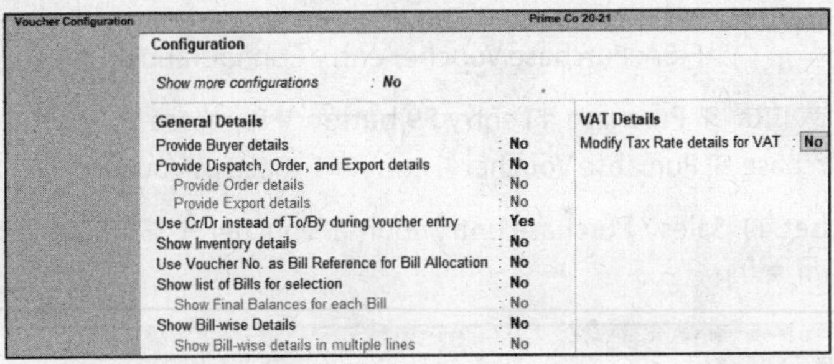

F-7A: Sales Voucher Configuration

Tally में हर तरह के Sales का entry F8 Button से Sales Voucher में होता है। Cash sales भी Sales Voucher में entry करे (Receipt Voucher में नहीं)।

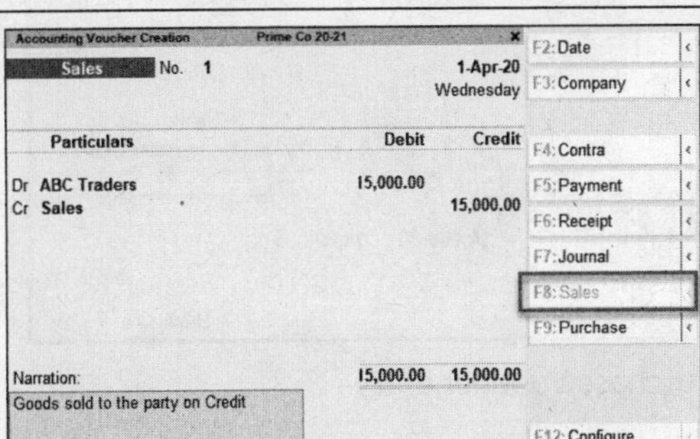

F-7B: Sales Voucher

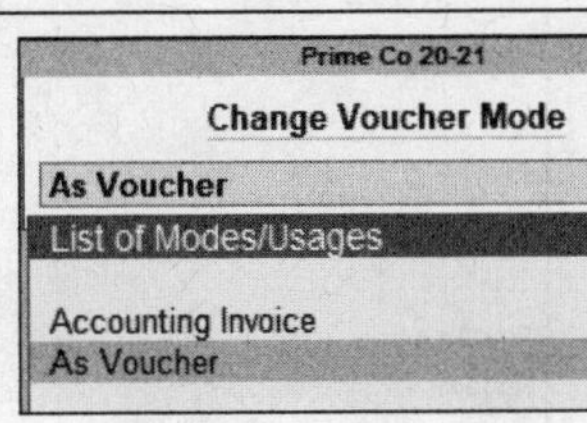

F-7C: Voucher Entry Mode selection

Purchase Voucher: Purchase Voucher (click *F9:Purchase*) is created (F-7A) to record all sorts of Purchase Transactions (Cash Purchase or Credit Purchase). At first ledger, you must select a Party Account (for Credit Purchase) or Cash / Bank A/c (for Cash Purchase) to be Credited. The next ledger account would be a Ledger under Purchase Group and must be Debited. In Purchase Voucher, a ledger account under Sales Group cannot be transacted.

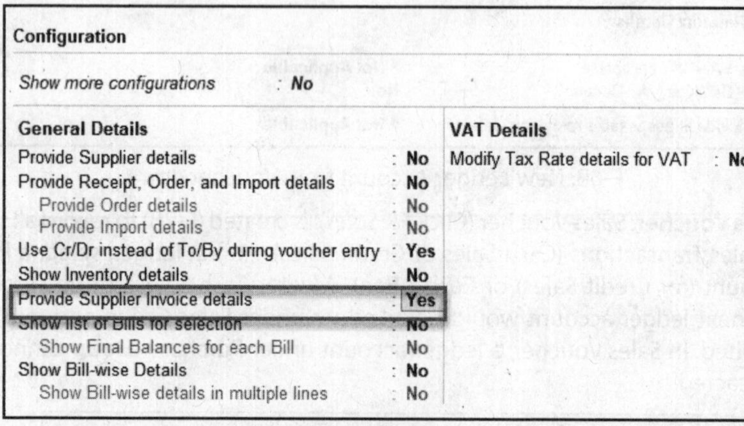

F-8A: Purchase Voucher entry Configuration

Tally में हर तरह के Purchase का entry F9 button से Purchase Voucher में होता है। Cash Purchase भी Purcahse Voucher में entry करे (Receipt Voucher में नहीं)।

Fixed Asset का Sales / Purchase entry Journal Voucher में करे (Sales / Purchase Voucher में नहीं)।

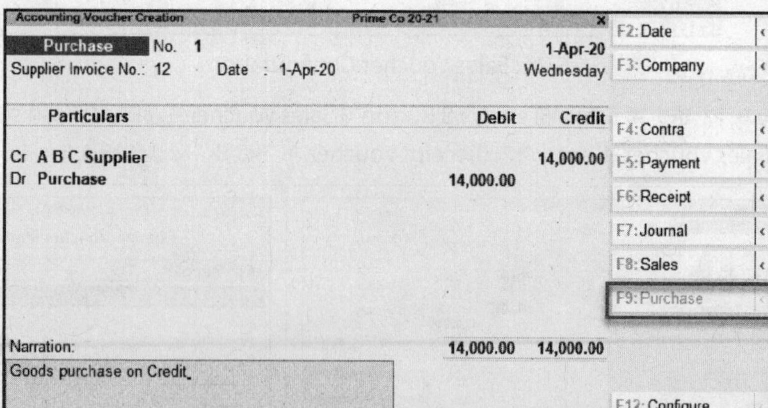

F-8B: Purchase Voucher entry

03 Debit / Credit Note voucher

Debit & Credit note voucher are normally used for adjustment, supplementary bills, rebates, goods returns, etc.

- **Debit Note Voucher Entry:** To enter Debit Note Voucher, at Voucher Entry screen, press Alt+F5 (or Click *F10:Other Voucher* button and select Debit note from the list of Vouchers).
- **Credit Note Voucher Entry**: To enter Credit Note Voucher, at Voucher Entry screen, press Alt+F6 (or Click F10: Other Voucher button and select Credit Note from the list of Vouchers).

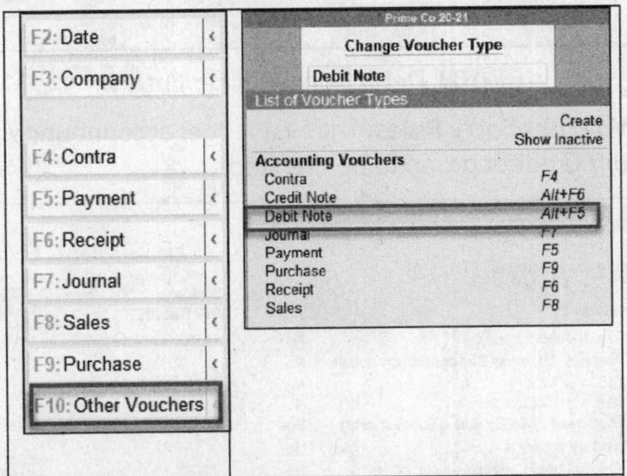

F-9A: Debit / Credit Note Voucher Type selection

Debit Note Voucher Entry Rules: The First ledger account under Cash / Bank, Sundry Debtor / Creditor group to be Debited.

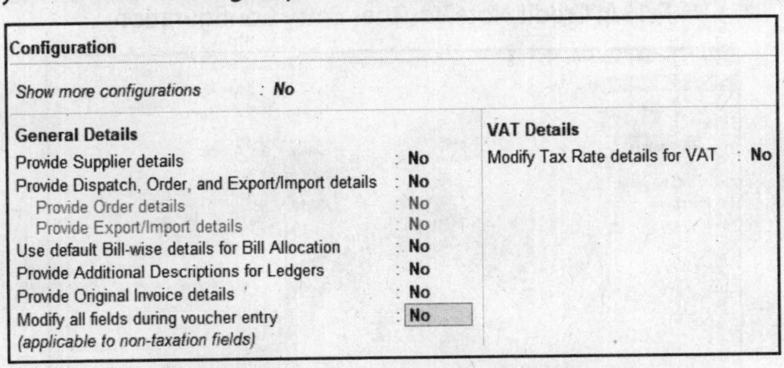

F-10A: Debit Note Voucher Entry Configuration

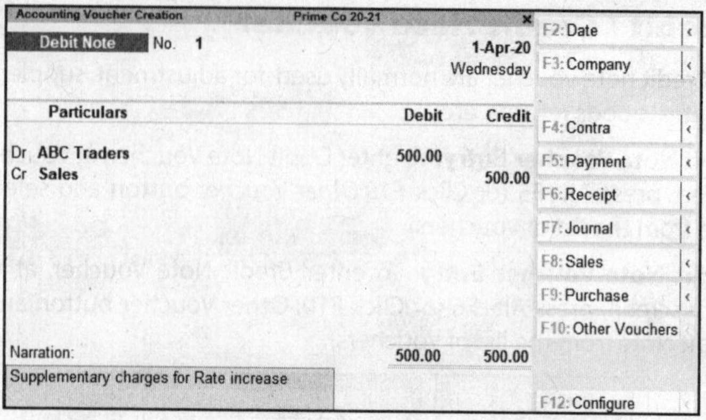

F-10B: Debit Note Voucher Entry

Credit Note Voucher Entry Rules: The First ledger account under Cash / Bank, Sundry Debtor / Creditor group to be Credited.

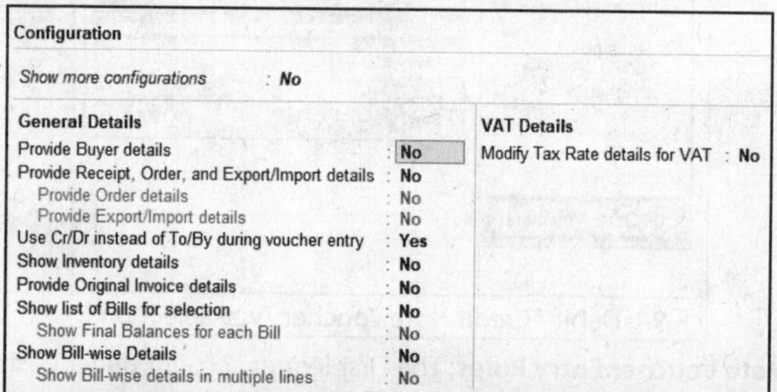

F-11A: Credit Note Voucher Entry Configuration

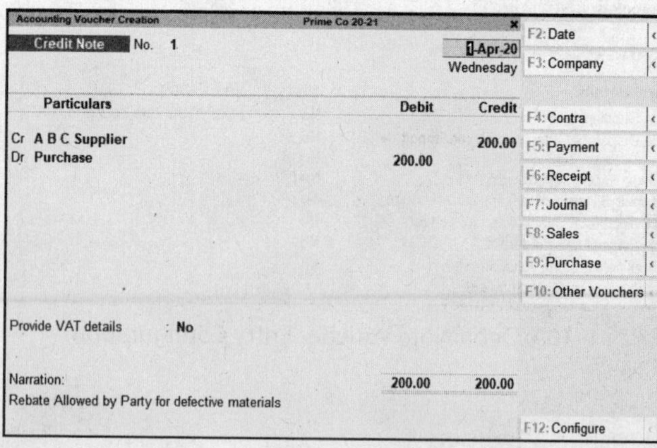

F-11B: Credit Note Voucher Entry

Sales Bill के सम्बंधित Additional Charge के लिए Seller Alt+F5 से Debit Note issue करते हैं। Seller के books में Buyer का Account Debit होता है; दूसरी तरफ, Buyer अपने Accounts में Seller को Alt+F6 से Credit Note issue करते हैं। Buyer के books में Seller का Account क्रेडिट होता है।

Goods Return करने वाली Party Goods पानेवाली Party के ऊपर Debit Note issue करते है। Goods Return पाने वाली Party Goods Return करने वाली Party के favour में Credit Note issue करते हैं।

04 Components of Voucher Entry Screen

Tally provides a standard Accounts Voucher entry Form for all types of Accounts Vouchers. We have described the rules of Voucher Entry (Account Heads, Debit / Credit) for each Voucher Type.

The Basic Accounts Voucher entry screen may be broadly divided into 3 areas :

Voucher Header	Ledger Details	Voucher Footer
Voucher Type/Number Voucher Date/Day	To/By(or Dr/Cr) Ledger Account Ledger Amount	Voucher Narration Voucher Amount

Voucher Header

At Voucher Header, you enter the following :

- **Voucher Number**: In automatic voucher numbering system, Tally auto generates voucher number in chronological order, for each Voucher type. In such case, you do not to manually enter Voucher Number.
- **Voucher Date**: The Current Date is carried at this field as Date of Voucher. To change the Voucher Date, press *F2: Date* button. The next Date is carried as default Voucher Date would be shown as Current Date as explained in earlier chapter. You may change it as needed. Alternatively, you may press Shift+Tab to get back to the Date field and enter the Voucher Date, without changing the Current Date.

Voucher Ledger Account details

This is a tabular area where each Ledger Transaction data is entered .

- **Ledger Sign:** At first column, Type D (for Debit) or C (for Credit) at first column to indicate Debit or Credit the ledger that you select at *Particulars* Column. The Debit or Credit nature of the first Ledger Account in the Voucher is pre-determined by Tally according to Voucher Type. So, you have to enter D/C only from second entry onwards.

- **Ledger Account:** At Particulars field, select the Ledger Account from List of Ledgers pop-up.
- **Ledger Amount:** As per Dr/Cr entry in the first column, the cursor would move to Debit or Credit column. Type the Amount for the Ledger Account.

New Ledger Accounts creation during voucher entry: During voucher entry, if the ledger account to be transacted is not yet created, press Alt+C at the ledger account (Particulars) column to get Ledger Accounts entry screen, without exiting from the current voucher. Now create the new ledger account as usual (F-4A / F-5B / F-6B). You will get back the voucher entry screen at the same point. Select the ledger account in the voucher entry screen.

This way, you may enter many Debit and Credit entries in a voucher. The Ledger entries will be terminated as soon as the total of *Debit* and *Credit* is equal.

Voucher Narration

Enter Voucher Narration, describing the voucher transactions briefly (upto 3 lines), but writing the essential details for future reference.

Saving Voucher Data: After complete entry of the voucher, you get *Save Y/N* box to save the voucher,

- **Saving the Voucher:** Press <Enter> or type Y at Accept*? Yes or No* to save the voucher. The current voucher will be saved.

  To modify any data before saving, type N (or No) to go back to the top field, edit as desired and then save the voucher.

- **Quit without Saving:** To close the voucher entry screen without saving the current voucher being entered, press *Q: Quit* button at the bottom of the screen (or press Ctrl+Q).
- **Quick Saving:** To save the current voucher quickly (without confirmation), press *A: Accept* button at the bottom of the screen (or press Ctrl+A).

Continuing Voucher Entry: After saving the current voucher, a blank Voucher entry screen would appear to continue voucher entry. To terminate voucher entry, press <Esc>. Type *Yes* at *Quit? Yes or No.* to quit . To enter any other type of Voucher, click the respective voucher type button.

Voucher के Header में Voucher Number और Voucher Date entry होता है। Ledger Details section में हर Ledger Account और Amount (Debit / Credit) entry होती है। Voucher के अंत में पूरे Voucher का विवरण (Narration) entry किया जाता है।

Voucher Entry के दौरान, गैर-मौजूदा (Non – existing) Ledger Account (यानि जो Ledger Account create नहीं है), create करने के लिए, Alt+C press कर, उस Ledger Account को भी create कर Voucher entry पूरा कर सकते हैं।

05 Voucher Alteration & Deletion

To *View / Alter or Delete* any saved Voucher, select *Day Book*, Click *F2:Date* (if you know the voucher date) or *F2:Period*. Enter the Voucher Date (at *F2:Date* prompt) or the Period (at *F2:Period* prompt) to get the list of the Vouchers (Day Book) for the selected Voucher Type for the selected Date / Period. At Day Book, drill down through the desired voucher (place the cursor on the voucher record and double click or press <enter>) to get the Voucher Alteration screen (similar to voucher entry screen). At Voucher Alteration screen:

- **Voucher Alteration:** Take the cursor on the desired field and make necessary alteration of data, as desired.
- **Voucher Deletion:** Press Alt+D and type Y to confirm deletion of the voucher. (you can view the entire voucher before confirming deletion)

Voucher entry के बाद Voucher में कोई alteration के लिए Day Book या दूसरे Report से drill down कर Voucher select करे। Voucher के Data Alter करे (जिस तरह data entry किया गया है), और Voucher save करे। Voucher Deletion के लिए Voucher Alteration screen में Alt+D press करे और Yes type कर Deletion confirm करे।

06 Dormant Vouchers

We have so far discussed about vouchers which makes immediate effect in accounts. So, the entry is reflected immediately in ledger accounts, Trial Balance, Final Accounts etc. However, tally provides following Dormant vouchers, which do not affect the accounts immediately.

– **Optional (L:Optional):** These voucher are created to make provisional entry, to be regularized later on. Click L:Optional toggle button to convert to Optional and vice versa

– **Post Dated (T:Post dated):** Entered in advance of the date of transaction. Often traders give post dated cheques, which are regularized when Banked. Click T:Post Dated toggle button to convert to Post dated and vice versa

Tally में Regular Voucher entry होते ही उसका effect Reports में automatic मिलेगा। कोई Posting की जरूरत नहीं। Optional Voucher को Regular me परिवर्तित करने के बाद ही उसका effect रिर्पोट में मिलेगा। Outstanding Report में Post Dated Voucher का Information दिखता है; लेकिन Post dated Voucher को Regular में परिवर्तन के बाद ही उसका effect Report में मिलेगा।

07 Single Mode Voucher Entry

You may, alternatively enter Cash Vouchers (Receipt, Payment & Contra) in Single Mode. As explained earlier, at Voucher Entry screen click *H:Change Mode* and select *Single Entry / Accounting Invoice* from the list of options.

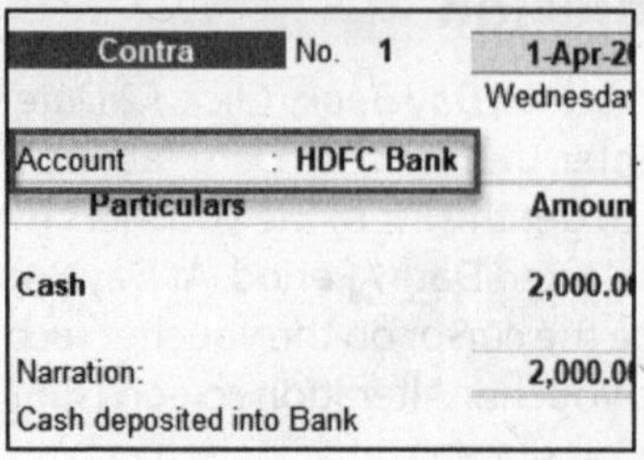

F-12A: Contra Voucher-Single Mode Entry

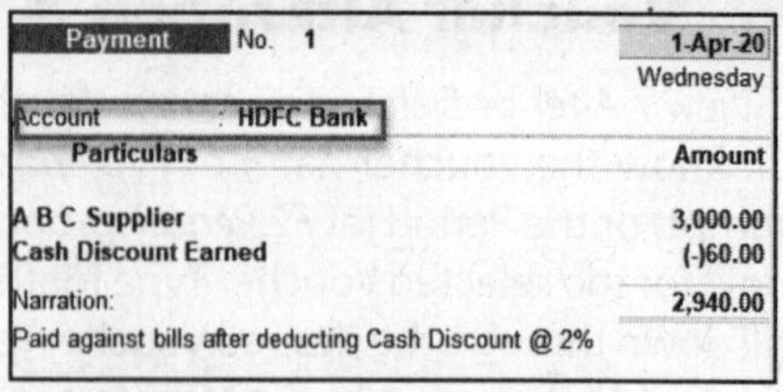

F-12B: Payment Voucher-Single Mode Entry

In Single Mode, enter Cash / Bank Account in Header and other Accounts in detail line. There is no Debit / Credit column in Single mode voucher entry. Tally internally sets the Dr / Cr sign for each entry according to the position (Header / Detail Line) and Voucher Types (F-12A to F-12C). So, Single Mode is easier to understand by Non Accountants.

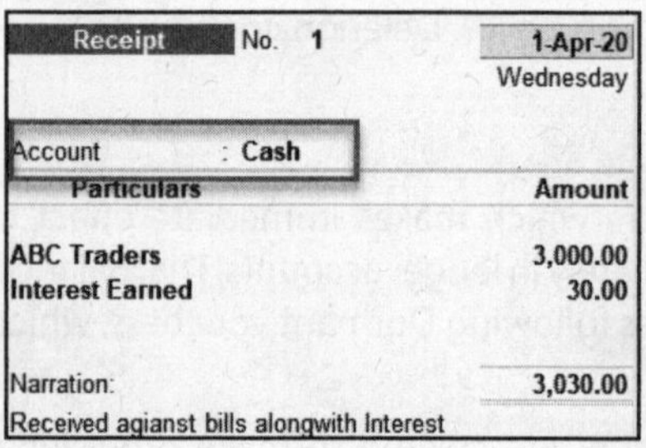

F-12C: Receipt Voucher-Single Mode Entry

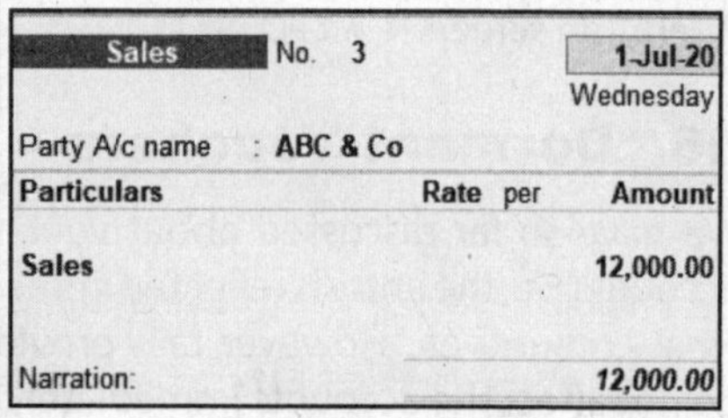

F-12D: Sales Voucher as Accounting Invoice

Tally stores the voucher in same manner, whether entered in Normal or Single Mode. You may edit / display a voucher in any mode, irrespective of the mode in which the voucher was created.

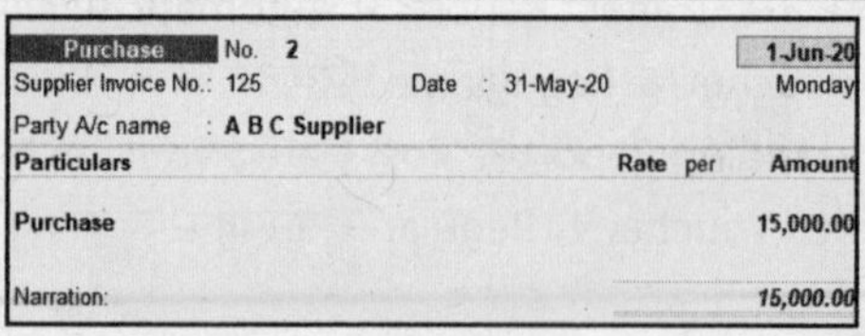

F-12E: Purchase Voucher as Accounting Invoice

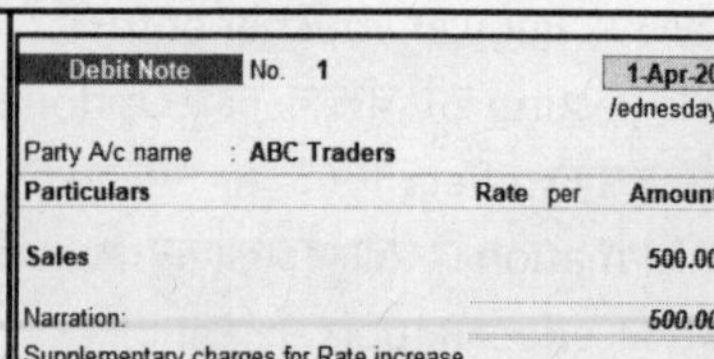

F-12F: Debit Note as Accounting Invoice

Single Mode Voucher entry Non-Accountants के लिए समझने में सरल है क्योंकि इसमें Debit Credit नहीं होता (F-12A to F-12F)। इसलिए, Single Mode entry का प्रचलन हुआ

है। Voucher entry चाहे Dr / Cr mode में हो, या Single Mode में, उसका Accounting effect एक ही है।

Single Entry mode के लिए Voucher entry screen में H:Change Mode click कर Single Entry (Payment, Receipt, Contra Voucher के लिए) / Accounting Invoice (Sale , Purchase, Debit Note, Credit Note) के लिए select करे।

08 Account Vouchers - Key Points

- सारे Accounts Voucher entry एक ही जैसे है। Voucher entry screen में अपने Hot key से Voucher type के अनुसार voucher entry करे।
- Tally द्वारा create किए गए voucher type उपयोग कर Voucher entry करे. जरूरत के अनुसार, Tally created Voucher Type के नया voucher type create कर, entry कर सकते हैं।
- Automatic numbering system में, हर voucher type में अपने serial से Tally द्वारा Voucher का Number हो जाता है। इसलिए, Back date का Voucher Delete या Insert करने से, उसके बाद date के सारे voucher number अपने आप change हो सकते हैं। इसे ध्यान रखे और Tally के इस विचित्र system को पहले से अच्छी तरह समझ ले, ताकि आपको परेशानी न हो। Back Date का Voucher Date change न करे, Back Date का voucher Delete न करे (Voucher Cancel करे, ताकि Voucher Number change न हो!)।
- Single Entry / Accounting Invoice me में Debit / Credit column नहीं होता। एक mode में entry कर दूसरे mode में voucher open कर सकते हैं; क्योंकि किसी भी mode में entry करे , Tally के अंदर Voucher data, एक ही तरह save होगा।
- Sales, Purchase, Debit और Credit Note voucher, As Voucher या Accounting Invoice mode में entry कर सकते हैं। As Voucher mode entry में हर Ledger Account के amount Debit या Credit column में entry होता है। Accounting Invoice mode में Debit / Credit column नहीं होता। Party (या Cash /Bank) Ledger Account header में entry होता है, बाकी सभी Ledger Account details area में entry होते हैं।

Accounts Reports 01-05

01 Accounts Reports Menu

As soon as you enter a voucher, its effect is immediately reflected in the respective places and you may view any report on screen or print on paper at any point of time to get the updated figures.

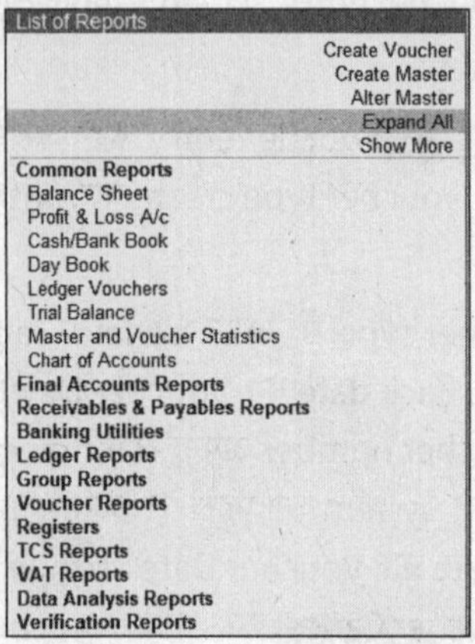

F-1A: Go-To menu Reports

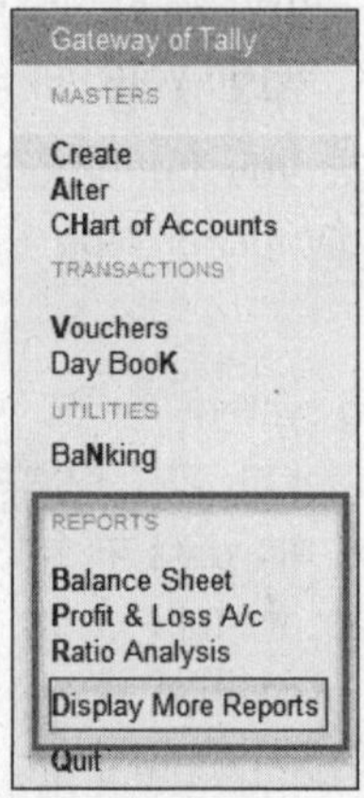

F-2A: Main Menu Reports

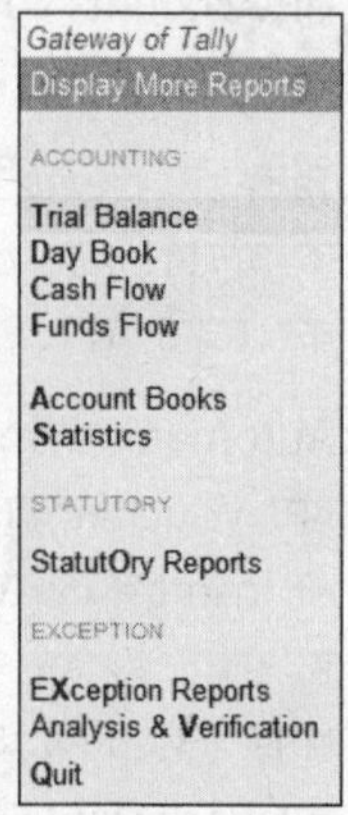

F-2B:Display Menu Reports

- **GoTo Report list:** To access any report, click on Go To option in GoT, to get the list of Main Reports. To get list of all Reports, click *Expand All* option at the top right of the Menu List (F-1A).
- **Reports Menu:** You may also access Reports from GoT Menu. The top level reports like Balance Sheet, Profit & Loss Statement, Ratio Analysis, etc. and Day Book, are available at *Main Menu* of Gateway of Tally (F-2A). Click *Display More Reports* to get sub menu for all other reports (F-2B). Click on the respective option in the sub menu.

Reports Drill Down & Trace Back: From any on-screen report, press <enter>at any record to drill down, level-by-level to view the intermediary reports and ultimately reach to the vouchers list (you may also edit any selected Voucher therefrom). Press <Esc> key to trace back (to the higher level report) in the same path through which you drilled down.

ERP 9 की तरह Prime में भी Main Menu से काम करे (F-2A)। सारे Masters और Voucher Entry option सिर्फ Main menu में ही है (F-2A / F-3B)। लेकिन Main Menu (F-2A / F-3B) या Go To Tabs (F-1A), दोनों जगह से Reports पा सकते है। एक साथ कई Reports open रख सकते हैं और Open Reports switch कर सकते हैं (F-1A)।

02 Reports Printing

At any Menu screen, Click P:Print button at the top menu bar (or Alt+P) to get Print Menu with following options (F-3A):

– **Others:** To select any other Report for printing
– **Configuration:** To set Report Printing General Configuration (F-4B). The options set would be applicable to all Reports for the Company. Select the option (F-4A) and press <enter> to change the values (Yes / No values are toggled and changed)

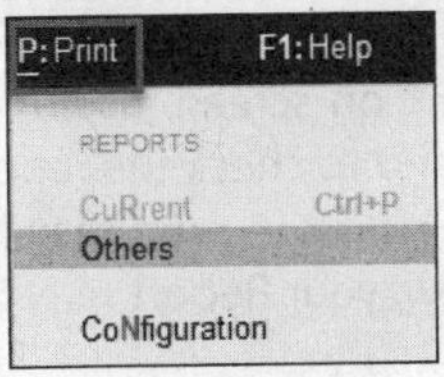

F-3A: Print Menu options

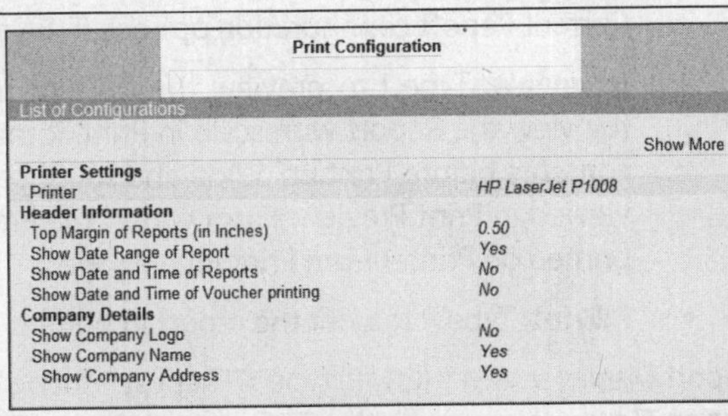

F-4A: General Printing Configuration

– Print Menu (F-3A) से Other option(F-3A) से Report select कर selected Report Print करे (F-6A)। Configuration option (F-3A) से General Configuration set करे (F-4A)।
– कोई भी Report Display में F12 : Configuration से current report का Display Configuration मिलेगा। हर Report का Display Configuration options अलग है हर Report Display में उस Report के Display Configuration show किए है।

03 Printing of Selected Report

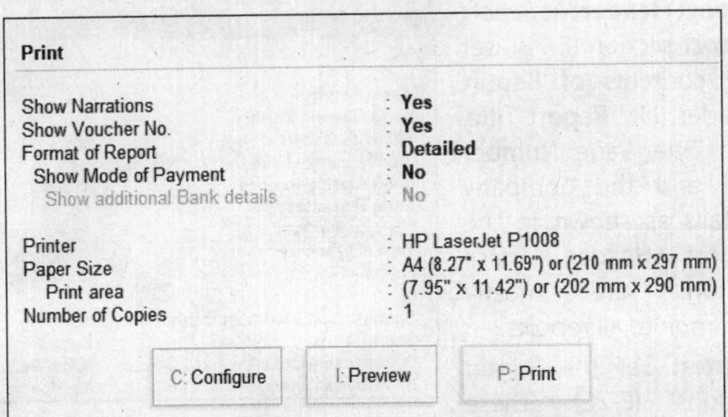

F-5A: Selected Report Printing options

At the current Report display screen, click (Ctl+P) to get Current Report Printing screen (F-5A), having 2 sections:

- **Important Configuration Options Display:** The current configuration main options as set at display configuration are displayed for info. To change the options, click C:Configure button as explained next
- **Buttons:** Below the important configuration options, the following buttons appear:
  - **C:Configure:** Type C or click F12:Configure button (or press F12) to set Current Report configuration options (F-6A to F-6C).
  - **I:Preview:** Type I to preview the Current report on screen, useful to the view the Report with scale in Print Format and to check the report contents before Printing. Wide and multi page report in print may be viewed in Print Preview. From within the Preview, your Report may be printed on Printer from Print Preview also.
  - **P:Print:** Type P to print the report in printer.

Report Display screen में (Ctl+P) type कर Report Printing screen (F-5A) से C:Configure button से current report printing का Configuration set करे, I:preview button से Report preview करे, P:print button से Report printer में print करे।

04 Current Report Printing Configuration

At Current report printing screen click *C:Configure* button or click *F12:Configure* button (or press F12) to get Current Report Configuration screen, which may be broadly divided into following sections (F-6A to F-6C):

– **Report Details:** At *Report Details* section (F-7A), set the options to configure the detail contents of the report. These options are report specific and vary according to the selected report.

– **Report Header:** At *Report Header* section (F-7B), set the contents of Report Header (like Report Title, Sub Title, Page Number etc) and the Company Details as shown in the Report Header. These options are mostly common to all reports.

– **Printer:** Set the Printer options (F-7C). These options are mostly common to all reports.

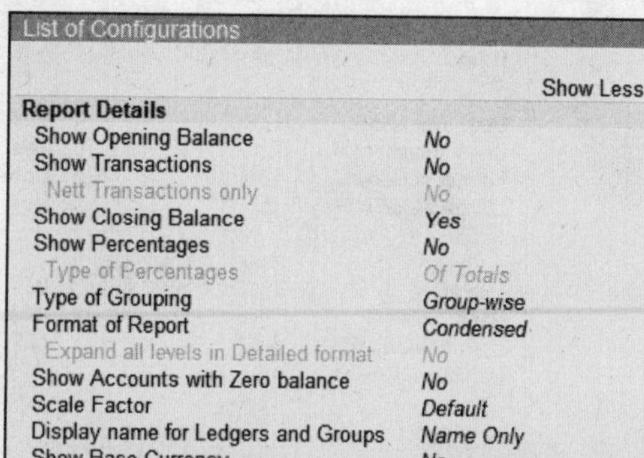

F-6A: Report Details set up

–

Header Information	
Title	Trial Balance
Subtitle (if any)	
Show Page Number	Yes
Company Details	
Show Company Name	Yes
Show Company Address	Yes
Type of Address	♦ Primary
Show Phone No.	No
Show Website	No
Show CIN	No

F-6B: Report Header set up

Printer Settings	
Print Format	Neat Mode
Printer	HP LaserJet P1008
Paper Type	Plain Paper
Show Language	English
Number of copies	1
Number to start from first page	1
Page Range	All

F-6C: Printer set up

Report Printing screen में C:Configure button click कर (या C type कर), या F12:Configure button click कर (या F12 type कर), Current Report Configuration (F-6A to F-6C) set करे।

05 Account Reports - Key Points

- **Report Display:** कुछ खास report (जैसे Balance Sheet, P L Statement, Ratio Analysis) का option GoT Main menu में मिलेंगे. बाकी सभी Reports GoT के Display More Reports option के Sub Menus से मिलेंगे।
- **Current Report Display Configuration:** कोई भी Reports Display screen में F12:Configure click कर उस Report के Display configuration set करे।
- **Reports Printing General Configuration:** कोई भी menu screen में Alt+P type कर Configuration option से Report Printing General Configuration set करे, जो सारे Report पर applicable होगा।
- **Current Report Printing options:** कोई भी Report Display screen में Ctl+P type कर Current Report Printing options के button से:

- **Current Report Printing Configuration:** C: Configure button से current report का printing Configuration set करे, जो Current Report के लिए applicable होगा।
- **Current Report Print Preview:** I: Preview button से Print Preview में scale के साथ Report view करे, Long report pan / scroll करे, Report Zoom कर view करे, Print link से Report Printer पर Print करे।
- **Current Report Printing:** P:Print button से Current Report Printer में print करे।

Report Display में F12:Configure set कर Report के contents set करे। Display में F12: Configure से set किया हुआ option Report Printing screen में carry होता है। Report printing screen के C:Configure button का Configuration बहुत ही लम्बा और complicated है; उससे हर Report configure करना आसान नहीं है; इसलिए Report Display के F12:Configuration से option set करे. *C:Configure* button, सिर्फ खास जरूरत पर ही click करें।

Cash Bank Book 01-06

01 Cash / Bank Book Display

Cash / Bank Book (normally referred as *Cash Book*) is a special composite Journal Book cum Cash / Bank Account Ledger Book, containing chronological records of all Receipts & Payments during the period & Closing Balance of Cash / Bank Account (like a Ledger Book).

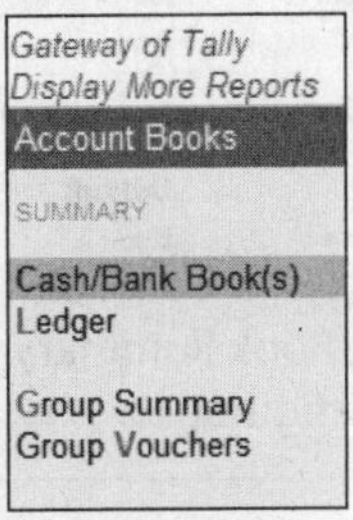

F-1A: Cash/ Bank Book from GoT>Display> Accounts Books

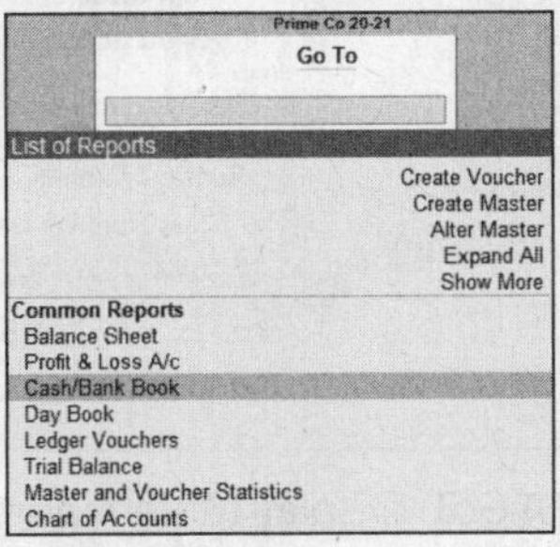

F-2A: Cash/Bank Book from GoTo Menu

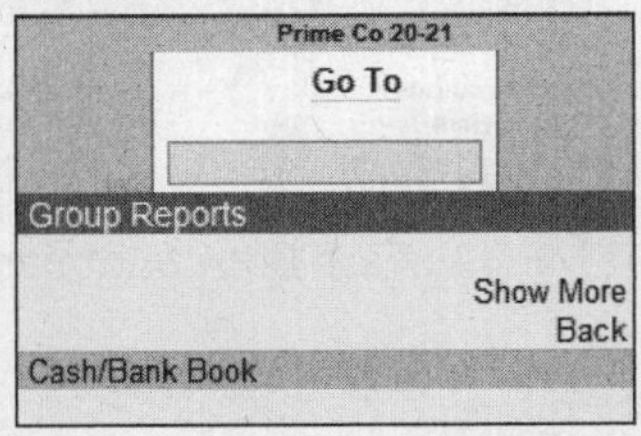

F-2B: Cash/Bank Book from GoTo>Group Reports list

Accessing Cash / Bank Books: Cash/ Bank Books may be accessed from GoT Main Menu or from GoTo Menu, as explained earlier.

- **GoT Main Menu:** Select *GoT>Display More Reports>Account Books* to get Accounts Book Menu. Select Cash / Bank Books to get list of Cash / Bank Accounts to display respective Cash / Bank Book
- **Go To Menu Bar:**
  - From GoTo Reports list, select *Cash / Bank Book* and then select the desired Cash Bank Account
  - From GoTo Reports list, select *Group Reports> Cash / Bank Book* and then select the desired Cash Bank Account

Cash / Bank Summary: The first screen shows the summary of each of the Cash Bank Accounts (Cash Bank Summary : F-3A)

- At Cash Bank Summary (F-3A), Click F12:Configure and set the Cash Bank Summary Configuration options (F-3B). At Cash Bank Summary (F-3A), click on (Drill down) any Cash or Bank Account to get Ledger Monthly

Summary (Ledger Monthly Summary) for the selected Cash / Bank Account

- At Ledger Monthly Summary, select a month to display Cash/Bank Account for the selected month
- Click *F2:Period* and set the Period to get the Cash Book for the desired period (F-4A)

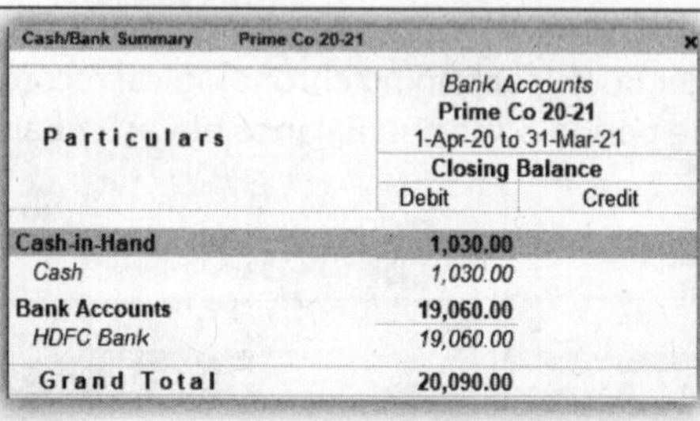

F-3A : Cash Book Summary Dislplay

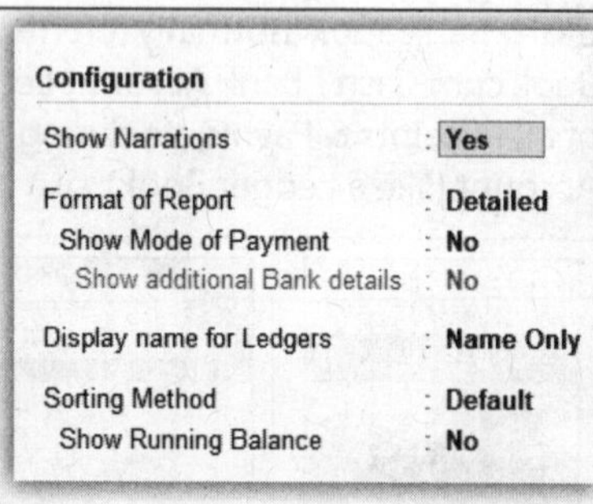

F-3B: Cash/Bank Book Summary Display Configuration

Cash/ Bank Book Report के लिए GoT>Display More reports>Accounts Books> Cash Bank Book, या Go To>Cash Bank Book>Group Reports>Cash/ Bank Books select करे (F-2A / F-2B)। पहले Cash / Bank Summary मिलेगा।

02 Contents of Cash / Bank Book

The Cash Book (Ledger Voucher) display shows the following details, for the selected Cash / Bank Account (F-4A).

- **Voucher Details:** All transactions involving the selected Cash / Bank account, and complementary Ledger accounts in the voucher
- **Opening Balance:** Opening Balance of Cash & Bank Accounts for the specified period, at the bottom of the Report
- **Current Total:** Total of debits / Credits of the transaction for the selected period, in respective Debit / Credit column
- **Closing Balance:** Closing balance for the end of the period, either in the Debit / Credit column, as per computed Closing Balance (normally at Debit column for Cash & Bank Accounts, Credit column for Bank OCC/OD Accounts).

Additional details are displayed as per configuration options set.

Ledger Vouchers Prime Co 20-21

Ledger: **Cash** 1-Apr-20 to 30-Apr-20

Date	Particulars		Vch Type	Vch No.	Debit	Credit
1-Apr-20	**HDFC Bank**		**Contra**	1		**2,000.00**
	Cash deposited into Bank					
1-Apr-20	**(as per details)**		**Receipt**	1	**3,030.00**	
	ABC Traders	**3,000.00 Cr**				
	Interest Earned	**30.00 Cr**				
	Received agianst bills alongwith Interest					
				Opening Balance :		
				Current Total :	**3,030.00**	**2,000.00**
				Closing Balance :	**1,030.00**	

F-4A: Cash / Bank Book Display

Report Display में Cash Bank Book के नाम का कोई report नहीं है। Cash Bank Account के Ledger Voucher display (F-4A) ही Cash Bank Book के जैसे हैं।

Cash / Bank Summary Dsiplay (F-3A) से Cash / Bank Ledger Account select करे; Selected Cash / Bank Account के monthly summary मिलेगा (F-3A)। उससे month select करे. Selected month के Ledger Voucher list मिलेगा (F-4A), जिसे Tally में Cash Bank Book कहा जाता है; Selected period के Cash Bank Book के लिए F2:Period set करे. Cash Bank Book असल में Cash Bank Ledger Report की तरह ही है।

03 Cash Bank Book Printing

At Cash / Bank Book Display (F-4A), Click *P:Print* button to get Cash / Bank Book Printing screen (F-5A). Click C:Configure (to set Printing Configuration options / I:preview (to preview the Report on screen) / P:Print (to preview the Report on screen : F-5B)

Print

Report Type	: **Ledger Accounts**
Show Narrations	: **Yes**
Show Voucher No.	: **Yes**
Format of Report	: **Detailed**
Show Mode of Payment	: **No**
Show additional Bank details	: **No**
Printer	: HP LaserJet P1008
Paper Size	: A4 (8.27" x 11.69") or (210 mm x 297 mm)
Print area	: (7.95" x 11.42") or (202 mm x 290 mm)
Number of Copies	: 1

C: Configure | I: Preview | P: Print

F-5A: Cash / Bank Book Printing

The printed Format of Cash / Bank Book shows Opening Balance at the beginning, followed by transactions and finally the Totals / Closing Balance (F-5B), while in Display format, the Transactions are shown first and Totals / Balance shown at the end (F-4A).

Prime Co

HDFC Bank Book

1-Apr-20 to 30-Apr-20

Page 1

Date		Particulars	Vch Type		Vch No.	Debit	Credit
1-Apr-20	Cr	**Opening Balance**				**20,000.00**	
1-Apr-20	Cr	**Cash** *Cash deposited into Bank*	**Contra**		1	2,000.00	
	Dr	**(as per details)** **A B C Supplier** **Cash Discount Earned** *Paid against bills after deducting Cash Discount @ 2%*	**Payment**	 **3,000.00 Dr** **60.00 Cr**	1		2,940.00
	Cr	**(as per details)** **ABC Traders** **Interest Earned** *Received agianst bills alongwith Interest*	**Receipt**	 **3,000.00 Cr** **30.00 Cr**	1	3,030.00	
						25,030.00	2,940.00
	Dr	**Closing Balance**					22,090.00
						25,030.00	**25,030.00**

F-5B: Cash / Bank Book in Print

जैसे कि Report Printing में बताया गया है, Cash Bank Ledger Voucher report (F-4A) में Ctl+P Type कर Cash / Bank Book Printing (F-5A) से (C:Configure) कर (F-5B) P:Print button से Printer में Cash Bank Book Print करे (F-5B)।

04 Cash Bank Book - Key Points

- Cash / Bank Book एक तरह का Cash / Bank Account Ledger Book ही है; इसलिए, Cash Bank Book को Ledger Book option से भी Print कर सकते है।
- Display Format में Cash / Bank Account के Ledger Voucher दिखता है, जिसमें पहले Transactions दिखता है, Total और Closing Balance last में दिखता है. लेकिन Print Format में सही तरीके से Opening Balance, फिर Transactions और अंत में Total / Closing Balance दिखता है।

Journal Books 01-07

01 Journal Books

Journal Books show list of Non-Cash Vouchers (other than Contra, Payment & Receipt vouchers). Here we discuss about following types of Journal Books:

- **Journal Register:** List of Journal Vouchers (Journal Proper : F-2B / F-3B)
- **Purchase Register:** List of Purchase Vouchers (F-6B/ F-7B)
- **Debit Note Register:** List of Debit Note Vouchers (F-4B/ F-5B)
- **Debit Note Register:** List of Debit Note Vouchers (F-8B/ F-9B)
- **Credit Note Register:** List of Credit Note Vouchers (F-10B/ F-11B)

Accessing Journal Books: Journal Books me be accessed as follows:

- **GoT Main Menu:** Select *GoT>Display More Reports>Account Books* to get Accounts Book Menu (F-1A). All types of Journal Books may be displayed from Account Books Menu.
- **Go To Menu Bar:** From GoTo Reports list, select *Register* (F-1B). Select *Show More* to show list of all types of Registers Now select the desired Register from the list (F-1C)

F-1A: Account Books Menu

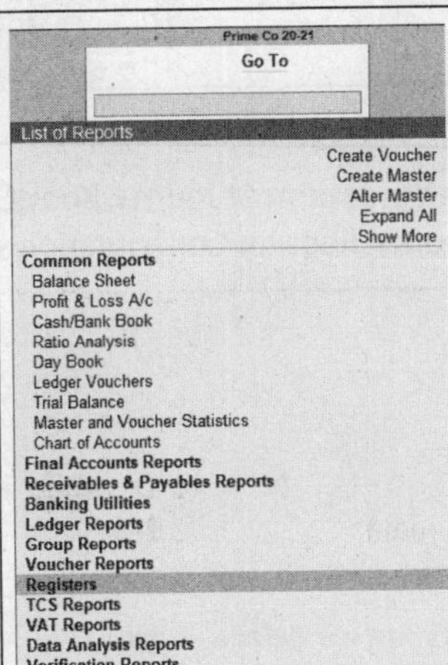

F-1B: Registers option in GoTo Menu

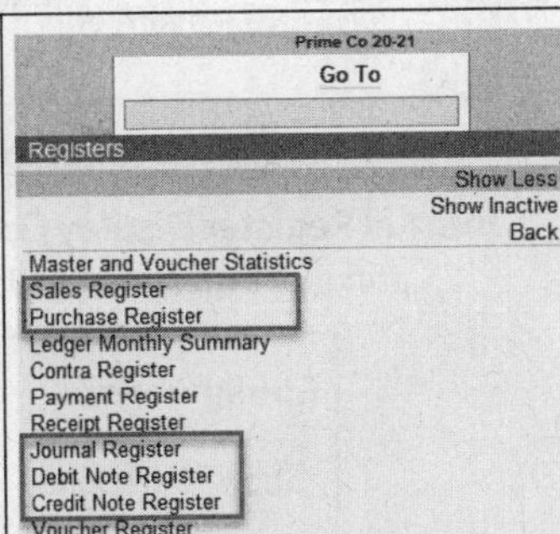

F-1C: Registers in GoTo > Regsiters list

Day Book में हर Type के Voucher होते है। Cash / Bank Account संबंधित Vouchers के अलावा सारे voucher Journal Books के अंतर्गत होते है। काम की सुविधा के लिए, Journal

Book को कई Books में बाँट दिया जाता है (Sales, Purchase, Debit Note, Purchase, Debit Note, Credit Note और Journal Proper : F-1A)। Tally में Journal Proper को Journal Register कहते हैं।

02 Journal Register

Journal Register (also referred as Journal proper), shows the list of Journal Voucher (Non cash Vouchers, i.e other than Contra, Payment & Receipt Voucher), and Non-Trade Vouchers (like Sales, Purchase, Debit Note & Credit Note : F-1A). So, Journal Register contains only Journal Vouchers (Accounting Adjustment vouchers other than Contra, Payment, Receipt, Debit Note, Purchase, Debit Note & Credit Note vouchers).

- **Journal Register Display**: On selection of Journal Register (F-1A / F-1C) as explained, you get Journal Register showing the monthwise voucher numbers / Amount figures. Drill down through any month to get list of Journal Vouchers for the selected month. Click *Alt+F2* and enter the period to get the Journal Register showing list of all Journal Vouchers for the specified period (F-2B).

Voucher Register — Prime Co 20-21

List of All Journal Vouchers — 1-Mar-21 to 31-Mar-21

Date	Particulars		Vch Type	Vch No.	Debit Amount	Credit Amount
31-Mar-21	**Depreciation**		**Journal**	1	2,000.00	
	Furniture	2,000.00 Cr				
	Depreciation on 20000 @10%					
				Total:	2,000.00	

F-2B: Journal Regsiter Display

- **Journal Register Display Configuration:** At Journal Book Display (F-2B), click *F12:Configure* button to get Journal Regsiter Configuration screen (F-2A).

Configuration

Show Narrations	: **Yes**
Format of Report	: **Detailed**
Show Mode of Payment	: **No**
Show additional Bank details	: No
Show Supplementary Invoice details	: **No**
Display name for Ledgers	: **Name Only**
Sorting Method	: **Default**

F-2A:Journal Register Configuration

- **Journal Register Printing:** At *Journal Book Display* (F-1A), press Ctrl+P to get Journal Register Printing screen (F-3A). Set the options (mostly similar to Journal Book Configuration screen (F-2A). Click P:Print button (or type P) to print Journal Register (F-3B).

Print

Report Type	: **Vouchers**
Show Narrations	: **Yes**
Show Voucher No.	: **Yes**
Format of Report	: **Detailed**
Show Mode of Payment	: **No**
Show additional Bank details	: **No**
Printer	: HP LaserJet P1008
Paper Size	: A4 (8.27" x 11.69") or (210 mm x 297 mm)
Print area	: (7.95" x 11.42") or (202 mm x 290 mm)
Number of Copies	: 1

C: Configure | I: Preview | P: Print

F-3A: Journal Register Printing

Journal Register
1-Mar-21 to 31-Mar-21

Page 1

Date	Particulars	Vch Type	Vch No.	Debit Amount	Credit Amount
31-Mar-21	**Depreciation**	**Journal**	1	**2,000.00**	
	Furniture				**2,000.00**
	Depreciation on 20000 @10%				
			Total:	**2,000.00**	

F-3B: Journal Register in Print

03 Sales Register

Like Journal Register, Sales Register (F-4B) is chronological list of Sales Vouchers for the specified period.

- **Sales Register Display:** At Account Books Menu (F-1A) / Go To Tab (F-1C), select *Sales Register* to get Sales Register showing the Monthly Summary. Drill down through any month to get Sales Register showing list of Sales Voucher for the selected month. Click Alt+F2, set the Period to get the Sales Register showing list of Sales Vouchers for the specified period (F-4B).

Voucher Register — Prime Co 20-21

List of All Sales Vouchers — 1-Apr-20 to 30-Apr-20

Date	Particulars		Vch Type	Vch No.	Debit Amount	Credit Amount
1-Apr-20	**ABC Traders**		**Sales**	1	**15,000.00**	
	Sales	**15,000.00 Cr**				
	Goods sold to the party on Credit					
				Total:	**15,000.00**	

F-4B: Sales Register Display

- **Sales Register Display Configuration:** At Sales Register Display, click *F12:Configure* button and set the Configuration options (F-4A) for Sales Register Display (F-4A).

Configuration

		List of Formats
Show Narrations	: **Yes**	
Format of Report	: **Detailed**	Condensed
Show Mode of Payment	: **No**	Detailed
Show additional Bank details	: No	
Show Supplementary Invoice details	: **No**	
Display name for Ledgers	: **Name Only**	
Sorting Method	: **Default**	

F-4A:Sales Register Display Configuration

- **Sales Register Printing:** At *Sales Register Display* (F-4B), press Ctrl+P to get Sales Register Printing screen (F-5A). Click *C:Configure* (to set Printing Configuration) / *I:Preview* (to Preview the Print Report on screen) / *P:Print* button (to print Sales Register on Printer :F-5B).

Print

Report Type	: **Vouchers**
Show Narrations	: **Yes**
Show Voucher No.	: **Yes**
Format of Report	: **Detailed**
Show Mode of Payment	: **No**
Show additional Bank details	: No
Printer	: HP LaserJet P1008
Paper Size	: A4 (8.27" x 11.69") or (210 mm x 297 mm)
Print area	: (7.95" x 11.42") or (202 mm x 290 mm)
Number of Copies	: 1

C: Configure | I: Preview | P: Print

F-5A: Sales Register Printing

Sales Register
1-Apr-20 to 30-Apr-20

Page 1

Date	Particulars	Vch Type	Vch No.	Debit Amount	Credit Amount
1-Apr-20	**ABC Traders**	**Sales**	1	**15,000.00**	
	Sales				**15,000.00**
	Goods sold to the party on Credit				
			Total:	**15,000.00**	

F-5B: Sales Register in Print

04 Purchase Register

Like Sales Register, Purchase Register shows chronological list of Purchase Vouchers for the specified period.

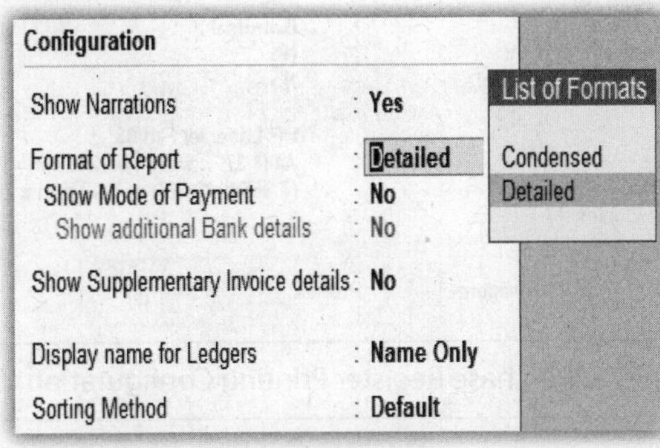

F-6A: Purchase Register Display Configuration

- **Purchase Register Display:** At Account Books Menu (F-1A) / Go To Tab (F-1C), select *Purchase Register* to get Purchase Register showing the Monthly Summary. Drill down through any month to get Purchase Register showing list of Purchase Voucher for the selected month. Set the Period (F2) to get the Purchase Register showing list of Purchase Vouchers for the specified period (F-6B).

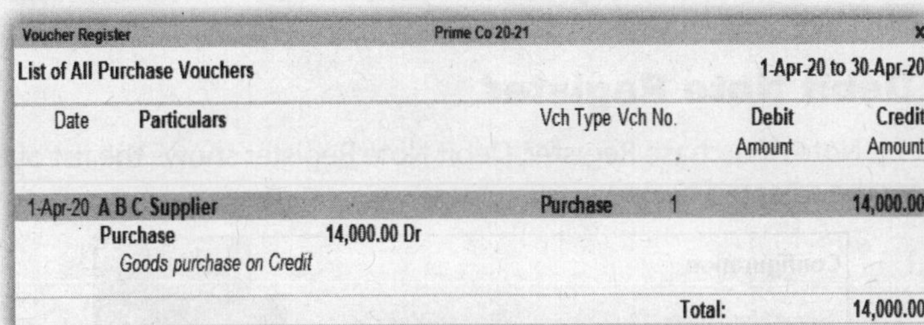

F-6B:Purchase Register Display

- **Purchase Register Display Configuration:** At Purchase Register Display, click F12:Configure button, and set the Configuration options (F-6A) for Purchase Register Display (F-6B).

- **Purchase Register Printing:** At Purchase Register *Display*, press Ctrl+P to get Purchase Register Printing screen (F-7A). Click *C:Configure* (to set Printing Configuration) / *I:Preview* (to Preview the Print Report on screen) / *P:Print* button (to print Purchase Register on Printer :F-7B).

Print

Report Type	: **Vouchers**
Show Narrations	: **Yes**
Show Voucher No.	: **Yes**
Format of Report	: **Detailed**
Show Mode of Payment	: **No**
Show additional Bank details	: No
Printer	: HP LaserJet P1008
Paper Size	: A4 (8.27" x 11.69") or (210 mm x 297 mm)
Print area	: (7.95" x 11.42") or (202 mm x 290 mm)
Number of Copies	: 1

C: Configure | I: Preview | P: Print

F-7A: Purchase Register Printing Configuration

Purchase Register
1-Apr-20 to 30-Apr-20

Page 1

Date	Particulars	Vch Type	Vch No.	Debit Amount	Credit Amount
1-Apr-20	**A B C Supplier**	**Purchase**	1		**14,000.00**
	Purchase			**14,000.00**	
	Goods purchase on Credit				
			Total:		**14,000.00**

F-7B: Purchase Register in Print

05 Debit Note Register

Like Debit Note / Purchase Register, Debit Note Register shows the list of Debit Notes for the selected period.

Configuration

Show Narrations	: **Yes**
Format of Report	: **Detailed**
Show Mode of Payment	: **No**
Show additional Bank details	: **No**
Show Supplementary Invoice details	: **No**
Display name for Ledgers	: **Name Only**
Sorting Method	: **Default**

List of Formats: Condensed, Detailed

F-8A: Debit Note Register Display Configuration

– **Debit Note Register Display:** At Account Books Menu (F-1A) / Go To Tab (F-1C), select *Debit Note Register* to get Debit Note Register showing Monthly Number of Voucher Statistics. Drill down through any month to get Debit Note Register showing list of Debit Note Voucher for the selected month. Set the Period (F2) to get the Debit Note Register showing list of Debit Note Vouchers for the specified period (F-8B).

Voucher Register — Prime Co 20-21

List of All Debit Note Vouchers — 1-Apr-20 to 30-Apr-20

Date	Particulars		Vch Type	Vch No.	Debit Amount	Credit Amount
1-Apr-20	ABC Traders		Debit Note	1	500.00	
	Sales	500.00 Cr				
	Supplementary charges for Rate increase					
				Total:	500.00	

F-8B: Debit Note Register Display

- **Debit Note Register Display Configuration:** At Debit Note Register Display (F-8B), click F12:Configure button, and set the Configuration options (F-8A) for Debit Note Register Display (F-8B).
- **Debit Note Register Printing:** At Debit Note Register *Display*, press Ctrl+P to get Debit Note Register Printing screen (F-9A). Click *C:Configure* (to set Printing Configuration) / *I:Preview* (to Preview the Print Report on screen) / *P:Print* button (to print Debit Note Register on Printer :F-9B).

Print

Report Type	: **Vouchers**
Show Narrations	: **Yes**
Show Voucher No.	: **Yes**
Format of Report	: **Detailed**
Show Mode of Payment	: **No**
Show additional Bank details	: **No**
Printer	: HP LaserJet P1008
Paper Size	: A4 (8.27" x 11.69") or (210 mm x 297 mm)
Print area	: (7.95" x 11.42") or (202 mm x 290 mm)
Number of Copies	: 1

C: Configure | I: Preview | P: Print

F-9A: Debit Note Register Printing Configuration

Debit Note Register

1-Apr-20 to 30-Apr-20

Page 1

Date	Particulars	Vch Type	Vch No.	Debit Amount	Credit Amount
1-Apr-20	ABC Traders	Debit Note	1	500.00	
	Sales				500.00
	Supplementary charges for Rate increase				
			Total:	500.00	

F-9B: Debit Note Register in Print

06 Credit Note Register

Like Debit Note / Purchase Register, Credit Note Register shows the list of Credit Notes for the selected period.

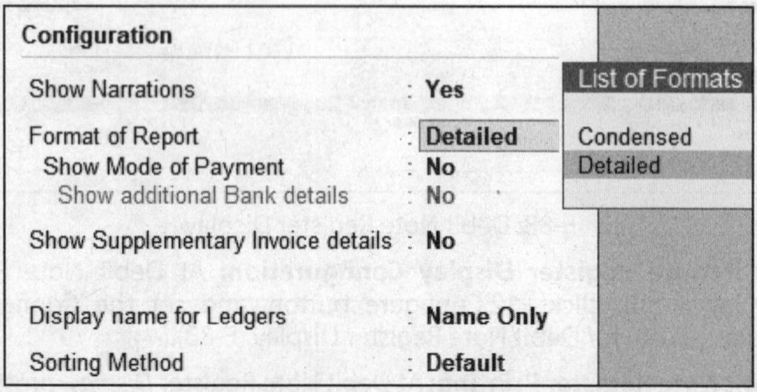

F-10A: Credit Note Register Display Configuration

- **Credit Note Register Display:** At Account Books Menu (F-1A) / Go To Tab (F-1C), select Credit Note Register to get Credit Note Register showing Monthly Number of Voucher Statistics. Drill down through any month to get list of Credit Note Vouchers for the selected month. Click Alt+F2 and enter the period to get Credit Note Register showing list of all Credit Note Vouchers for the specified period (F-10B).

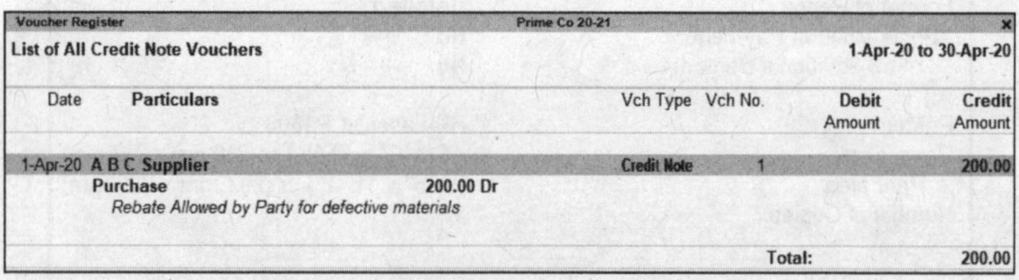
Voucher Register — Prime Co 20-21

List of All Credit Note Vouchers — 1-Apr-20 to 30-Apr-20

Date	Particulars		Vch Type	Vch No.	Debit Amount	Credit Amount
1-Apr-20	A B C Supplier		Credit Note	1		200.00
	Purchase	200.00 Dr				
	Rebate Allowed by Party for defective materials					
				Total:		200.00

F-10B:Credit Note Register Display

- **Credit Note Register Display Configuration:** At Credit Note Register Display (F-10B), click F12:Configure button to get Credit Note Register Configuration to set Credit Note Register Display (F-10B)
- **Credit Note Register Printing:** At Credit Note Register *Display* (F-10B), press Ctrl+P to get Credit Note Register Printing screen (F-11A). Click *C:Configure* (to set Printing Configuration) / *I:Preview* (to Preview the Print Report on screen) / *P:Print* button (to print Credit Note Register on Printer :F-11B).

Print

Report Type	: **Vouchers**
Show Narrations	: **Yes**
Show Voucher No.	: **Yes**
Format of Report	: **Detailed**
Show Mode of Payment	: **No**
Show additional Bank details	: No
Printer	: HP LaserJet P1008
Paper Size	: A4 (8.27" x 11.69") or (210 mm x 297 mm)
Print area	: (7.95" x 11.42") or (202 mm x 290 mm)
Number of Copies	: 1

C: Configure | I: Preview | P: Print

F-11A: Credit Note Register Printing Configuration

Credit Note Register
1-Apr-20 to 30-Apr-20
Page 1

Date	Particulars	Vch Type	Vch No.	Debit Amount	Credit Amount
1-Apr-20	**A B C Supplier**	**Credit Note**	**1**		**200.00**
	Purchase			**200.00**	
	Rebate Allowed by Party for defective materials				
			Total:		**200.00**

F-11B: Credit Note Register in Print

07 Journal Books - Key Points

- Journal Register, Debit Note Register और Credit Note Register Display में Register सीधा नहीं मिलता। पहले monthwise Voucher Number statistics मिलता है। फिर सिर्फ selected एक महीना का Register मिलता है। फिर F2 period से selected period का Regsiter मिलेगा। कोई भी Period का Report display करने के लिए पहले कोई month select कर फिर Alt+F2 से period set करना होगा।
- Debit Note Register और Purchase Register Display में पहले monthwise Voucher Summary मिलता है। फिर सिर्फ selected एक महीना का Register मिलता है। फिर F2 period से selected period का Register मिलेगा।
- Journal Books Display में हर Voucher का सिर्फ पहला account का Amount Debit Column में दिखेगा. बाकी सभी account का Amount inner column में Debit / Credit sign के साथ मिलेगा। Credit column में कोई भी figure नहीं दिखेगा. सिर्फ Debit Column का Total दिखेगा (क्योंकि Debit और Credit column का Total बराबर होता है!)।
- Journal Books Print में Debit और Credit column में हर ledger account का amount मिलेगा, लेकिन Total figure सिर्फ एक ही column (Debit या Credit Column) में दिखेगा।

Ledger Book 01-08

01 Ledger Book

Ledger Book is a report of assorted transactions related to a specified ledger account (F-2B). It shows Opening / Closing Balance & Transactions of the ledger account in chronological order, for the specified period.

Accessing Ledger Account: Ledger Account may be accessed from GoT Main Menu or from GoTo Menu, as explained earlier.

- **GoT Main Menu:** Select *GoT>Display More Reports>Account Books>Ledger* (F-1A) and then select the Ledger Account from the list (F-1B)
- **Go To Menu Bar:** Select GoTo>Ledger Vouchers, or select GoTo>Ledger Reports>Ledger Vouchers (F-1C) and then select Ledger account from the list (F-1B)

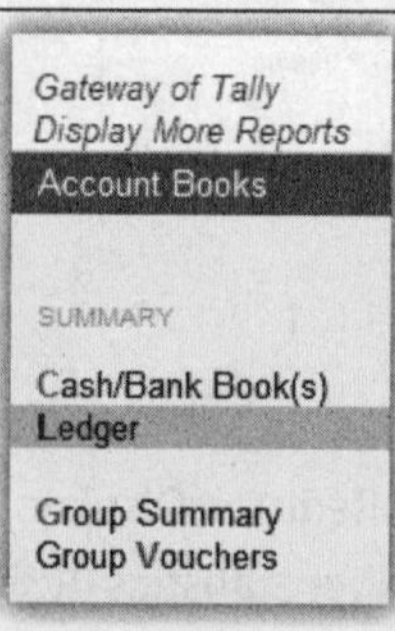

F-1A: Ledger from GoT Main Menu

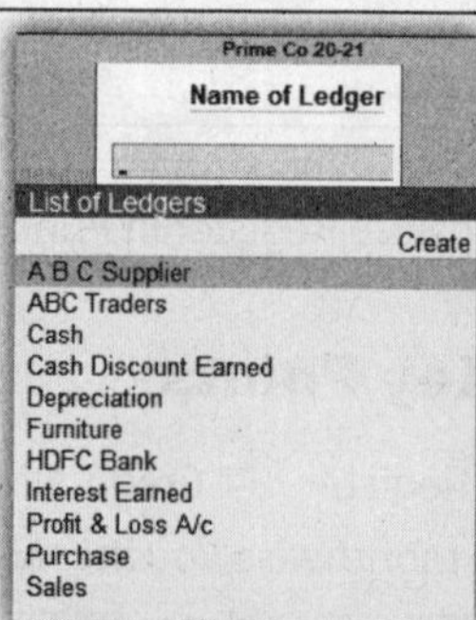

F-1B: Selection of Ledger Accout from List of Ledgers

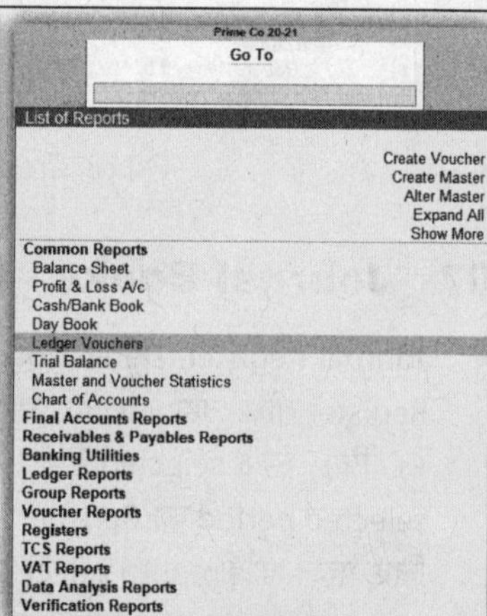

F-1C: Ledger from GoTo Menu Bar

02 Ledger Book Display

Select the Ledger Account from the Menu / List (F-1B) to get Ledger Vouchers Display (F-2B) as Ledger Book of the selected Ledger Account showing :

- **Ledger Account transactions & Amount:** Amount of the Ledger Account in respective Debit / Credit column in first line, followed by complementary Ledger Account and amount with Dr/Cr Sign (in Detail mode)

- **Opening Balance:** Opening Balance of Ledger Account in respective column.
- **Closing Balance:** Closing Balance for the end of the period, in respective column.

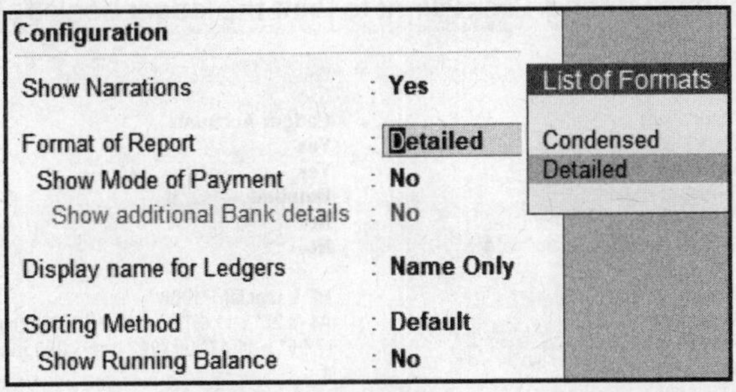

F-2A: Ledger Book Display Configuration

Ledger Display Configuration: At Ledger Account Display (F-1B), click *F12: Configure* to get *Ledger Display Configuration* screen (F-2A), to set the options.

- GoT Menu या Go To Tab, दोनों से ही कई step में Ledger Account select करे (F-1B)। Ledger Vouchers Display मिलेगा (F-2B) जिसे हम Ledger Book कहते हैं।
- Ledger Account Display के Top Header line में Ledger Account Name दिखेगा (F-2B)। Main Body Part में selected Ledger Account संबंधित सभी transactions दिखेंगे। Report के Footer Part में Opening Balance, Transaction Total और Closing Balance दिखेंगे। Transaction से drill down करने से Voucher Alteration screen मिलेगा।
- Cash / Bank Ledger select करने से Cash / Bank Book मिलेगा, जो पहले ही explain कर चुके हैं।

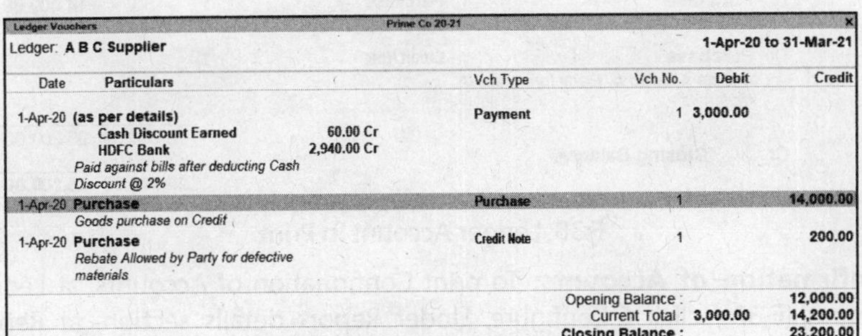

Ledger Vouchers — Prime Co 20-21

Ledger: **A B C Supplier** — 1-Apr-20 to 31-Mar-21

Date	Particulars		Vch Type	Vch No.	Debit	Credit
1-Apr-20	**(as per details)**		Payment	1	3,000.00	
	Cash Discount Earned	60.00 Cr				
	HDFC Bank	2,940.00 Cr				
	Paid against bills after deducting Cash Discount @ 2%					
1-Apr-20	**Purchase**		Purchase	1		14,000.00
	Goods purchase on Credit					
1-Apr-20	**Purchase**		Credit Note	1		200.00
	Rebate Allowed by Party for defective materials					
				Opening Balance :		12,000.00
				Current Total :	3,000.00	14,200.00
				Closing Balance :		23,200.00

F-2B: Ledger Book Display

03 Ledger Book Printing

At Ledger Display screen (F-2B), press Alt+P to get Ledger Book Printing Screen (F-3A). Click C:Configure (or type C) to get Ledger printing Configuration screen to set the options to show the contents of Ledger Account. Click I:Preview to preview the ledger book before Printing. Click P:Print to Print the ledger book (F-3B).

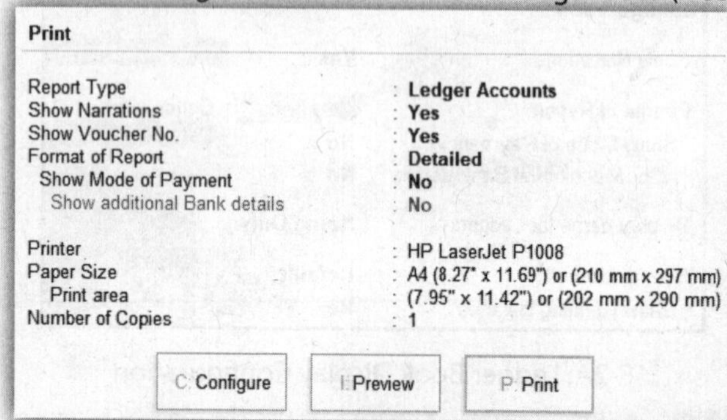

F:3A : Ledger printing

Ledger Report Display में Ctrl+P press कर Ledger Printing screen पाए (F-3A)। P:Print button से current Ledger Account Print करे (F-3B)। Printed Ledger में पहले opening Balance, फिर transactions और अंत में Closing Balance print होता है (F-3B)।

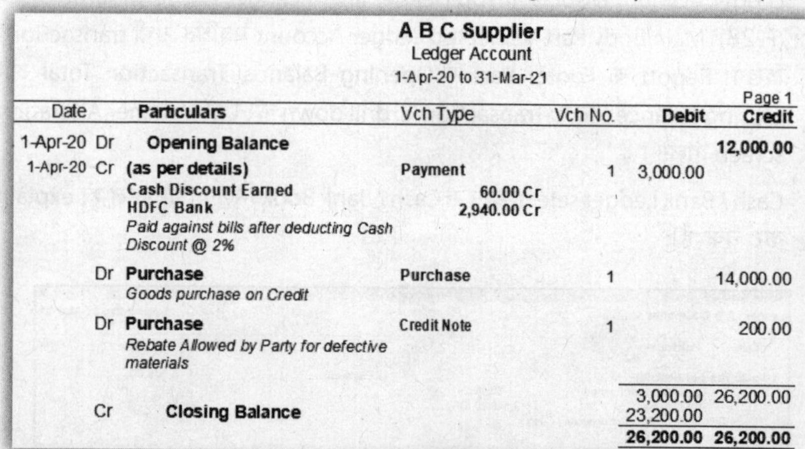

A B C Supplier
Ledger Account
1-Apr-20 to 31-Mar-21

Page 1

Date		Particulars	Vch Type	Vch No.	Debit	Credit
1-Apr-20	Dr	**Opening Balance**				**12,000.00**
1-Apr-20	Cr	**(as per details)** **Cash Discount Earned** 60.00 Cr **HDFC Bank** 2,940.00 Cr *Paid against bills after deducting Cash Discount @ 2%*	**Payment**	1	3,000.00	
	Dr	**Purchase** *Goods purchase on Credit*	**Purchase**	1		14,000.00
	Dr	**Purchase** *Rebate Allowed by Party for defective materials*	**Credit Note**	1		200.00
					3,000.00	26,200.00
	Cr	**Closing Balance**			23,200.00	
					26,200.00	**26,200.00**

F:3B: Ledger Account in Print

Confirmation of Accounts: To print Confirmation of Accounts, at Ledger Printing (F-3A), click C:Configure. Under Report details section, at Report Type, select Confirmation of Accounts (F-3C). Now click P:Print button to print Confirmation of Accounts.

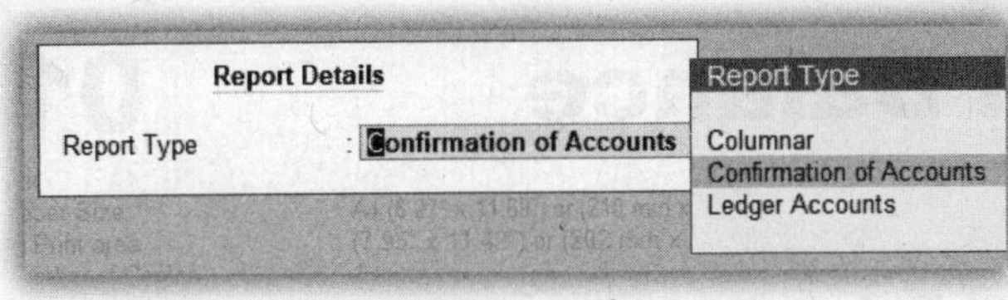

F-3C:Confirmation of Accounts

04 Ledger Books - Key Points

- Ledger Display में पहले Ledger Account के Amount Debit या Credit column में Display होते हैं। Voucher के बाकी सभी ledger account के figure inner column में Dr / Cr sign से display होते हैं। अंत में Opening Balance, Totals और Closing Balance display होते हैं।
- Ledger Print में पहले Ledger Opening Balance print होते है। फिर voucher से Ledger Account के Amount Debit या Credit column में Print होते है। Voucher के बाकि ledger accounts के figure inner column में Dr / Cr sign से print होते हैं. अंत में Totals और Closing Balance print होते हैं।
- Cash / Bank Book और Cash Bank Ledger, एक ही Report है. इसलिए Cash / Bank Ledger select कर Cash Bank Book भी Ledger Book से Display / Print कर सकते हैं।

Trial Balance 01-09

01 Trial Balance

Trial Balance is an important summary Statement showing the Net Balance of all Ledger Accounts. Trial Balance serves 2 major objectives:

- **Accuracy of Accounts:** To check the arithmetic accuracy of Trial Balance ensuring Total Debits & Credits are equal (so the name Trial Balance). If the opening Balance of Ledger Accounts are not correctly and completely entered, Trial Balance will not tally, and the difference will be shown at the end as *Difference in Trial Balance*. Just check the Opening Balance entry, rectify mistakes, and get the Trial Balance agreed.
- **Financial Statements:** Trial Balance figures are used in various Financial Statements and Final Accounts (Profit & Loss & Balance Sheet) statements.

Trial Balance Ledger Accounts की summary है. Trial Balance से Accounts की यर्थाथता (correctness) check होता है। इसके अलावा, Trial Balance से Profit Loss, Balance Sheet और Financial statements prepare करने में उपयोग किया जाता है।

02 Trial Balance Display

Accessing Ledger Account: Trial Balance may be accessed from GoT Main Menu or from GoTo Menu, as explained earlier.

- **GoT Main Menu**: Select *GoT>Display More Reports>Trial Balance* (F-1A)
- **Go To Menu Bar**: Select GoTo> *Trial Balance* (F-1B)

Initially the Trial Balance Displays the Major Accounts Groups and the Closing Balance as at the end of the Period.

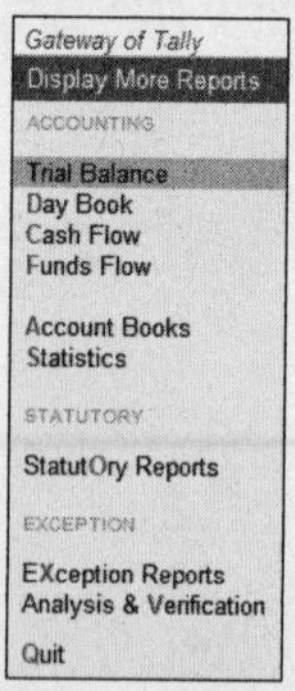

F-1A: Trial Balance from GoT Main Menu

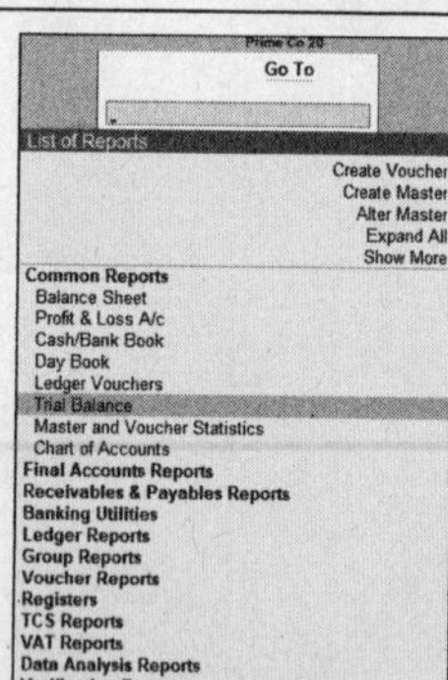

F-1B: Trial Balance from GoTo List

- **Trial Balance Configuration**: At Trial Balance Display (F-3A), Click F12:Configure button and set the Configuration options (F-2A)
- **Trial Balance Structure**: Through *F5:Ledgewise / Groupwise* toggle button, you may get a flat list of all Ledger Accounts / Groupwise hierarchical structure.

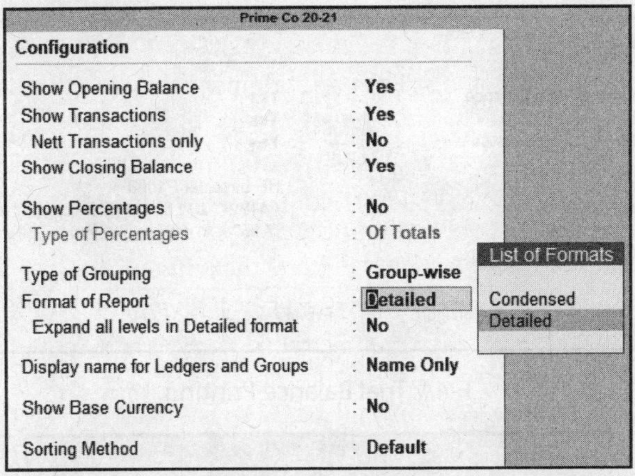

F-2A: Trial Balance Display Configuration

GoT>Display More Reports>Trial Balance (F-1A) या GoTo> Trial Balance (F-1B) select कर, F12 से Configuration set कर (F-2A), Trial Balance Display करे (F-3A)। F5:Ledgewise / Groupwise button से Ledgerwise list या Account Group / Ledger structure में Trial balance display कर सकते हैं।

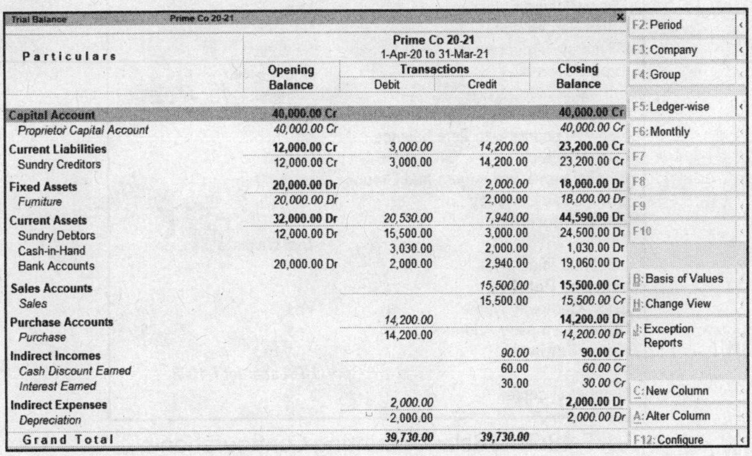

Trial Balance — Prime Co 20-21

Particulars	Prime Co 20-21 1-Apr-20 to 31-Mar-21 Opening Balance	Transactions Debit	Transactions Credit	Closing Balance
Capital Account	**40,000.00 Cr**			**40,000.00 Cr**
Proprietor Capital Account	*40,000.00 Cr*			*40,000.00 Cr*
Current Liabilities	**12,000.00 Cr**	*3,000.00*	*14,200.00*	**23,200.00 Cr**
Sundry Creditors	12,000.00 Cr	3,000.00	14,200.00	23,200.00 Cr
Fixed Assets	**20,000.00 Dr**		*2,000.00*	**18,000.00 Dr**
Furniture	*20,000.00 Dr*		2,000.00	*18,000.00 Dr*
Current Assets	**32,000.00 Dr**	*20,530.00*	*7,940.00*	**44,590.00 Dr**
Sundry Debtors	12,000.00 Dr	15,500.00	3,000.00	24,500.00 Dr
Cash-in-Hand		3,030.00	2,000.00	1,030.00 Dr
Bank Accounts	20,000.00 Dr	2,000.00	2,940.00	19,060.00 Dr
Sales Accounts			*15,500.00*	**15,500.00 Cr**
Sales			15,500.00	*15,500.00 Cr*
Purchase Accounts		*14,200.00*		**14,200.00 Dr**
Purchase		14,200.00		*14,200.00 Dr*
Indirect Incomes			*90.00*	**90.00 Cr**
Cash Discount Earned			60.00	*60.00 Cr*
Interest Earned			30.00	*30.00 Cr*
Indirect Expenses		*2,000.00*		**2,000.00 Dr**
Depreciation		2,000.00		*2,000.00 Dr*
Grand Total		***39,730.00***	***39,730.00***	

F-3A: Trial Balance Display

03 Trial Balance Printing

At Trial Balance Display (F-3A), press Ctl+P to get Trail Balance printing screen (F-4A). Click C:Configure to set the Printing options (F-4B). Click I:Preview to preview the Report before Printing. Click P:Print to print the report on printer (F-4C).

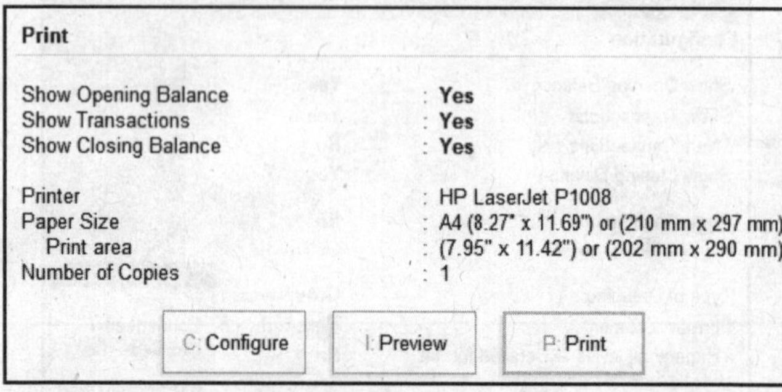

Print

Show Opening Balance	: **Yes**
Show Transactions	: **Yes**
Show Closing Balance	: **Yes**
Printer	: HP LaserJet P1008
Paper Size	: A4 (8.27" x 11.69") or (210 mm x 297 mm)
Print area	: (7.95" x 11.42") or (202 mm x 290 mm)
Number of Copies	: 1

C: Configure   I: Preview   P: Print

F-4A: Trial Balance Printing

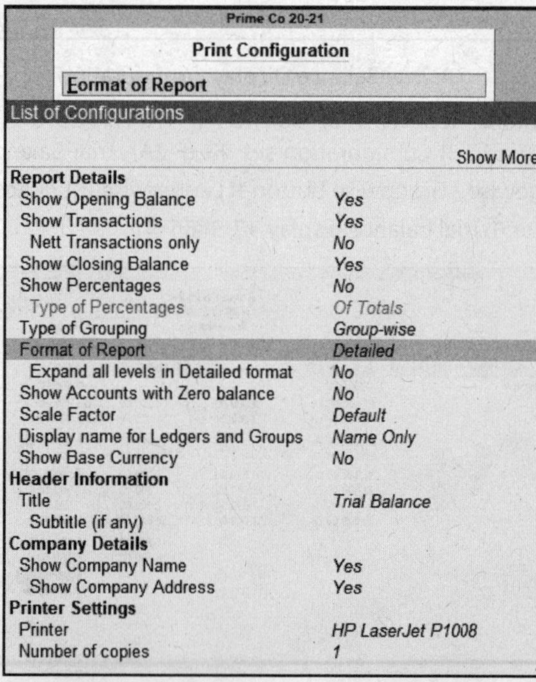

Prime Co 20-21

Print Configuration

Format of Report

List of Configurations

Show More

Report Details	
Show Opening Balance	*Yes*
Show Transactions	*Yes*
Nett Transactions only	*No*
Show Closing Balance	*Yes*
Show Percentages	*No*
Type of Percentages	*Of Totals*
Type of Grouping	*Group-wise*
Format of Report	*Detailed*
Expand all levels in Detailed format	*No*
Show Accounts with Zero balance	*No*
Scale Factor	*Default*
Display name for Ledgers and Groups	*Name Only*
Show Base Currency	*No*
Header Information	
Title	*Trial Balance*
Subtitle (if any)	
Company Details	
Show Company Name	*Yes*
Show Company Address	*Yes*
Printer Settings	
Printer	*HP LaserJet P1008*
Number of copies	*1*

F-4B: Trial Balance Printing Configuration

Trial Balance Display (F-3A) में Ctrl+P press कर Trial Balance printing screen (F-4A) से Trial Balance Print करे(F-4C)।

Prime Co

Trial Balance

1-Apr-20 to 31-Mar-21

Page 1

Particulars	Opening Balance	Transactions		Closing Balance
		Debit	Credit	
Capital Account	**50,000.00 Cr**			**50,000.00 Cr**
Proprietor Capital Account	*50,000.00 Cr*			*50,000.00 Cr*
Current Liabilities	**12,000.00 Cr**	*3,000.00*	*14,200.00*	**23,200.00 Cr**
Sundry Creditors	12,000.00 Cr	3,000.00	14,200.00	23,200.00 Cr
Fixed Assets	**20,000.00 Dr**		*2,000.00*	**18,000.00 Dr**
Furniture	*20,000.00 Dr*		2,000.00	*18,000.00 Dr*
Current Assets	**47,000.00 Dr**	*33,530.00*	*14,940.00*	**65,590.00 Dr**
Opening Stock	10,000.00 Dr			10,000.00 Dr
Stock of Materials	10,000.00 Dr	*6,000.00*		10,000.00 Dr
Sundry Debtors	17,000.00 Dr	24,500.00	3,000.00	38,500.00 Dr
Cash-in-Hand		4,000.00	2,000.00	2,000.00 Dr
Cash		*4,000.00*	*2,000.00*	2,000.00 Dr
Bank Accounts	20,000.00 Dr	5,030.00	9,940.00	15,090.00 Dr
HDFC Bank	20,000.00 Dr	*5,030.00*	*9,940.00*	15,090.00 Dr
Sales Accounts			*21,500.00*	**21,500.00 Cr**
Sales			21,500.00	*21,500.00 Cr*
Purchase Accounts		*14,200.00*		**14,200.00 Dr**
Purchase		14,200.00		*14,200.00 Dr*
Indirect Incomes			*90.00*	**90.00 Cr**
Cash Discount Earned			60.00	*60.00 Cr*

F-4C: Extended Trial Balance in Print

04 Extended Trial Balance

Normally Trial Balance shows Closing Balance as on the specified period end date. However, you may optionally include Opening Balance & Transaction details (separate Debit / Credit or Net), through the Trial Balance Configuration option (F-4B). This is very useful report giving a concise summarised view of Opening, Transactions & Closing Balance, very useful in practical working, and to check Opening Balance of Ledger Accounts.

साधारणतया Trial balance में Ledger Accounts का closing Balance का figure ही होता है। लेकिन Trial Balance Configuration option set कर Opening, Transaction और Closing Balance figure सहित Trial Balance (जिसे Extended Trial Balance कहते हैं) print कर सकते हैं; जो Financial Reports prepare करने में काफी उपयोगी होता है।

05 Ledger Opening Balance Statement

Tally does not provide Opening Balance entered in Ledger Account Master List. To get the list of Ledger Accounts, print the Trial with Opening Balance, setting the Configuration Options.

In your desired sequence (Groupwise Hierarchical, or flat alphabetical Ledger List), to check the correctness of Ledger Opening Balance entered in Ledger Accounts. However, in detailed mode, you get only the next level details.

Ledger Account का Opening Balance का Statement print करने के लिए Trial Balance Printing Configuration (F-4B) में सिर्फ Opening Balance option में Yes कर Trial Balance print करें।

06 Trial Balance - Key Points

- Ledger Accounts के Opening Balance का Debit और Credit Total match नहीं करने से Trial Balance और Balance Sheet के अंत में Opening Balance difference का figure दिखेगा। ऐसे स्थिति में Opening Balance check करने के लिए सिर्फ Opening Balance का Trial balance print करे।
- सिर्फ Closing balance का Trial Balance print के बजाय Extended Trial Balance print करे. यह report कई मायने में ज्यादा उपयोगी होता है।
- Alphabetic Ledger Accountwise Trial Balance Display / Print करने के लिए Trial Balance Display में F5:Ledgwise button क्लिक करे।
- Chart of Accounts में Ledger Opening Balance print नहीं होता। Ledger Opening Balance check करने के लिए F:Configure में सिर्फ Opening Balance figure में Yes set कर Trial Balance print करे।

Profit & Loss Statement 01-10

Profit & Loss Account

Profit & Loss Account shows the heads of all Nominal Accounts (Income & Expenses) and the net Profit / Loss, for the specified period (F-1A), the result of performance of the enterprise.

Profit & Loss Account Business के लिए एक महत्वपूर्ण Report है, क्योंकि इससे business की आमदनी (Income), खर्चे (Expenses), और लाभ नुकसान (Profit / Loss) का हिसाब (Account) मिलता है।

01 Stock Ledger Account

Profit & Loss Account includes Opening Stock Value (at Debit Side) and Closing Stock value (at Credit Side). These figures are carried from the Stock Ledger Account created under Stock-in-Hand Group.

Ledger Account creation and Opening Balance entry in Ledger Accounts has been explained earlier. Select *GoT>Create>Ledger* to create Stock Ledger Account (F-1A). At *Under* field, select Stock-in-Hand Group. Enter Opening Stock value at Opening Balance of the Ledger Account (F-2B).

Ledger Creation		Prime Co 20-21
Name	: Stock of Materials	
		Tax Registration Details
Under	Stock-in-Hand *(Current Assets)*	PAN/IT No.
	Opening Balance (on 1-Apr-20) :	10,000.00 Dr

F-1A: Stock Ledger Account Creation

02 Closing Stock Value Entry

At the year end, do not create any Journal Voucher for Closing Stock (as done in Traditional Accounts), but enter the Closing Stock Value at Stock-in-Hand Ledger Account.

So, closing Stock is entered off the accounts and used on the fly during creation of P L Statement and Balance Sheet, and its value may be altered any moment any number of times, without creation or modification of any voucher.

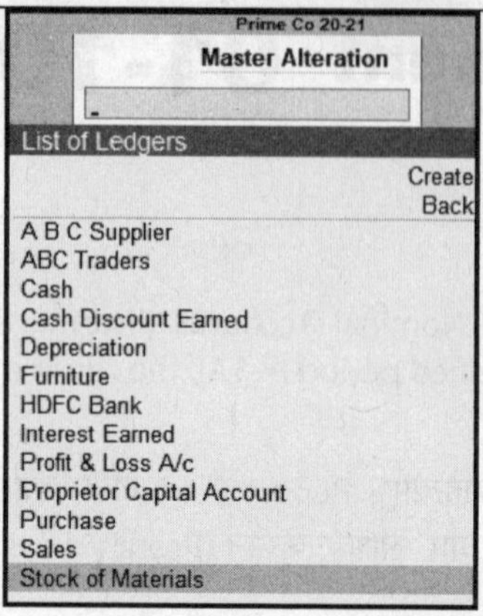

F-2A: Stock Ledger Account Alteration

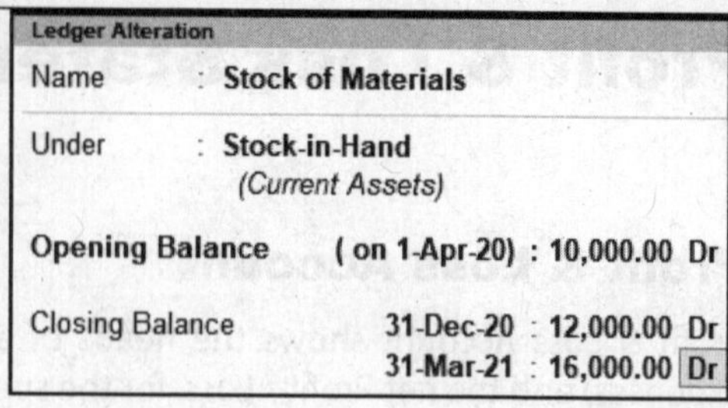

F-2B: Closing Stock Vaue entry in Stock Ledger Account

कोई period का सही Profit Loss Account पाने के लिए, period के अंत का Closing Stock value भी entry करना है। Tally में Closing Stock का Journal Voucher entry नहीं होता (जैसे की आपलोग Accounting के class में सीखे हैं)। Journal entry के बदले, Closing Stock का Value Closing Stock Ledger Account में entry करे, जेसे यहाँ बाद में explain किये हैं।

Entry of Closing Stock Value: Select *GoT>Alter>Ledger* and select *Stock Ledger* Account to get Leger Alteration screen (F-2B). Below the Opening Balance figures, enter Closing Stock Value for respective Date.

This way, you may enter several Dates and corresponding Stock Values for the respective Dates. This helps you to prepare PL Statement for any period and Balance Sheet for any Date.

Stock Ledger Account creation और उसमें Opening Stock Value entry पहले भी समझाया है। Stock Ledger Account में Closing Stock Value entry के लिए GoT>Alter>Ledger में Stock Ledger Account select कर Ledger Alteration में Opening value के नीचे Date और उस Date के Closing Stock value entry करें (F-2B)। इस तरह हर period end (जैसे Month End, Quarter End, Half Year End या Year End के Closing Stock Figure entry करे), ताकि कोई भी period के Profit Loss Statement कभी भी पा सके. पूरे साल के Profit Loss Statement पाने के लिए Financial Year End Date की Closing Balance entry जरूरी है।

03 Profit & Loss Statement

The Profit & Loss Statement contains 2 parts, showing details of Expenses & Income Accounts, divided by a vertical line.

- **Expenses Side** (or Debit Side): The Left Part shows the top level Expenses Groups (Direct & Indirect Expenses). The figures represent the total of Net Amount of all Ledger Accounts under the respective Group.
- **Incomes Side** (or Credit Side): The Right Part contains the top level Income Groups (Direct & Indirect Incomes). The figures represent the total of Net Amount of all Ledger Accounts under the respective Group.

Net Profit / Loss: The Net Profit / Loss is computed as difference between Total of Income figures (Direct Income & Indirect Income) and the Total of Expenses figures (Direct Expense & Indirect Income).

- If the *Total of Income* figures is greater than *Total of Expense* figures, the difference is computed as *Net Profit* and is shown at left side of the Profit & Loss Statement.
- If the *Total of Expense* figures is greater than *Total of Income* figures, the difference is computed as *Net Loss* and is shown at right side of the Profit & Loss Statement.

Profit & Loss Statement के left part me expenses और Right Part में Income के figure होता है। Total Income और Total expenses का अंतर (difference), यानि Net Profit या Net Loss अंत में show होता है।

04 Profit & Loss Statement Display

Having entered the Closing Stock Value, you may display/ print Profit & Loss Statement.

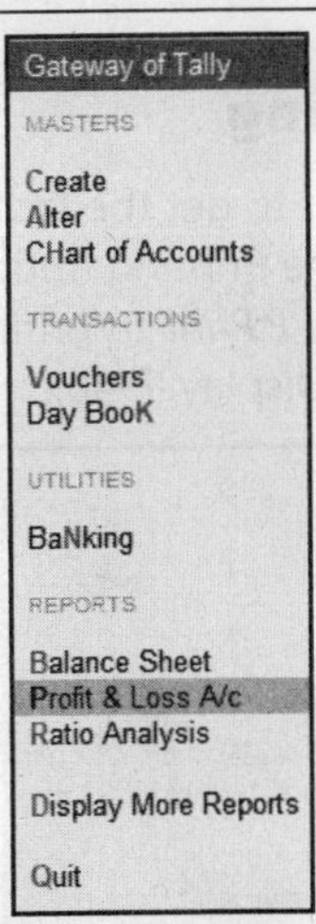

F-3A: P L Statement from GoT Main Menu

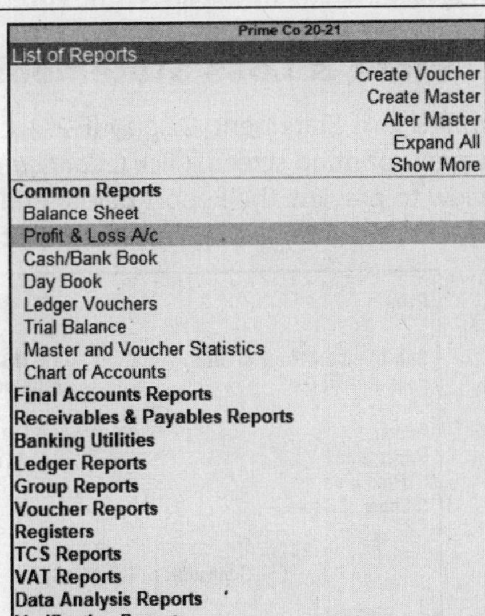

F-3B: P L Statement from GoTo Bar List

Select *GoT > Profit & Loss Account* (F-3A) / *Go To > Profit & Loss Account* (F-3B) to get Profit & Loss Statement for the specified period (F-4B). Click F12:Configure button and set the Configuration options (F-4A) to set up the contents of Profit & Loss Statement (F-4B).

Configuration	
Show Percentages	: No
Exclude Accounts with zero Closing Balance	: No
Format of Report	: Detailed
Show Vertical Profit & Loss A/c	: No
Show Gross Profit	: No
Display name for Ledgers and Groups	: Name Only
Show Base Currency	: No

List of Formats
Condensed
Detailed

F-4A: P L Statement Display Configuration

Profit & Loss A/c — Prime Co 20-21

Particulars		Prime Co 20-21 1-Apr-20 to 31-Mar-21	Particulars		Prime Co 20-21 1-Apr-20 to 31-Mar-21
Opening Stock		**10,000.00**	**Sales Accounts**		**15,500.00**
Stock of Materials	*10,000.00*		*Sales*	*15,500.00*	
Purchase Accounts		**14,200.00**	**Indirect Incomes**		**90.00**
Purchase	*14,200.00*		*Cash Discount Earned*	*60.00*	
Indirect Expenses		**2,000.00**	*Interest Earned*	*30.00*	
Depreciation	*2,000.00*		**Closing Stock**		**16,000.00**
Nett Profit		***5,390.00***	*Stock of Materials*	*16,000.00*	
Total		**31,590.00**	**Total**		**31,590.00**

F-4B: P L Statement Display

Closing Stock value entry (F-2B) के बाद, *GoT>Profit & Loss Account* (F-3A) या *Go To >Profit & Loss Account* (F-3B) select कर F12 से Configuration set कर (F-4A) Profit & Loss Statement display करे (F-4B)।

05 Profit & Loss Statement Printing

At Profit & Loss Statement Display (F-2A), click *P:Print* to get the Profit & Loss Statement printing screen. Click *C:Configure* to set the Printing options. Click I:Preview to preview the Report before Printing. Click *P:Print* to print the P L Statement on printer (F-5B), similar to P L Statement Display (F-4B).

Print	
Show Vertical Profit & Loss A/c	: **No**
Format of Report	: **Detailed**
Printer	: HP LaserJet P1008
Paper Size	: A4 (8.27" x 11.69") or (210 mm x 297 mm)
Print area	: (8.27" x 11.69") or (210 mm x 297 mm)
Number of Copies	: 1

C: Configure | I: Preview | P: Print

F-5A: P L Statement Printing

Profit Loss Statement Display में Alt+P type कर C:Configuration click कर Configuration option set up करें (अगर जरूरत हो तो) और फिर *P:Print* click कर Printer में P L Statement (F-5B) Print करे।

Prime Co

Profit & Loss A/c

1-Apr-20 to 31-Mar-21

Particulars		1-Apr-20 to 31-Mar-21	**Particulars**		1-Apr-20 to 31-Mar-21
Opening Stock		**10,000.00**	**Sales Accounts**		**21,500.00**
Stock of Materials	*10,000.00*		*Sales*	*21,500.00*	
Purchase Accounts		**14,200.00**	**Indirect Incomes**		**90.00**
Purchase	*14,200.00*		*Cash Discount Earned*	*60.00*	
			Interest Earned	*30.00*	
Indirect Expenses		**2,000.00**	Closing Stock		**16,000.00**
Depreciation	*2,000.00*		*Stock of Materials*	*16,000.00*	
Nett Profit		***11,390.00***			
Total		**37,590.00**	**Total**		**37,590.00**

F:5B: P L Statement in Print

06 Profit & Loss Account - Key Points

- Stock Ledger account में under field में *Stock-in-Hand* Account Group select करे।
- सही P L Statement पाने के लिए Closing Stock Value और बाकी adjustments Journal Entries पहले कर ले। Closing Stock की entry Stock Ledger Account में करे, Journal Voucher में नहीं. Multiple Date के Stock value entry कर कोई भी Period के Profit Loss Account Display / Print कर सकते हैं।
- Closing Stock Value का Figure Trial Balance में नहीं दिखेगा (लेकिन Trial Balance में Opening Stock value, Stock Ledger के Opening Balance column में दिखेगा)।

Balance Sheet 01-11

01 Balance Sheet

Balance Sheet shows all the Assets & Liabilities at the close of the specified Date. The Balance Sheet contains 2 major parts, Liabilities & Assets, divided by a vertical line (F-2B).

- **Liabilities** (or Credit Side): The Left Part shows the top level Groups of Capital (Funds *Owned*, by the organisation, like Capital & Reserves) & Liabilities (Funds *Owed*, by the organization, like Loans & other Liabilities).
- **Assets** (or Debit Side): The Right Part contains the top Assets Groups (all Assets possessed by the organization, like Fixed Assets, Investments & Current Assets).

The figures represent the Major Account Group totals of Net Amount of all Ledger Accounts under the respective Group.

Current Year Profit Loss: The current year net Profit / Loss carried from P L Statement is shown separately at the end.

Balance Sheet के left part में Liabilities (Capital और outside Liabilities) और Right side में Assets के Accounts detail होते हैं (F-2B)। Left side अंत में Current Year Profit / Loss अलग से दिखता है।

02 Balance Sheet Display

Select *GoT* > *Balance Sheet* (F-1A), *or* select *Go To* > *Balance Sheet* (F-1B) to get Balance Sheet (F-2B) as at end of the Current Period.

F-1A: Balance Sheet from GoT main Menu

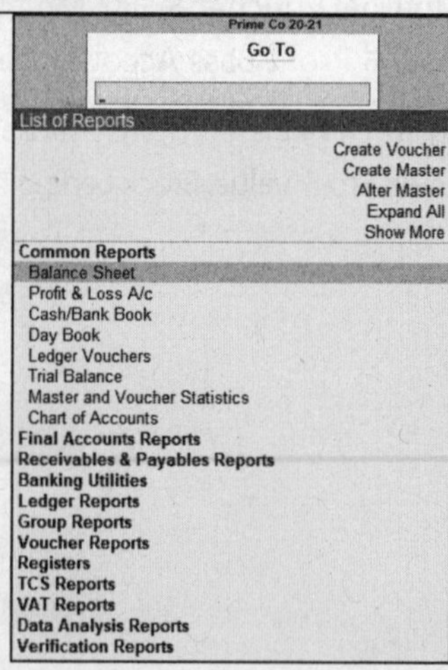

F-1B: Balance Sheet from Go To Menu list

Balance Sheet Display Configuration: At Balance Sheet display (F-2B), click F12:Configure and set up the options for contents of Balance Sheet (F-2A).

Configuration

		List of Formats
Show Percentages	: No	
Exclude Accounts with zero Closing Balance	: Yes	
Format of Report	: Detailed	Condensed
Show Vertical Balance Sheet	: No	Detailed
Show Loss also under Liabilities	: No	
Method of showing Balance Sheet	: Liabilities / Assets	
Display name for Ledgers and Groups	: Name Only	
Show Base Currency	: No	

F-2A: Balance Sheet Display Configuration

GoT > Balance Sheet (F-1A), या Go To > Balance Sheet (F-1B) select कर F12 से Configuration set कर (F-2A) Balance Sheet Display करे (F-2B)।

Balance Sheet — Prime Co 20-21

Liabilities	Prime Co 20-21 as at 31-Mar-21		Assets	Prime Co 20-21 as at 31-Mar-21	
Capital Account		50,000.00	**Fixed Assets**		18,000.00
Proprietor Capital Account	*50,000.00*		*Furniture*	*18,000.00*	
Current Liabilities		23,200.00	**Current Assets**		60,590.00
Sundry Creditors	*23,200.00*		Closing Stock	*16,000.00*	
Profit & Loss A/c		5,390.00	Sundry Debtors	*24,500.00*	
Opening Balance			Cash-in-Hand	*1,030.00*	
Current Period	*5,390.00*		Bank Accounts	*19,060.00*	
Total		78,590.00	**Total**		78,590.00

F-2B: Balance Sheet Display

03 Balance Sheet Printing

At Balance Sheet Display (F-2B), click *P:Print* to get the Balance Sheet printing screen (F-3A). Click C:Configure to set the Printing options. Click I:Preview to preview the Report before Printing. Click P:Print to print the report on printer. The Format & Contents of Balance in Print (F-3A) is similar to Balance Sheet Display (F-2B)

Print

Format of Report	: Detailed
Show Vertical Balance Sheet	: No
Include Working Capital	: No
Printer	: HP LaserJet P1008
Paper Size	: A4 (8.27" x 11.69") or (210 mm x 297 mm)
Print area	: (7.95" x 11.42") or (202 mm x 290 mm)
Number of Copies	: 1

C: Configure | I: Preview | P: Print

F-3A: Balance Sheet Printing

जैसे पहले Report Printing में बताया है, Balance Sheet Display (F-3A) में Ctrl+P type कर Balance Sheet Printing (F-3A) से Balance Sheet Configuration, Preview और Printer से Print करे (F-3B)।

Balance Sheet
1-Apr-20 to 31-Mar-21

Liabilities		as at 31-Mar-21	Assets		as at 31-Mar-21
Capital Account		**50,000.00**	**Fixed Assets**		**18,000.00**
Proprietor Capital Account	*50,000.00*		*Furniture*	*18,000.00*	
Current Liabilities		**23,200.00**	**Current Assets**		**60,590.00**
Sundry Creditors	*23,200.00*		Closing Stock	*16,000.00*	
			Sundry Debtors	*24,500.00*	
Profit & Loss A/c		**5,390.00**	Cash-in-Hand	*1,030.00*	
Opening Balance			Bank Accounts	*19,060.00*	
Current Period	*5,390.00*				
Total		**78,590.00**	**Total**		**78,590.00**

F-3B: Balance Sheet in Print

04 Ratio Analysis

To display key performance ratios, select *GoT>Ratio Analysis* to get Ratio Analysis Report (F-4B). Click *F12:Configure* and set Configuration options (F-4A). You may further drill down to related reports through any of the figures in Ratio Analysis.

Configuration

Show Explanation	: **Yes**
Show Vertical Analysis	: **No**

F-4A : Ratio Analysis Display Configuration

GoT>Ratio Analysis से Ratio Analysis Display (F-4B) में F12 से Configure कर (F-4A) key ratio और percentage देखे (F-4B). किसी भी Item से drill down कर related detail figure भी देख सकते हैं।

Ratio Analysis — Prime Co 20-21

Principal Groups	Prime Co 20-21 1-Apr-20 to 31-Mar-21	Principal Ratios	Prime Co 20-21 1-Apr-20 to 31-Mar-21
Working Capital *(Current Assets-Current Liabilities)*	37,390.00 Dr	**Current Ratio** *(Current Assets : Current Liabilities)*	2.61 : 1
Cash-in-Hand	1,030.00 Dr	**Quick Ratio** *(Current Assets-Stock-in-Hand : Current Liabilities)*	1.92 : 1
Bank Accounts	19,060.00 Dr		
Bank OD A/c		**Debt/Equity Ratio** *(Loans (Liability) : Capital Account + Nett Profit)*	0.00 : 1
Sundry Debtors	24,500.00 Dr		
Sundry Creditors	23,200.00 Cr	**Gross Profit %**	47.10 %
Sales Accounts	15,500.00 Cr	**Nett Profit %**	34.77 %
Purchase Accounts	14,200.00 Dr	**Operating Cost %** *(as percentage of Sales Accounts)*	65.23 %
Stock-in-Hand	16,000.00 Dr		
Nett Profit	5,390.00 Cr	**Recv. Turnover in days** *(payment performance of Debtors)*	576.93 days
Wkg. Capital Turnover *(Sales Accounts / Working Capital)*	0.41	**Return on Investment %** *(Nett Profit / Capital Account + Nett Profit)*	9.73 %
Inventory Turnover *(Sales Accounts / Closing Stock)*	0.97	**Return on Wkg. Capital %** *(Nett Profit / Working Capital) %*	14.42 %

F-4B : Ratio Analysis

05 Balance Sheet - Key Points

- Balance Sheet printing के पहले, Closing Stock Value और सारे Journal Adjustment entry कर ले।
- Configuration में या Printing में Show Vertical Balance Sheet में Yes कर Vertical Format में Display / Print करे।
- Balance Sheet Printing में Show Vertical Balance Sheet में Yes कर Working Capital details print करे। Working Capital Display का कोई option नहीं, लेकिन Print Preview से Working Capital view कर सकते हैं।
- Ratio Analysis Display में कोई भी Item drill down कर उसका details देख सकते हैं। F12:Configuration options (F-4A) set कर Ratio Analysis के Formula भी Display कर सकते हैं।

Accounts Receivables Payables 01-12

01 Accounts Receivables & Payables

Most of the business is done through Credit sale. The buyer pays on a future specified date (called Bill Due Date) after the sale. So, the Seller has to keep track on Receivable Dues and Buyer has to manage Payables (known as Debtors & Creditors Management). Accounts Receivables & Payables module deals with detailed records of Trade Transactions with Suppliers & Customers and Open Accounts (Outstanding Dues) for Party Analysis & Performance, tracking & control of Receivables & Payables in time.

हर business को, Credit Sale के Customer Dues का Accounts maintain करना, customer से due bill का payment Collect करना, Credit Sales / Purchase का Accounts maintain करना, supplier के due bills का payment करना, Outstanding Due Bills को track करना और सही समय पर Outstanding Bills payment करना होता है। Accounts Receivables / Payables system में accounts के इस तरह के details maintain होते हैं।

02 Bill Reference Activation for Company

To activate the Bill Reference Features (A/R A/P) and maintain Billwise Details of Outstanding of Parties, at K:Company Menu Bar (F-1A), select *Features* (or press F11 button) to get Company Features (F-2A) screen. Under the section Accounting, at *Enable Billwise Entry,* set Yes (F-2A), to Activate Bill Ref Features, for Traders Accounts (Sundry Debtors & Creditors).

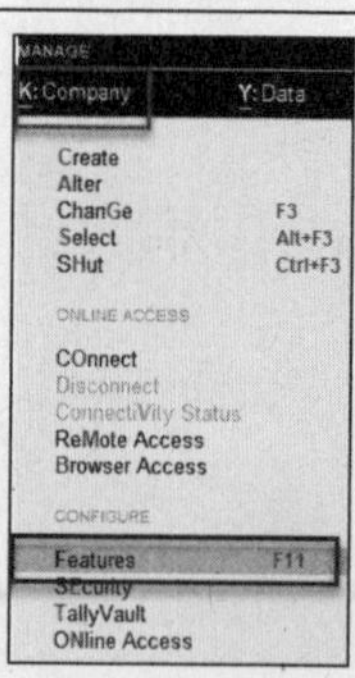

F-1A: Company Features set up

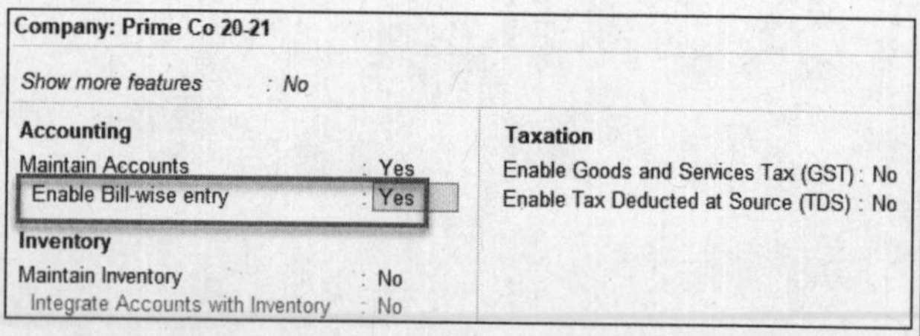

F-2A: Company Features set up for AR/AP

Accounts Receivables / Payables system के Bill Details maintain करने के लिए पहले F11 click कर Company Features में *Enable Bill wise Entry* में Yes set करे (F-2A)।

03 Bill Reference Activation for Ledger Accounts

Ledger Creation / Alteration of Customers (under *Sundry Debtors*) and Suppliers (under *Sundry Creditors*) have already been explained. To maintain Receivables & Payables system, Bill Details features should be set for Ledger Accounts under the Groups Sundry Debtors, Sundry Creditors, Loans & Advance and Branch Accounts.

Having activated the Billwise Features for the Company as explained above, at Ledger Account Creation / Alteration (*GoT>Create> Ledger* or *GoT>Alter Ledger*), set as follows (F-3A/F-4A):

- Click F12:Configuration and set the options (F-3A). Enter relevant details (like *Mailing Details* etc – F-4A)
- At *Maintain Balances Bill By Bill*, set *Yes* (F-3A / F-4A) to activate Bill Reference Feature for the Ledger Account. You may further set up the Default Credit period (F-4A).

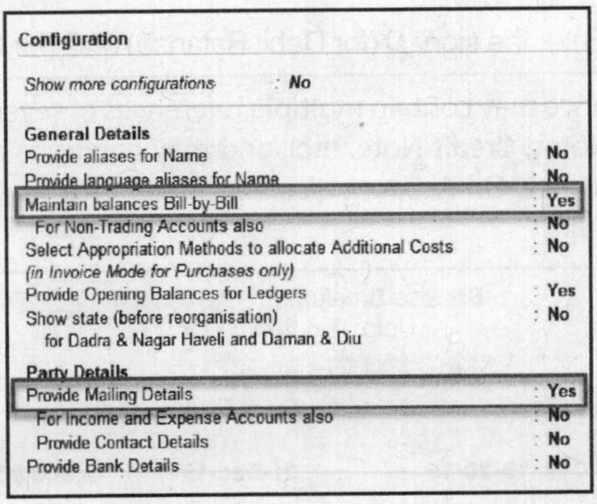

F-3A: Party Ledger Entry configuration

Customer/ Supplier Ledger में F12 से Maintain Balances Bill By Bill में Yes set करे (F-3A / F-4A). Party Ledger में Mailing Details entry करे (F-4A)।

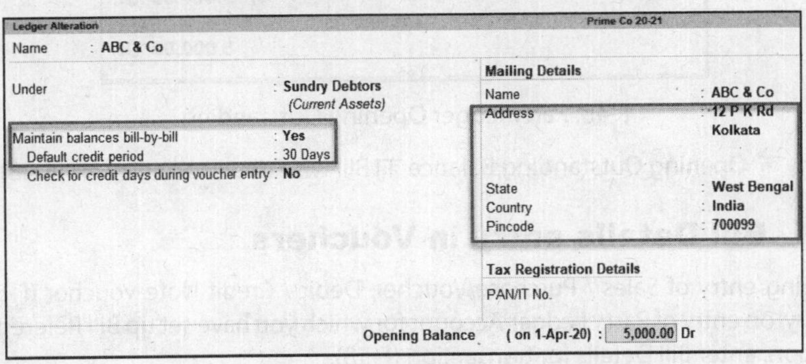

F-4A: Party Ledger Entry / Alteration

Opening Outstanding Bill Details Entry for Ledger Accounts : After entry of Opening Balance for the Ledger Accounts (for which Maintain balances Bill by Bill is set to *Yes*- F-3A/F-4A), enter outstanding Bill details for Opening Balance entered in Ledger Account Master, at Bill wise break up screen (F-4B), enter following details:

Date	Enter Date of Bill (Prior to *Books Beginning From* date)
Name	Enter Bill Reference (normally Bill No.) or Advance (as the case be)
Due Date / Credit Days	Enter the *Due Date* of the Bill or *Credit Days* – Bill Due Date would be arrived at by adding the Credit Days from Date of Bill
Amount	Enter the Opening Outstanding Bill Amount (not original bill amount, if part paid).
Dr / Cr	Enter the sign, *D* (for Debit Balance) or *C* (for Credit Balance).

The Opening Balance may contain multiple references of several voucher types (like Bills, Debit Notes, Credit Note, etc). and may comprise of Bill References of Open Bills, Advance, On Account also. Each reference would be entered in separate row (F-4B).

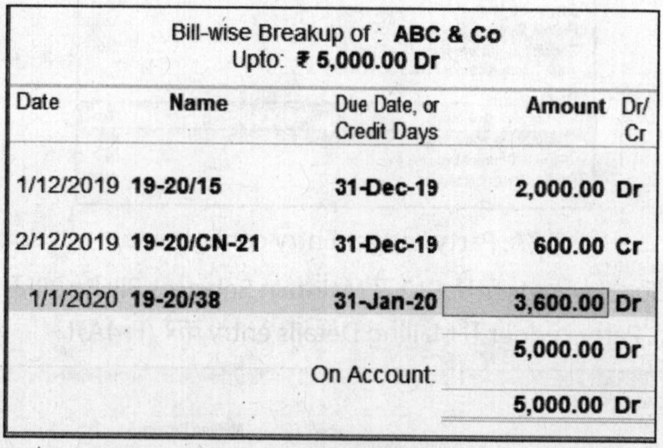
Bill-wise Breakup of : **ABC & Co**
Upto: **₹ 5,000.00 Dr**

Date	Name	Due Date, or Credit Days	Amount	Dr/ Cr
1/12/2019	**19-20/15**	**31-Dec-19**	**2,000.00**	**Dr**
2/12/2019	**19-20/CN-21**	**31-Dec-19**	**600.00**	**Cr**
1/1/2020	**19-20/38**	**31-Jan-20**	**3,600.00**	**Dr**
			5,000.00	**Dr**
		On Account:		
			5,000.00	**Dr**

F-4B: Party ledger Opening Outstanding

Party के Opening Outstanding Balance का Bill wise details भी entry करे (F-4B)।

04 Bill Details entry in Vouchers

During entry of Sales / Purchase Voucher, Debit / Credit Note voucher (F-5A) entry, on entry of Party Ledger Account for which you have set up Bill Reference option, enter Bill Details for transaction (F-5B):

- **Bill Ref Type**: Select the Bill Ref Type from the List (F-5C), as described next
- **Bill Reference Number**: Enter / Select the Reference Number, as described next
- **Credit Period / Due Date**: Enter Credit Period or Due Date for New Reference (when Credit Period is entered, the Due date is computed from the Voucher Date & Credit Period and shown)
- **Bill Reference Amount**: Enter the Amount for the respective Bill Reference Number. In case of *Against Reference*, the Balance amount of Reference is auto carried (which may be changed)

The entry process of each of these elements are explained below in details.

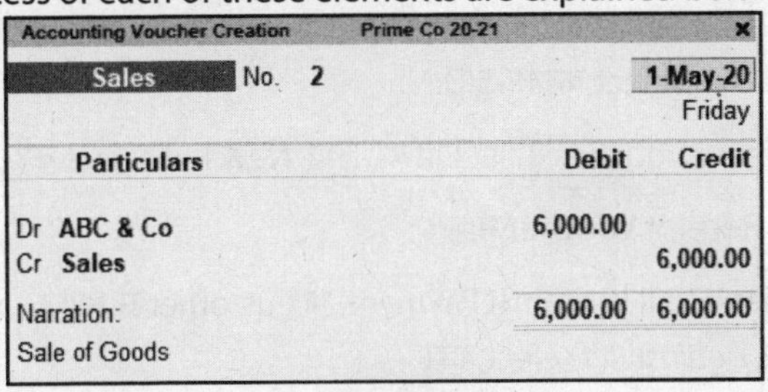

F-5A: Voucher Entry

Bill Reference Type: At Bill Details screen (F-5B), Select the relevant Type of Bill Reference at *Type of Ref* (F-5B), from the list (F-5C):

- **New Ref.**: Select it when a new Ref is created (normally a Sales or Purchase Voucher). Consequently, At *Name* field, the Ref Number from the voucher would be auto carried, which you may change.
- **Against Ref.**: Select it when the transaction is for adjustment of an existing reference (like payment is received or made against any existing Ref). All existing references are listed from which select the *Ref* to which the current entry relates.
- **Advance**: Select it when you make / get Advance Payment (which would be adjusted against a reference later on).
- **On Account**: Select it (this option does not appear in Sales / Purchase Voucher) when payment is received or made but not against specific Bill or Advance (or Bill reference is not known). *On Account* amounts are not reflected in Interest Statement, Outstanding (Open Bills) Statements or Age Analysis Statement.

In this way, you may make multiple entries of Bill Reference. However, the total net amount of all references (F-5B) must be equal to the net amount of debit / credit in the respective ledger account of the party, as entered in main voucher entry screen (F-5A).

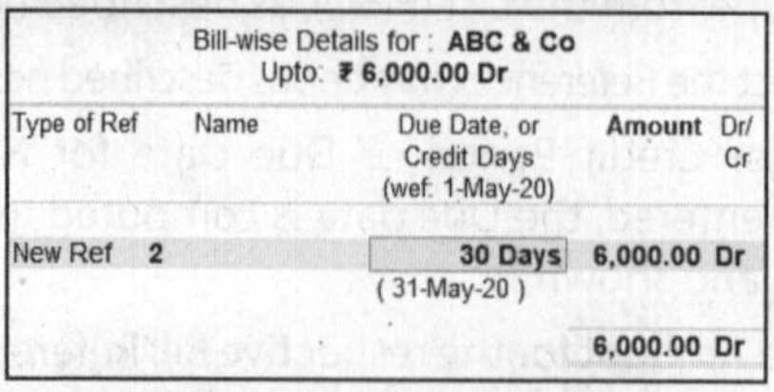

F-5B: Bill details in Voucher entry

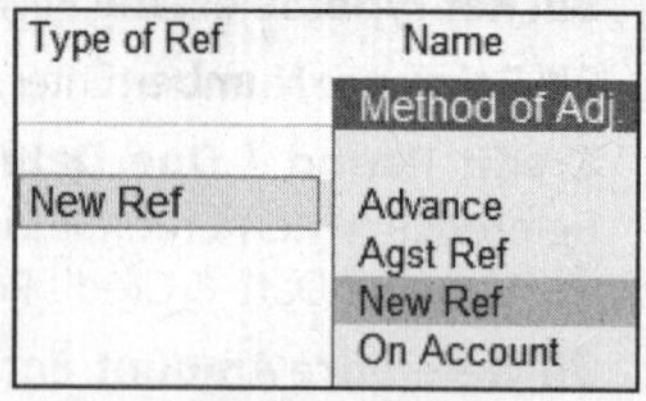

F-5C: Type of Reference List

Bill Details maintain करने के लिए, Voucher में Party के Ledger Account entry करने के बाद (F-5A), *Bill wise Details* screen में Bill Details entry करे (F-5B). Type of Ref column में इस प्रकार select करे (F-5C):

- Sale / Purchase voucher में नए Bill के लिए New Ref select करे.
- Payment / Receipt Voucher में:
  - Supplier को Bill के against Payment, या Customer से Bill के against Receipt के लिए, *Against Ref* select करे।
  - Customer से Advance मिलने, या Supplier को Advance Payment के लिए *Advance* select करे।
  - Customer / Supplier को On Account Payment के लिए *On Account* select करे।

05 Outstanding Reports Menu

Having entered the Voucher (F-5A) with Bill details (F-5B), you may print Outstanding Reports (List of Open Bills for which some amount is still due).

Accessing Outstanding Reports: Outstanding Reports may be accessed from GoT Main Menu (F-6A) or from GoTo Menu (F-7A).

- **GoT Main Menu**: Select *GoT>Display More Reports>Statement of Accounts> Outstandings* to get Outstandings menu (F-6A). Now select the option to get the respective Outstanding Report:
  - *Receivables* for Outstanding Bills Receivables (from Customers)
  - *Payables* for Outstanding Bills Payables (to Suppliers).
  - *Ledger* for Outstanding Bills for a selected Ledger Account
  - *Group* for Outstanding Bills for a selected Account Group
- **Go To Reports List**:
  - Select *Bills Receivable / Bills Payable* to get the respective report (F-7A)
  - Select *Receivables & Payables* (F-7A) to get *Receivables & Payables Reports*

list (F-7B), from which select the desired Report as follows:

- *Bills Receivables* for Outstanding Bills Receivables (from Customers)
- *Bills Payables* for Outstanding Bills Payables (to Suppliers).
- *Overdue Receivables* for Overdue Bills Receivables (from Customers)
- *Overdue Payable* for Overdue Bills Receivables (from Customers)

Select Ledger Reports (F-6A) and then select *Ledger Outstandings*

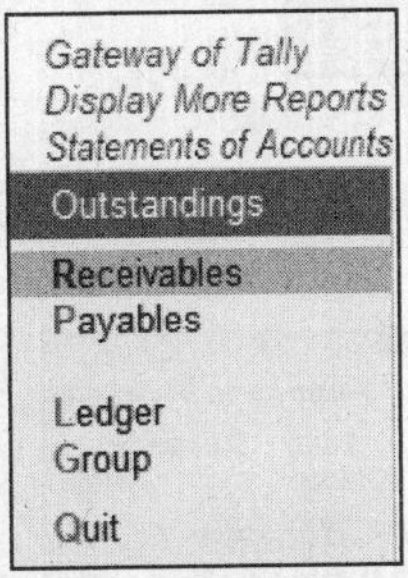

F-6A: Outstanding Reports from GoT Menu

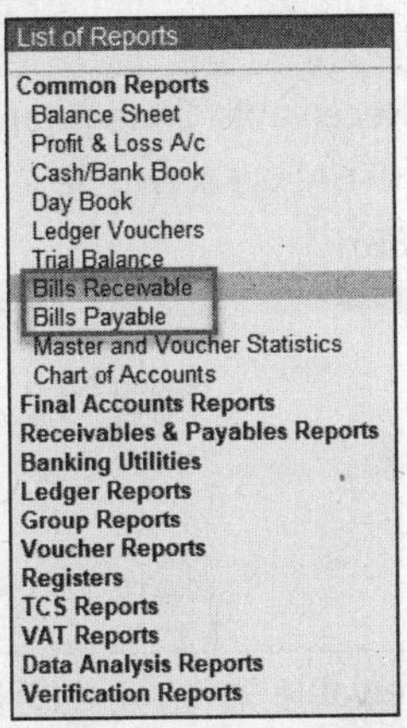

F-7A: Outstanding Reports from GoTo List

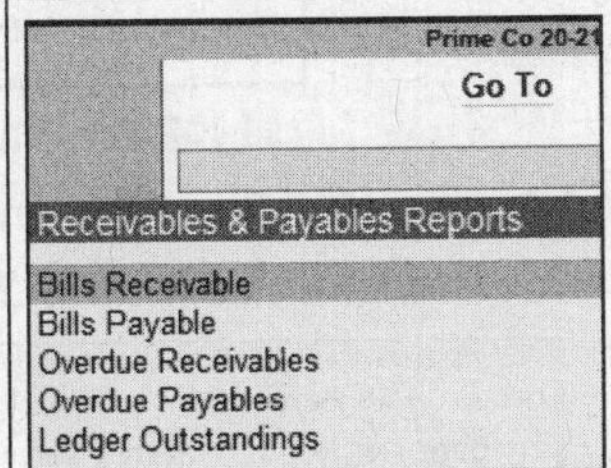

F-7B: Outstanding Reports from GoTo> Receivables & Paybales List

Bill Outstanding Report के लिए:

- **GoT Main Menu से**: GoT>Display More Reports>Statement of Accounts> Outstandings select करे (F-6A)। फिर Menu से option select कर Outstanding Report पायें।
- **Go To List से**: Bills Receivable / Bills Payable select कर (F-7A), Receivables & Payables Reports list से option select कर Outstanding Report पायें (F-7B)।

06 Outstanding Bills Report Display

The Outstanding Reports *Receivables* or *Payables*, as selected from the Menu / List, shows the Billwise details of Outstanding (F-8B / F-8C). Click F12:Configure and set the options(F-8A) as desired.

Configuration

Type of Grouping	:	**Ledger-wise Bills**
Show Opening Amount	:	**No**
Show Due On	:	**Yes**
Show Overdue Days/Bill age in Days	:	**Yes**
Show Overdue Days from Bill Date	:	**No**
Format of Report	:	**Detailed**
Show Narrations	:	**No**
Display name for Ledgers	:	**Name Only**
Sorting Method for Bills	:	**Default**
Sorting Method for Party	:	**Default**

Method of Info
- Bill-wise
- Ledger-wise Bills

F-8A: Bills Receivable Configuration

Outstanding Reports Menu (F-6A) से *Receivable* या *Payable* option select कर *Outstanding Reports* पाए (F-8B)।

Bills Receivable — Prime Co 20-21

Group : ♦ **All Items** — **1-Apr-20 to 31-Mar-21**

Date	Ref. No.	Party's Name	Pending Amount	*Post-Dated Amount*	Final Balance	Due on	*Overdue by days*
1-Dec-19	19-20/15	**ABC & Co**	2,000.00		2,000.00 Dr	31-Dec-19	*456*
1-Jan-20	19-20/38	**ABC & Co**	3,600.00		3,600.00 Dr	31-Jan-20	*425*
1-Feb-20	120	**ABC Traders**	7,000.00		7,000.00 Dr	1-Mar-20	*395*
1-Mar-20	127	**ABC Traders**	5,000.00		5,000.00 Dr	31-Mar-20	*365*
1-May-20	2	**ABC & Co**	6,000.00		6,000.00 Dr	31-May-20	*304*
			23,600.00		23,600.00 Dr		

F-8B: Bills Receivable Statement (Billwise)

Outstanding Reports Menu (F-6A) से Ledger option के बाद Party Ledger select कर Party Ledger Outstanding Report पायें (F-8C)।

F12:Configure button click कर अपने अनुसार Configuration option सेट करे (F-8A।

Bills Receivable — Prime Co 20-21

Group : ♦ **All Items** — **1-Apr-20 to 31-Mar-21**

Date	Ref. No.	Party's Name		Pending Amount	*Post-Dated Amount*	Final Balance	Due on	*Overdue by days*
		ABC & Co						
1-Dec-19	19-20/15			2,000.00		2,000.00 Dr	31-Dec-19	*456*
	1-Dec-19 Opening Balance		*2,000.00 Dr*					
1-Jan-20	19-20/38			3,600.00		3,600.00 Dr	31-Jan-20	*425*
	1-Jan-20 Opening Balance		*3,600.00 Dr*					
1-May-20	2			6,000.00		6,000.00 Dr	31-May-20	*304*
	1-May-20 Sales 2		*6,000.00 Dr*					
				11,600.00		11,600.00 Dr		
		ABC Traders						
1-Feb-20	120			7,000.00		7,000.00 Dr	1-Mar-20	*395*
	1-Feb-20 Opening Balance		*7,000.00 Dr*					
1-Mar-20	127			5,000.00		5,000.00 Dr	31-Mar-20	*365*
	1-Mar-20 Opening Balance		*5,000.00 Dr*					
				12,000.00		12,000.00 Dr		
				23,600.00		23,600.00 Dr		

F-8C: Bills Receivable Statement (Ledgerwise Bills)

07 Age Analysis Report

At Outstanding Report (Receivable or Payable), click *F6:Ageing Method* button (F-9D), set the Ageing Method (F-9A) and Analysis Slab (F-9B) to get display Age Analysis Report (F-9B), showing the Age slab wise details of outstanding Bills.

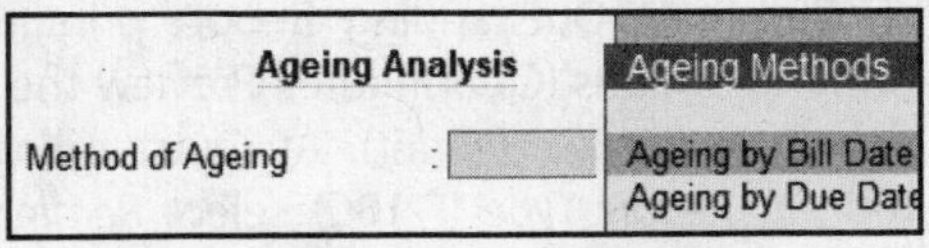

F-9A: Ageing Methods

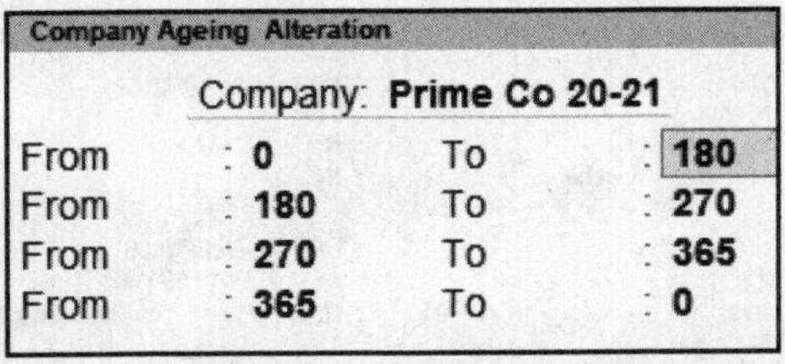

F-9B: Age Analysis Slab set up

Bill Outstanding Reports Buttons: At the right side Button Bar, you get various buttons (F-9D) to navigate through various Bill Outstanding / Age Analysis Reports:

- **F5:Bills Receivable / Bill Payable**: Click F5 to toggle between Bills Receivable & Bills Payable Reports. Click Alt+F5 to toggle between Detailed and Condensed report.
- **F6: Age Analysis**: Click F6 to get Ageing methods screen to set up Method of Ageing and Age Analysis Slab

F8:Bill wise / Ledger-wise Bills: Click F8 to toggle between Bill wise & Ledger-wise outstanding Bills Reports. Click Alt+F8 to toggle between *Including Post Dated & Excluding Post Dated* report.

At Age Analysis Report Display (F-9C), click Ctrl+P and Print *Age Analysis Report* (similar to Age Anslysis Display : F-9B), as explained for Report Printing.

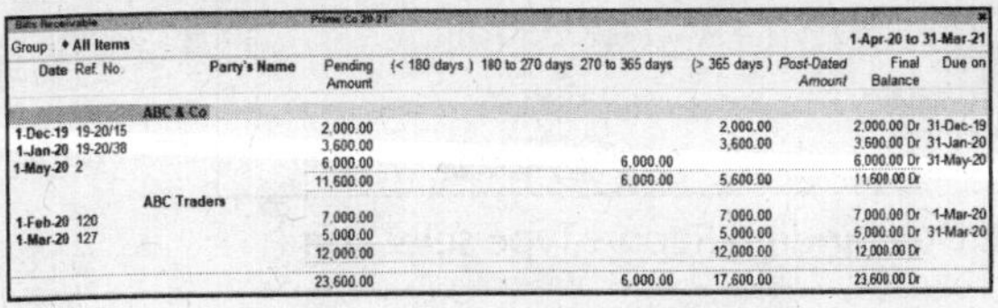

F-9C: Age Analysis Display

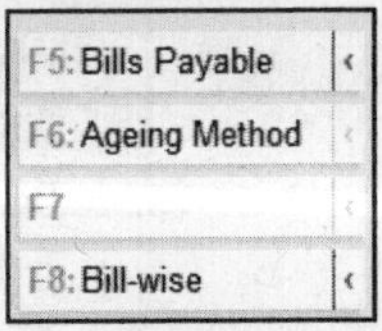

F-9D: Bills Outstanding Buttons

Outstanding Reports में F6: Ageing Method button (F-9A) से, Age Analysis Slab (F-9B) set कर Age Analysis Display करे (F-9C)। Ctrl+P कर P:Print Button से *Age Analysis Report* Configure / Preview / Print करे।

08 Outstanding Reports Printing

As explained earlier for Report Printing, at Outstanding Bill (F-8B/F-8C) display screen (F-9B), Click Ctrl+P. At Outstanding Report printing screen (F-10A), Configure Report Printing options (C:Configure), Preview the Report (I:Preview) and Print the Report on Printer (P:Print). At Outstanding Report Printing Configuration (F-10B), at *Report Type* (F-10C) select *Reminder Letter* to print Reminder Letter (F-11A) / *Bills Outstanding* to Print Party Outstanding Report.

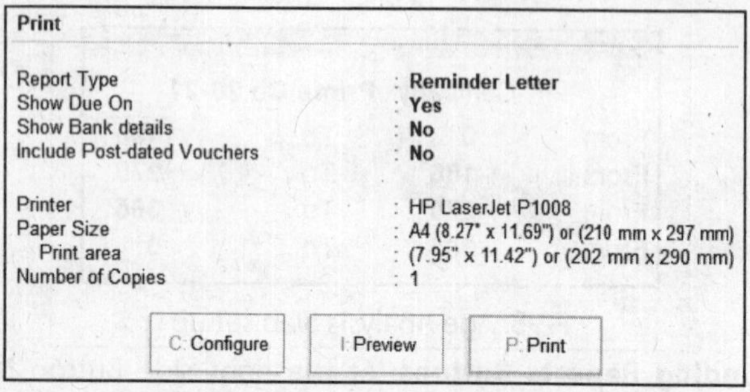

F-10A: Outstanding Report Printing

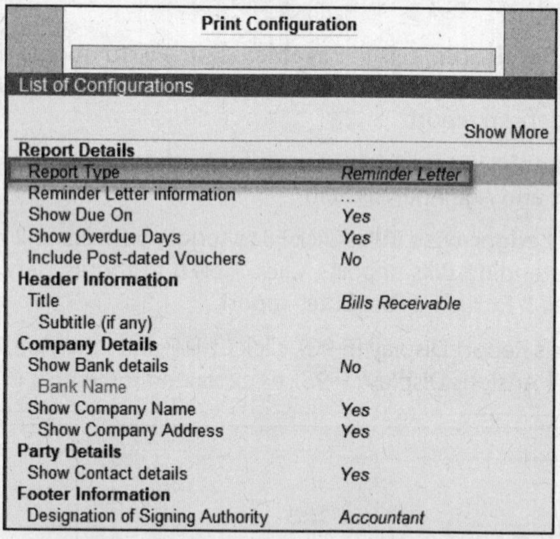

F-10B: Outstanding Report Type selection

जैसे पहले Report printing के बारे में बताये है, Outstanding Bill (F-8B/F-8C) में Ctrl+P type कर, Report Printing 10A) में Configure (C:Configure) , Report Preview करे (I:Preview), P:Print button से Printer में print करे। Report Printing Configuration (F-10B) में Report Type (F-10C) select कर Ledger Outstanding / Outstanding Reminder Print (F-11A) करे।

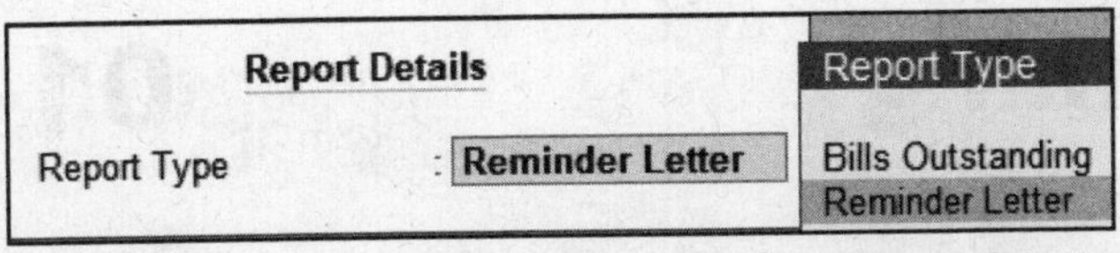

F-10C: Report Type seelction at Outstanding Report Printing

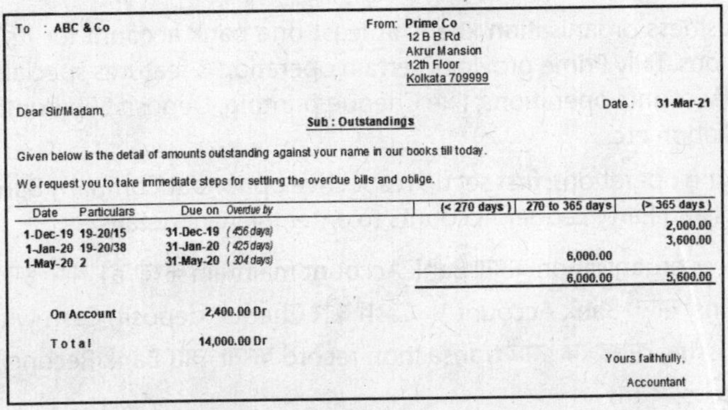

To : ABC & Co

From: Prime Co
12 B B Rd
Akrur Mansion
12th Floor
Kolkata 709999

Date : 31-Mar-21

Dear Sir/Madam,

Sub : Outstandings

Given below is the detail of amounts outstanding against your name in our books till today.

We request you to take immediate steps for settling the overdue bills and oblige.

Date	Particulars	Due on	*Overdue by*	(< 270 days)	270 to 365 days	(> 365 days)
1-Dec-19	19-20/15	31-Dec-19	*(456 days)*			2,000.00
1-Jan-20	19-20/38	31-Jan-20	*(425 days)*			3,600.00
1-May-20	2	31-May-20	*(304 days)*		6,000.00	
					6,000.00	5,600.00

On Account 2,400.00 Dr

Total 14,000.00 Dr

Yours faithfully,

Accountant

F-11A : Party Outstanding Reminder Letter in Print

09 Accounts Receivables Payables - Key Points

- Party के Bill wise Outstanding details maintain करने के लिए पहले Company Features में Enable Billwise Entry में Yes set करे।
- जिन party के Bill wise Details maintain करने है, सिर्फ उन Party ledger Account में Maintain Balance Bill by Bill में Yes set करे, और Party ledger के Opening Balance का Billwsie Details entry करे. Credit Period भी set कर सकते हैं (Credit Period zero नहीं हो सकता)।
- Voucher में Bill Details वाली Party Ledger के Bill Details screen में Bill Reference और amount entry करे।
- GoT main menu या Go To List से Bills Outstanding Receivable और Payables Report Display करे।
- Bills Outstanding Receivable और Payables Report Display में Ctrl+P से Print screen में C:Configure button से Outstanding Report Printing Configuration में Report Type select कर Party Outstanding Report या Party Outstanding Reminder print करे।
- Outstanding Report में F6 click कर Age Analysis slab set कर Age Analysis report Display / Print करे।

Banking 01-13

01 Bank Account Management

Every business organisation keeps at least one bank account for its business transactions. Tally Prime provides certain operation & features specially related to Bank Accounts operations, like Cheque printing, Deposit Slip Printing, Bank Reconciliation etc.

For Banking operations, first set up respective options at Company Bank Ledger Accounts and Party Ledger Accounts to enter relevant details.

हर business organisation अपना Bank Account maintain करते हैं। यहाँ हम Banking Operations, यानि Bank Account में Cash और Cheque deposit, Cash withdrawal, Cheque Issue, बगैरह के सारे transaction record करना और Bank Reconciliation के बारे में discuss करेंगे।

02 Bank Ledger Account set up

At the Bank Ledger Creation / Alteration (*GoT>Create>Ledger* or *GoT>Ledger>Ledger*) screen (F-1B), click *F12:Configure* and set the following options (F-1A):

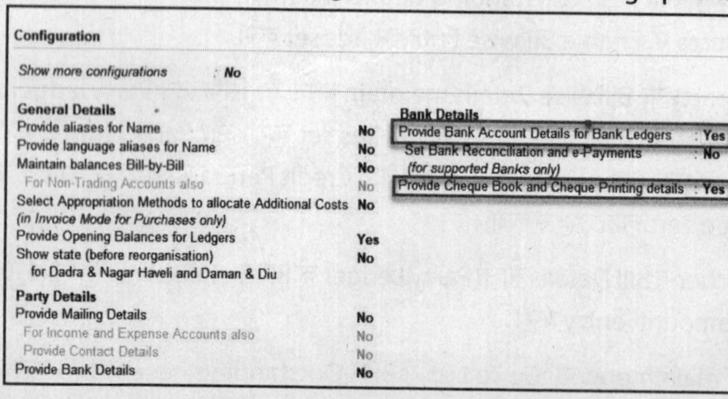

F-1A: Bank Ledger Account Configuration

- **Bank Ledger Details**: At Left part, at *Provide Bank Account Details*, set Yes.
- **Bank Details**: At Right Part, under *Bank Details* section, at *Provide Bank Account Details for Bank Ledgers*, set *Yes* to enable entry of Bank Accounts Details in Bank Ledger Account.
- **Cheque Details**: At *Provide Cheque Book* and *Cheque Printing Details*, set Yes to enable Cheque Printing.

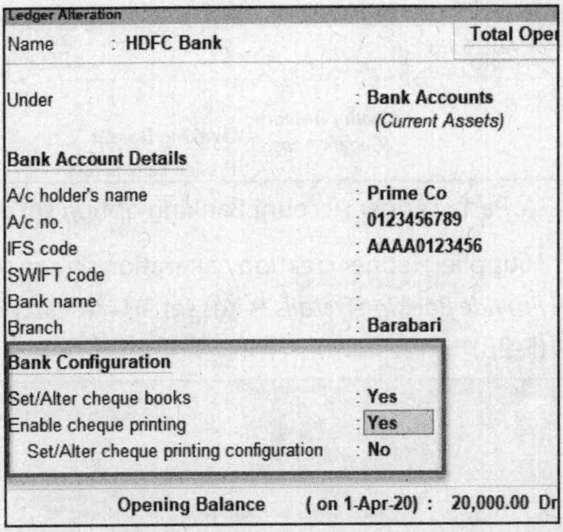

F-1B: Bank Ledger Account details for Banking Features

At Bank Ledger Account creation / Alteration screen, set the following options under Bank Configuration section (F-1B).

- At *Alter Cheque Books*, set *Yes* to enter Cheque Book details (F-1C)
- At *Enable Cheque Printing*, set *Yes* to activate Cheque Printing for the Bank Account. You may further set Yes at *Set Cheque Printing Configuration* to set up Customised Cheque Format.

Cheque Range for : HDFC Bank

From Number	To Number	Number of Cheques	Cheque Book Name
100001	100100	100	HDFC-1

F-1C: Cheque Book details

GoT>Create>Ledger / GoT>Ledger>Ledger screen (F-1B) से Bank Ledger Account Creation/ Alteration में F12 से Bank Details section में Configuration set करे (F-1A), Bank Ledger Account में Bank Configuration section के details (F-1B) और Cheue Book details entry करे (F-1C)।

03 Party Bank Account set up

Debtors & Creditors Ledger Account Creation / Alteration (*GoT>Create>Ledger* or *GoT>Ledger>Ledger*) screen (F-2A) have been explained earlier. At the Customer (under Sundry Debtor Group) / Supplier (under Sundry Creditor Group) Ledger Accounts (F-2A), set *Yes* at the option *Provide Bank Details*, to enable entry of Bank Account details. At Party Ledger Banking details (F-2B), select the Payment Mode from the list.

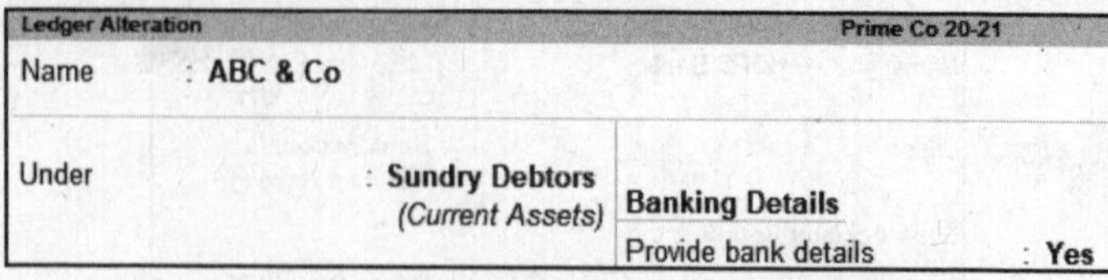

F-2A: Party Ledger Account Banking option set up

Party (Customer / Supplier) ledger creation / alteration screen (F-2A) में *Banking Details* section में *Provide Banking Details* में Yes set करे और Party के Bank Account Details entry करे (F-2B)।

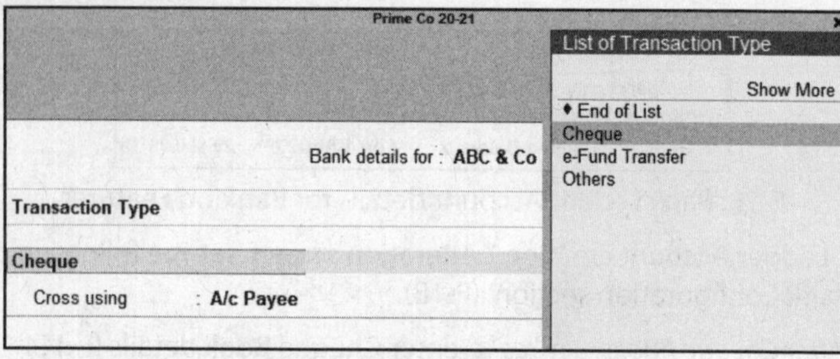

F-2B: Party Bank details set up

04 Banking Details entry in Voucher

We have already explained entry of Contra Voucher, Payment Voucher & Receipt Voucher. Here we explain additional details entry in respect Bank ledger transaction in such vouchers.

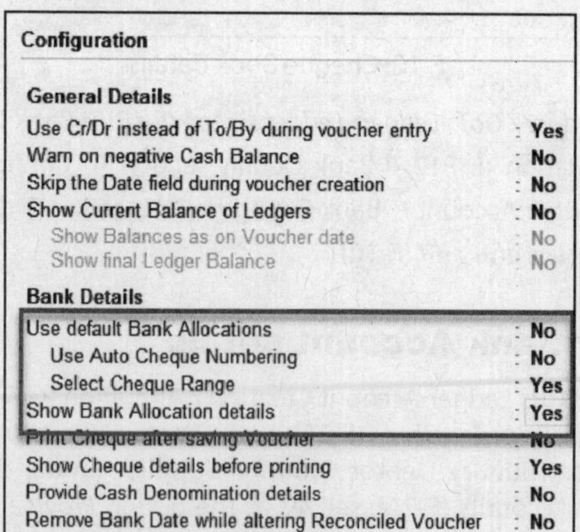

F-3A: Banking option set up in Voucher entry Configuration

At Voucher entry screen GoT>Vouchers (F-3B), click F12:Configure and set the Bank details option under Bank details section (F-3A). During Voucher entry, on selection of Bank Account and Amount, at Bank Allocation screen, enter the cheque Book details (F-3C).

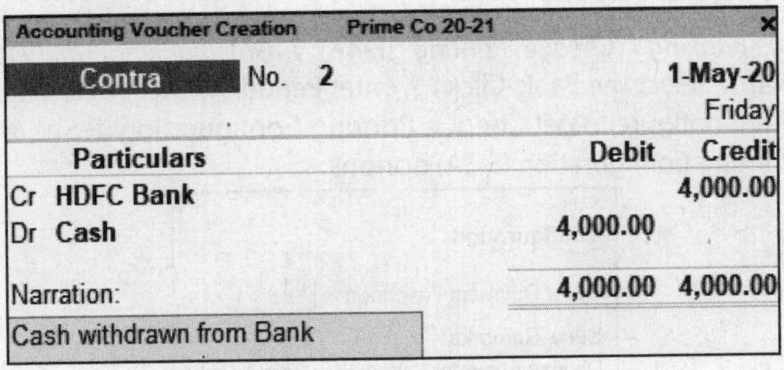

F-3B: Voucher entry for Bank transaction

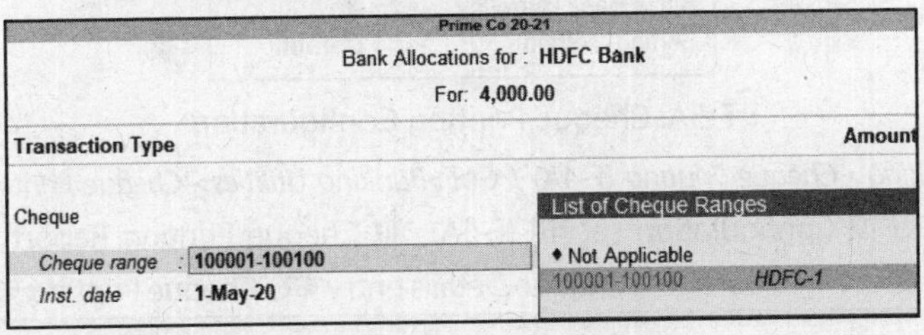

F-3C: Bank details in Voucher

05 Banking Menu

After Banking Option set up in Bank Ledgers (F-1A to F-1C) and Party Ledgers (F-2A / F-2B), to access Banking related task, select *GoT>Banking* (F-4A) / Go To > Banking Utilities (F-4B).

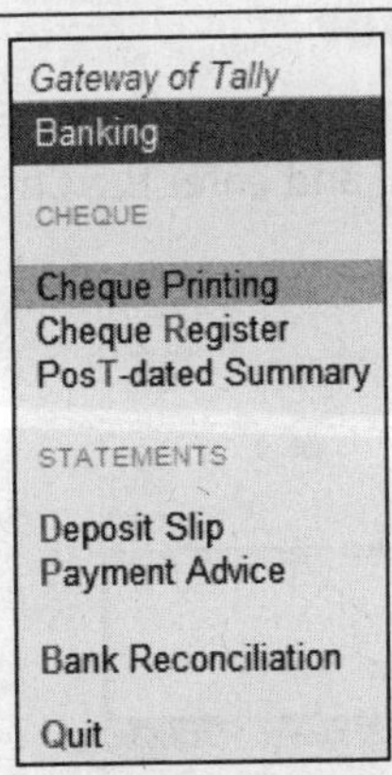

F-4A: Banking Menu from GoT

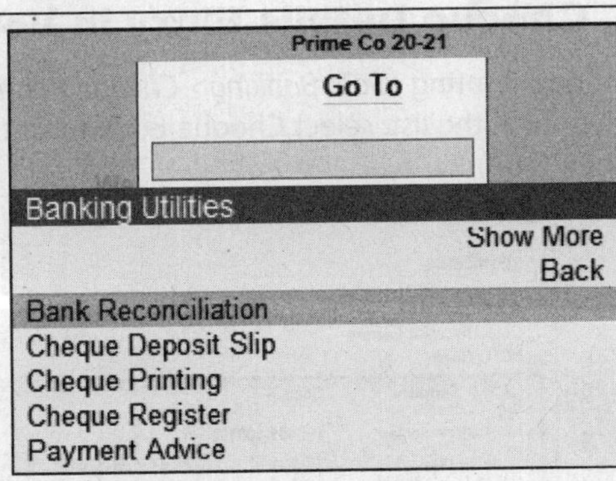

F-4B: Banking Utiliies from Go To list

GoT>Banking (F-4A) / Go To > Banking Utilities (F-4B) से सारे Banking Operation का options select करे।

06 Cheque Issue

Select *GoT>Banking> Cheque Printing* (F-4A) / *GoT>Banking Utilities> Cheque Printing* (F-4B). Select the Bank, Click F2, enter Period. At *Cheque Printing* screen(F-5B), click F12:Configure to get Cheque Printing Configuration (F-5A) and set the Cheque Printing Configuration (F-5A) oprions.

Configuration

Show Payment Favouring	: **Yes**
Show Remarks	: **No**
Display name for Ledgers	: **Name Only**
Show Base Currency	: **No**
Sorting Method	: **Default**

F-5A: Cheque Printing Configuration

GoT>Banking> Cheque Printing (F-4A) / *GoT>Banking Utilities> Cheque Printing* (F-4B) select कर F12 Configuration set करे (F-5A) और Cheque Printing Report से (F-5B) Voucher select कर Voucher में Cheque Details entry करे / Cheque Printing करे (F-6A)।

Cheque Printing — Prime Co 20-21

Ledger: **HDFC Bank** — *(Cheque Printing - All Cheques)* — 1-Apr-20 to 31-Mar-21

Date	Particulars	Favouring Name	Instrument No.	Instrument Date	Printed ?	Amount
1-Apr-20	**A B C Supplier**		100001	1-Apr-20	No	2,940.00
1-May-20	**Cash**	Prime Co	100002	1-May-20	No	4,000.00
1-Jun-20	**ABC & Co**		100003	1-Jun-20	No	3,000.00
Selected Total						
Grand Total						9,940.00

F-5B: Cheque Printing Report.

07 Cheque Details Entry in Voucher

At Cheque Printing (*GoT>Banking> Cheque Printing*) Report (F-5B), select the voucher from the list, select Cheque Book from the list and enter the Cheque Number (F-6A).

Payment No. 1 — 1-Apr-20, Wednesday

Particulars			Debit	Credit
Dr **A B C Supplier**			3,000.00	
Cr **Cash Discount Earned**				60.00
Cr **HDFC Bank**				2,940.00
A B C Supplier	Cheque	2,940.00		
Cheque range	: 100001-100100			
Inst. no.	: 100001	*Inst. date* : 1-Apr-20		
Narration:			3,000.00	3,000.00

Paid against bills after deducting Cash Discount @ 2%

F-6A: Cheque details entry in Voucher

Banking menu (F-4A) से Cheque Printing select कर Cheque Printing report (F-5B) से Voucher select कर Voucher में Cheque Details entry करे (F-6A)।

08 Cheque / Payment Advice Printing

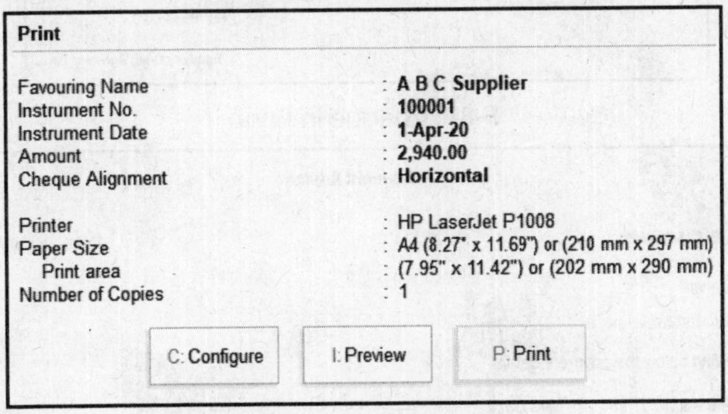

F-7B: Cheque Printing

Payment Voucher Printing: After Cheque Details entry in a voucher (F-6A), Click *P:Print* to Configure / Preview / Print the Voucher (F-7A), as explained in Reports Printing.

Payment Advice Printing: After Voucher Printing, at Payment Voucher printing (F-7A), click *C:Configure* and set Yes at *Print Payment Advice*, and then Click *P: Print* (F-7A) to print the Payment Advice (F-9A)

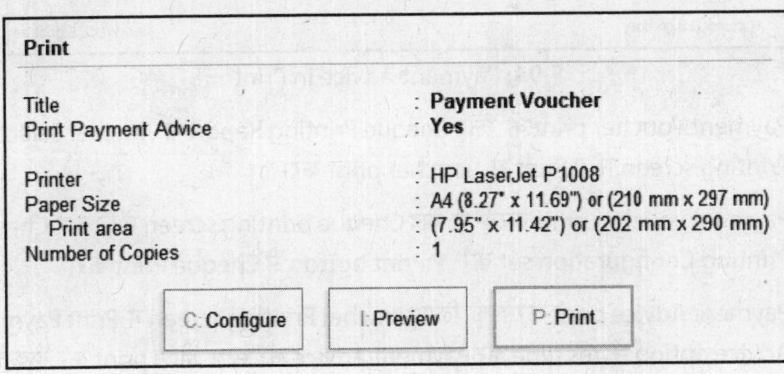

F-7A: Payment Voucher / Payment Advice Printing

Cheque Print: Having printed the Payment Voucher, you get the Cheque Printing details screen (F-7B),showing the Cheque details for information. Click C:Configure button to set up Cheque Configuration and then click *P:Print* to print the Cheque (F-8A).

A/c Payee 01042021

A B C Supplier

Two Thousand Nine Hundred Forty Only

**2,940.00

for Prime Co

Signatory One Signatory Two

F-8A: Cheque in Print

Payment Advice

M/s. A B C Supplier Date : **2-Apr-20**

West Bengal -

Dear Sir/Madam,

Please find below the payment details.

Bill Ref.	Bill Date	Amount
On Account		3,000.00
Less : Cash Discount Earned		(-)60.00
	Nett Amount	**₹ 2,940.00**

Payment Details

Payment Mode	Transferred to	Instrument Details	Issued From	Amount
Cheque		No.: 100001 Dt: 1-Apr-20	HDFC Bank	2,940.00
			Total	**₹ 2,940.00**

Kindly acknowledge the receipt.

Thanking You

Authorised Signatory Receiver's Signature

F-9A: Payment Advice in Print

- Payment Voucher print के लिए Cheque Printing Report से Voucher select कर Printing screen में P:Print से Voucher print करे।
- Payment voucher print करने के बाद Cheque printing screen में F12 से Cheque Printing Configuration set करे. P:Print button से Cheque Print करे।
- Payment Advice print करने के लिए Voucher Printing screen में Print Payment Advice option में Yes type कर Payment Advice भी साथ ही में print कर सकते है।

09 Deposit Slip Printing

At Banking menu (F-4A), select *Deposit Slip* and then select the Bank for which you like to print the deposit slip to get Deposit Slip screen (F-10D / F-10E). Click Ctrl+P to get Deposit Slip Printing screen (F-8C)

Configuration

Show Received From	: **Yes**
Show Remarks	: **No**
Display name for Ledgers	: **Name Only**
Show Base Currency	: **No**
Sorting Method	: **Default**

F-10A: Deposit Slip Printing

For Cash Deposit, during Voucher Entry / Alteration of the respective Contra Voucher, enter the Cash Denominations (F-11A). During Voucher Printing, set the options for Cash Deposit Slip Printing (F-10B) to Print Cash Deposit Slip (F-11D).

Print

Print Cash Deposit Slip	: **Yes**

F-10B: Cash Deposit Slip Printing

Print

Print Cheque Deposit Slip	: **Yes**
Print Customer's Copy	: **Yes**
Date of Print	: **16-Dec-20**
Printer	: HP LaserJet P1008
Paper Size	: A4 (8.27" x 11.69") or (210 mm x 297 mm)
Print area	: (7.95" x 11.42") or (202 mm x 290 mm)
Number of Copies	: 1

C: Configure | I: Preview | P: Print

F-10C: Cheque Deposit Slip Printing

– Bank में Deposit के लिए Banking Menu (F-4A) से Deposit Slip select करे, फिर Bank Account select करे। Alt+F2 से Report Period set कर Deposit Slip Register (F-10E) में Voucher select कर Deposit Slip Print करे।

Cash Deposit Slip — Prime Co 20-21

Ledger: **HDFC Bank** — **1-Apr-20 to 31-Mar-21**

Date	Particulars	Received From	Instrument Date	Printed ?	Amount
1-Apr-20	**Cash**		1-Apr-20	**No**	**2,000.00**
	Selected Total				
	Grand Total				**2,000.00**

F-10D: Cash Deposit Slip

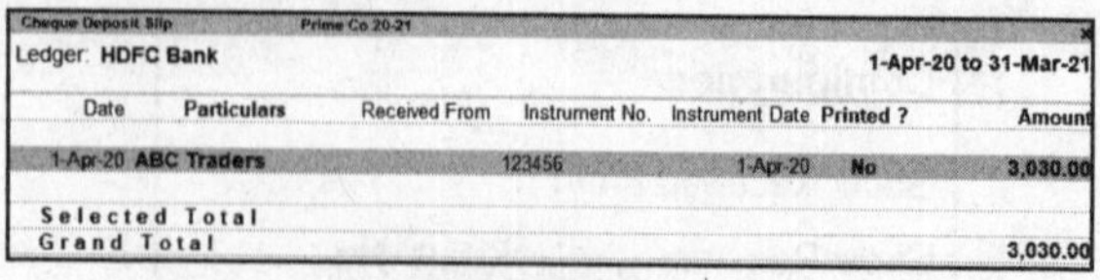

F-10E: Cheque Deposit Slip

- Cash Deposit के Contra Voucher में Cash Denomination entry करे (F-11A) I Ctrl+P type कर Printing screen (F-10B) में P:Print click कर Deposit Slip print (F-11D) करे.

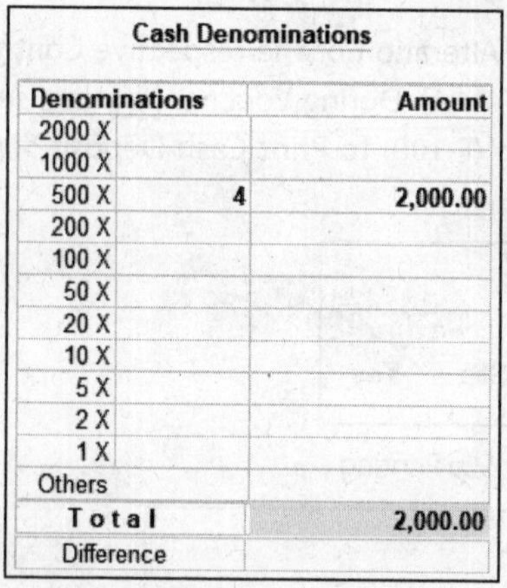

F-11A: Cash Deposit Slip Entry

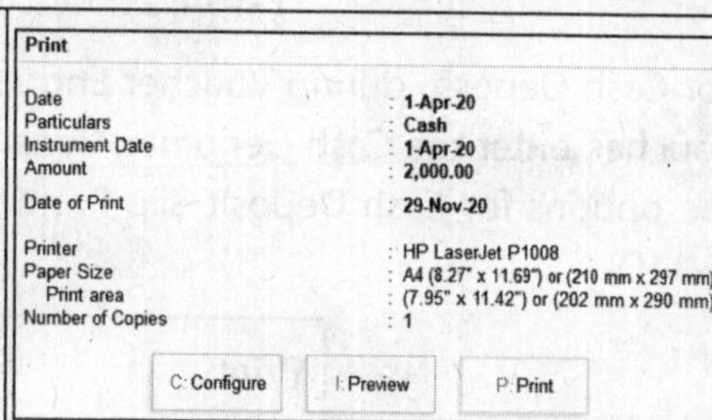

F-11B: Cash Deposit Slip Printing

- Bank का Deposit slip के लिए Bank का अपना printed slip होता है। Tally से printed Deposit slip का Bank द्वारा स्वीकृति (acceptance) पहले जाँच ले।

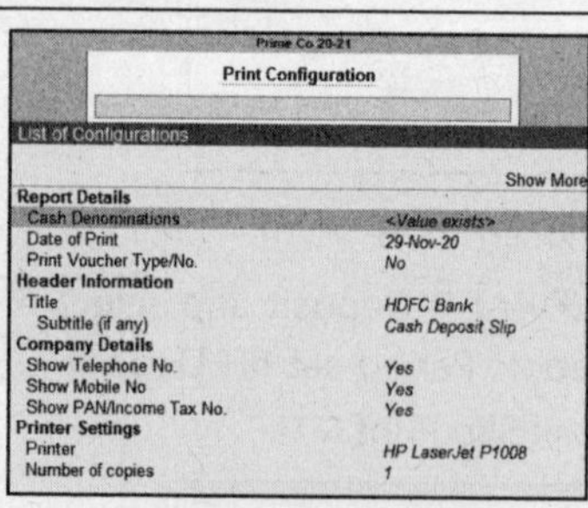

F-11C: Deposit Slip Printing Configuration

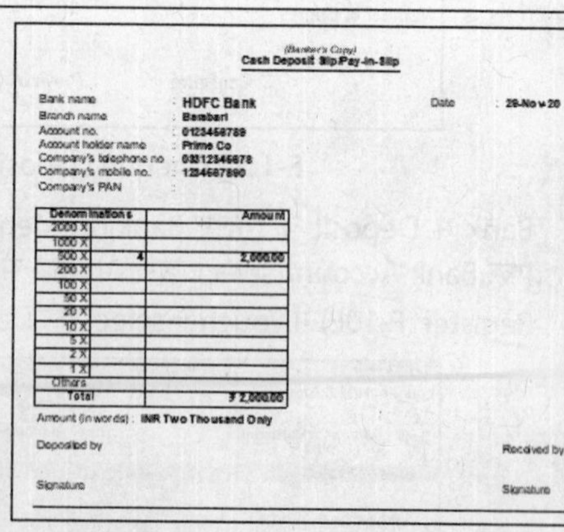

F-11D: Cash Deposit Slip in Print

10 Bank Reconciliation

Bank Reconciliation is the process of matching the entries between Bank Book & Pass Book) with Bank Pass Book) and tracing the unmatched entries in either of the books (Bank Book or the Pass Book), It is essential to ensure correctness of Bank Accounts.

Configuration

Show Narrations	: **Yes**
Show Favouring Name/Received From	: **Yes**
Show Remarks	: **Yes**
Allow Back-dated Reconciliation	: **Yes**

F-12A: Bank Reconciliation Configuration

Select *GoT>Banking > Bank Reconciliation* (F-4A) and select a *Bank Account* from the list to get Bank Reconciliation screen (F-12B).

Bank Reconciliation द्वारा Bank Book और Bank Statement (Pass Book) match करे. GoT> Banking > Bank Reconciliation select कर Alt+F2 से Period set कर Bank Reconciliation report पाएं.

Bank Reconciliation — Prime Co 20-21

Ledger: **HDFC Bank** — (Reconciliation) — **1-Apr-20 to 31-Mar-21**

Date	Particulars	Favouring Name / Received From	Vch Type	Transaction Type	Instrument No.	Instrument Date	Bank Date	Debit	Credit
1-Apr-20	**Cash** *Cash deposited into Bank*		**Contra**	Cash		1-Apr-20	*1-Apr-20*	**2,000.00**	
1-Apr-20	**A B C Supplier** *Paid against bills after deducting Cash Discount @ 2%*		**Payment**	Cheque	100001	1-Apr-20			**2,940.00**
1-May-20	**Cash** *Cash withdrawn from Bank*	Prime Co	**Contra**	Cheque	100002	1-May-20	*1-May-20*		**4,000.00**
1-Jun-20	**ABC & Co** *Paid to Party as Advance*		**Payment**	Cheque	100003	1-Jun-20			**3,000.00**
							Balance as per company books:	**12,060.00**	
							Amounts not reflected in bank:		**5,940.00**
							Balance as per bank:	**18,000.00**	

F-12B: Bank Reconciliation

At *Bank Reconcilitaion* screen (F-12B), click *F12:Configure* to get *Bank Reconciltaion Configurtaion* screen (F-12A) to set the options.

Pass Book Date Entry: Enter the Bank Pass Book Date of the matched Vouchers at bank date column in Bank Reconcilation Statement (F-12B) and print the Bank Reconcilation Showing unmatched Vouchers, to tally the Bank passbook balance with Bank Book Balance.

Bank Reconcilation screen (F-12B) के Bank Date column में Matched Entry के Bank Pass Book date entry कर Unmatched Entry के Bank Reconciliation Statement print करे, जिसमें Bank Pass Book और Bank Book के balance match होगा।

Bank Reconciliation Opening entries: To start Bank Reconciliation from a date having unreconciled entries, click <u>H</u>*: Opening BRS* button to get the Opening BRS screen, and enter the details of such opening unreconciled entries.

Bank Reconciliation Start करते वक्त के unmatched records की entry *H: Opening BRS* button click कर entry करें।

11 Banking - Key Points

- Banking Features activate करने के लिए Bank Ledger और Party Ledger के option set करें।
- Voucher entry में cheque details entry करें।
- Cheque Reports से voucher select कर Voucher / Cheque / Payment Advice print करें।
- Contra / Receipt Voucher entry में Cash Denomination entry कर Deposit slip print करें।
- Bank Reconciliation screen से Bank entry match कर Bank Reconciliation Statement (BRS) print करें।

Tally Data Maintenance

01-14

Tally Data Maintenance

Now we discuss briefly about maintenance of Tally Data like, Data Back Up, Data Restoration and Data Repair (Rewrite)

01 Data Backup

Through Data Backup, a copy of data is kept at another place for safety. If the current working data is lost or damaged, the Backed Data may be restored and continue working.

F-1A: Data Menu

Select *Y: Data* from top menu bar to get Data menu (F-1A). Select *Back Up* to get Back Up Companies screen (F-2A). The default Back Up location and the Companies at default data Path are shown for convenience (F-2A).

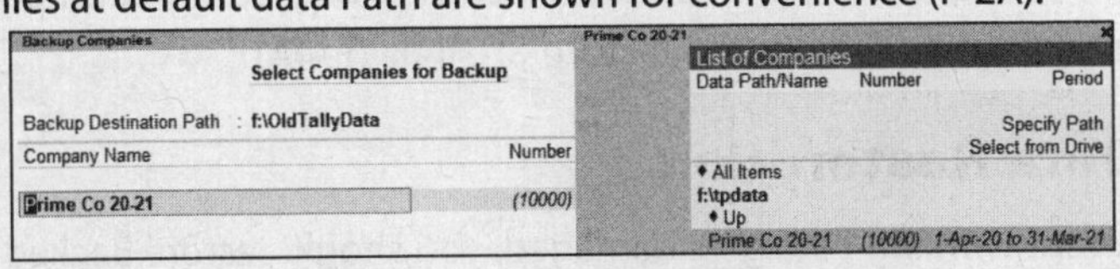

F-2A: Company Selection for Data Back Up

- **Source Data Back Up Locations**: To Back Up data from other locations, select the desired data path from the options *Specify Path* (when the data path is known) or *Select from drive*. All the Companies stored in the specified path will be listed, as explained earlier.
- **Selection of Companies for Back Up**: Now select the Company to Back Up from the list (F-2A). The selected Company will be listed left part (F-2A). This way, you may select multiple Companies for Back Up and finally press <enter> at blank line.

- **Data Back Up Locations**: At *Back Up Destination Path* (F-2A), the default Back Up path is sown at the top. To change it, click on the Data path and the select the Back Up Data path from the list of Folders. The selected path will appear at *Back Up Destination Path.*

F-3A: Data Back Up overwrite message

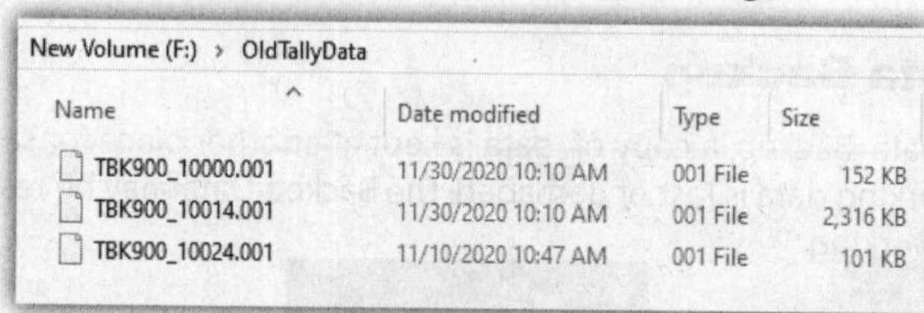

F-4A: Backed up data

Having set the Back Up Destination path and selection of Companies Data for Back Up (F-2A), Press Y at Accept Yes/ No to start the Back Up process (message of overwriting on Previous Back up may appear– F-3A). Backed Up Data of each of the selected Company will be stored in the specified Back Up Data Path (F-4A). The Back Up filename indicates the Company Number (F-4A).

Data Back up से चालू data की एक copy दूसरे folder या media में रखा जाता है, ताकि अगर चालू data कोई कारण खराब हो जाये, to Back up से Data वापस मिल जाये. Top Menu Bar Y: Data option से Back Up select करे (F-1A), Back Up Destination Path में Back Up Folder नाम entry करे (F-2A), और Back Up करने वाली Company Select करे (F-2A). Back up Destination path में Backed Up Company data Company Number के filename में store हो जायेगा (F-4A)।

02 Data Restoration

If the current working data gets damaged, you should restore Backed up data to get the data back in the current working directory, in functional condition.

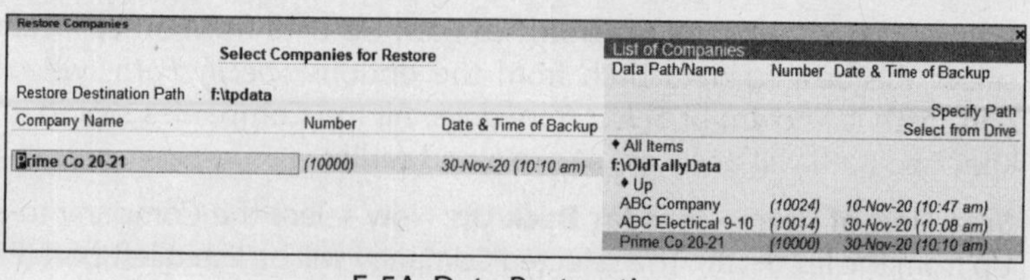

F-5A: Data Restoration

At Data Menu, select *Restore* from top *Y:Data* Menu Bar option (F-1A) to get *Restore Companies* screen (F-5A). At the Right Part of *Restore Companies* screen (F-5A), all the Back Up Data stored in the default Back Up Path along with date of data Back Up is shown (change the data path to Restore Back Up data from Different Directory). Select the file for Data Restoration. Selected file will be then shown in the left part (select End of List at end of selection). The default Data Path is also shown at Restore Destination path at the top. Overwriting on Restoration message will be displayed (F-5B). Type N and change the Data Path if you like to Restore in a different Data path, or Type Y to Restore Backed up Data in the current working directory.

F-5B: Data Restoration Message

चालू data कोई कारण से खराब होने से Back Up Data Restore करने के लिए Y:Data Menu Bar option (F-1A) से Restore select करे। Default Data Path में Back Up किये Company के list से Restore करने वाली Company select करे। Restoration message पर Yes type करे (F-5B)।

03 Data Re-writing (Data Repair)

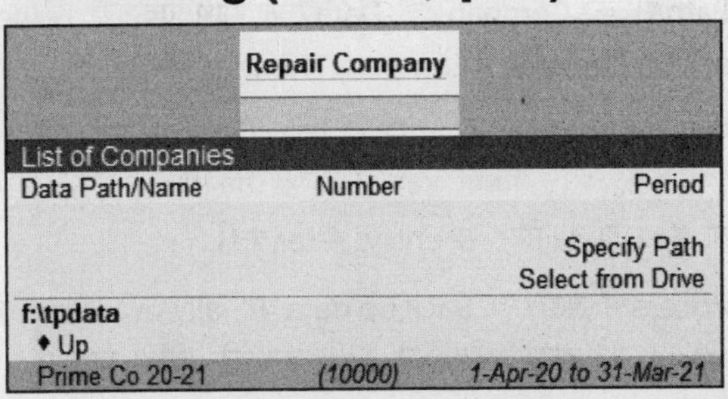

F-6A: Repair Company Screen

Sometimes, Tally fails to open a company (due to minor data problem or non-compatibility). In such instance, at GoT, press *Alt+Ctrl+R*. At Repair Company screen, select the Company whose data is to be repaired (F-6A). Click R:Repair button (F-6B). At Repair Message, click Y to Repair data (F-6C). After Repair, select the Company. If still the Company fails to Open, then there is damage in data and you need to Restore from Backed up Data as explained.

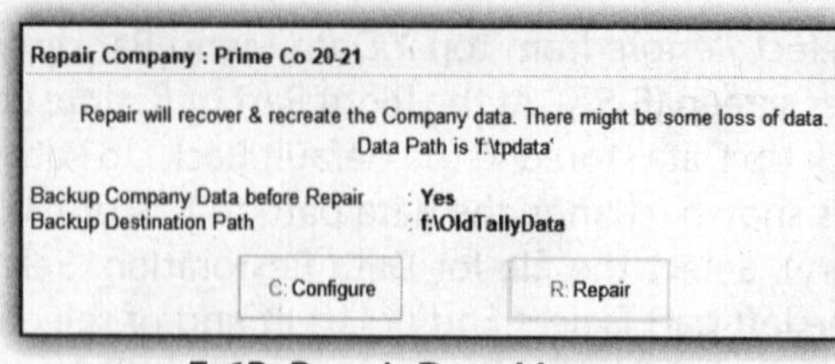

F-6B: Repair Data Message

Company Open नहीं हो पाने से Data Repair के लिए GoT में Alt+Ctrl+R type करे और Repair करने वाली Company select करे (F-6A)। Repair Company screen में R:Repair button click करे। GoT में F3:Select Company button से Company select करे। अगर Compny Open हो गयी तो ठीक है, नहीं तो Back Up से Data Restore करना होगा।

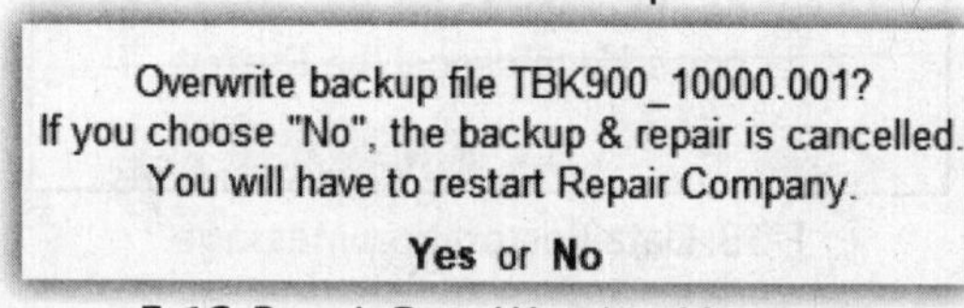

F-6C: Repair Data Warning Message

04 Tally Data Maintenance - Key Points

- Backed up data से ही Data Restore कर सकते हैं। Back up नहीं तो Restoration भी नहीं।
- एक Data Path से कई Company के Data एक साथ एक ही Folder में Back up कर सकते हैं। Back Up filename में Company Number और Back Up का Time दिखता है।
- Restore किया हुआ data current Data को overwrite कर देगा। इसलिए Backed Up data में last Back up किया हुआ data ही मिलेगा। Last back up के बाद entry / Alter किया हुआ Data फिर से entry/ Alter करे।
- Back up process में पहले के Back up data को Tally overwrite करता है, इसलिए, पहले के back up को दूसरे folder में copy कर ले, ताकि जरूरत हो तो पुराने back up data भी मिल सके. अगर datewise Voucher entry ना हुआ हो, backdated voucher alter, insert या Alter हुआ हो, Master modify हुआ हो, तो Restore कर बिल्कुल current स्थिति का data वापस पा सकने की कोई निश्चयता नहीं।
- अगर multiple directory में data रख रहे हैं तो हर directory में Company Number 10000 से start होता है। इसलिए, एक ही नंबर की कई Company create हो सकती है. Data Folder Name और Back Up data file नाम से Company का नंबर मालूम होता है लेकिन Company Name नहीं मालूम होता, ऐसे स्थिति में Data file mix हो सकता है, data overwrite हो सकता है. Careful रहे।

- Company Number के अनुसार Back up Data का filename होता है। अगर कई folder में Tally Data store करते हैं तो एक ही number की कई Company create होगी। इस स्थिति में, Back up भी उस अनुसार अलग folders में करे, नहीं तो एक Company के Back Up data दूसरी company के Back Up Data को overwrite करेगा।
- कभी-कभी version change या अन्य कारण से Company Open नहीं होता। ऐसे समय में Ctrl+ Alt+R से Company select कर Data Repair करे। Data Repair के बाद भी अगर Company Open नहीं हुई तो शायद आपको Back Up से data Restore करना होगा।
- पुराना Data Restore करने के पहले कोई expert से Data Recover करने की कोशिश करे।
- Data Back Up और Data Restoration अनुभवी staff पर ही सौंपे। यह एक sensitive काम है।

PART 2

Basic Invoicing & Inventory

So far we discussed about Financial Accounting (Accounting of Money). In this section, we discuss about Accounting of Materials, covering creation of Masters, Entry of Transactions, Printing of Invoices and various Inventory Reports.

अभी तक हमने Financial Accounting System के बारे में explain किया है. इस अध्याय में Inventory System और Invoicing के बारे में पढ़ेंगे।

Inventory Masters explains creation of Inventory Masters, like UoM, Stock Group, Stock Items, Stock Category and Godowns, to maintain Inventory System

Inventory Master में हर तरह के Inventory master, जैसे UoM, Stock Group, Stock Items, Godown, बगैरह के बारे में explain किया है।

Inventory Vouchers describes various types of transactions of materials. It describes how the Accounting & Inventory transactions (like in Sales, Purchase, Debit & Credit Notes) and Stock Journal Vouchers are recorded.

Inventory Voucher में माल (Materials) का लेन देन (जैसे Sales, Purchase, Debit & Credit Notes) के बारे में समझाया है।

Invoicing is the most important task of Inventory system, taking most of the time and volume of Inventory work. The finer aspect of essential Invoice Data Entry & Configuration are explained.

Invoicing में खरीद बिक्री (Sale/Purchase) के Invoice entry और Print करने का तरीका समझाया है।

Invoice Printing explains the process of configuring the contents of Invoice and printing the Invoice in various formats

Invoice Printing में अपने तरीके से Bill Printing समझाया है।

Inventory Reports describes scores of Inventory reports Display & Printing.

Inventory Reports में माल संबंधित सभी reports समझाया है।

Point of Sales describes quick entry printing of Retail Invoices.

Point of Sales में Cash Counter में खुदरा बिक्री की entry और तुरंत Cash memo Printing के बारे में समझाया है।

Inventory Masters 02-01

Inventory System

In previous part, we have explained Basic Accounting System, involving Financial Transactions (transaction represented in Money). Now we will discuss Basic Inventory System involving (transaction involving Materials) also. Without repeating what has already been explained, we discuss the additional aspects for maintaining Inventory System (Materials).

Accounts module में जो explain किये हैं, उसे repeat किये बगैर, अब हम Inventory module के additional options discuss करेंगे।

01 Inventory System Activation

To maintain Inventory system also, at Menu bar option *K:Company*, click *F11:-Features* (or press *F11* button). At *Company Features* screen (F-1A), set *Yes* at *Maintain Inventory*.

Company: Prime Co 20-21 (Inventory)			
Show more features	: No		
Accounting		**Taxation**	
Maintain Accounts	: Yes	Enable Goods and Services Tax (GST)	: No
Enable Bill-wise entry	: Yes	Enable Tax Deducted at Source (TDS)	: No
Inventory			
Maintain Inventory	: Yes		
Integrate Accounts with Inventory	: No		

F-1A: Accounting Features set up for Inventory & Invoicing

Inventory System Activate करने के लिए, F11:click कर *Maintain Inventory* option में Yes type करे (F-1A)।

02 Inventory Masters Menu

Having activated Inventory for the Company (F-1A), first you need to create the required Basic Inventory Masters like Unit of Measure (UoM) and Stock Item. You may optionally also create Stock Group, Stock Category, Godowns, where needed. Select *GoT>Create* to get Master Creation Menu (F-2A).

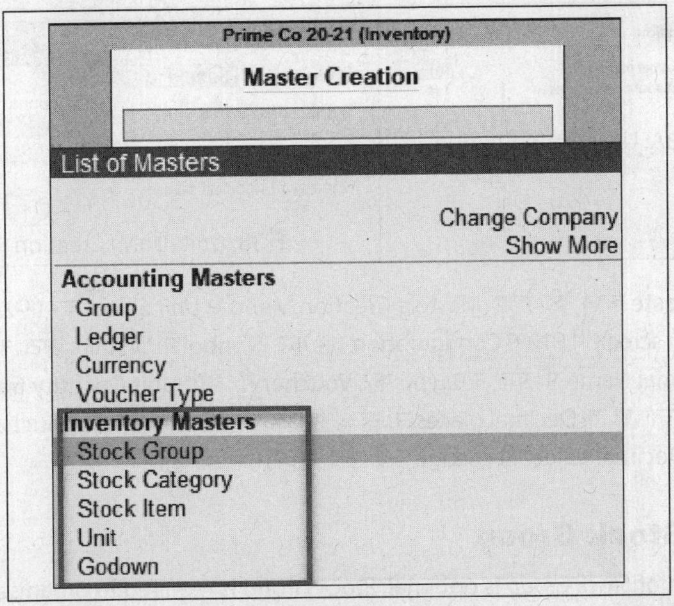

F- 2A : Masters creation Menu

Inventory Masters create करने के लिए *GoT>Create* select करे और फिर Inventory Masters के list से Master select करे (F-2A)।

03 Unit of Measure (UoM)

Every Stock Item must be measured in some specified Unit (Unit of Measurement or UoM). So, first create the necessary UoM. At Masters creation (*GoT>Create*) Menu (F-2A), select *Unit* to get Unit (UoM) Creation Screen (F-3B). Click F12:Configure button to get UoM Configuration screen (F-3A) and set the options. Now enter the following Particulars.

- **Type**: Cursor normally skips showing at *Type* field, with *Simple* as selected, to create a Simple Unit (otherwise press <shift+Tab> or <backspace> to get the cursor at *Type* field and select *Simple* (F-3B).
- **Symbol**: At *Symbol* field, enter the Short Name of the Unit (e.g., Kg. Ltr.). In all reports, the Unit Symbol appears along with Quantity, to indicate the UoM of the Quantity.
- **Formal Name**: Enter full Name of the Unit (e.g., Kilogram, Litre etc) different from UoM Symbol, for proper identification
- **Number of Decimal Places** : If the quantity is to be expressed in fractional values, enter the number of decimal places, to allow sufficient precision for accurate computation.

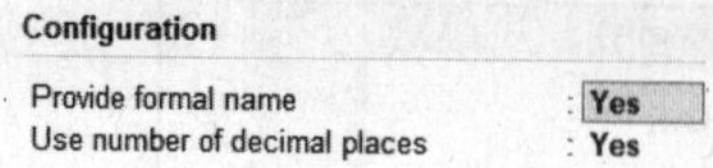

F-3A: UoM Configuration

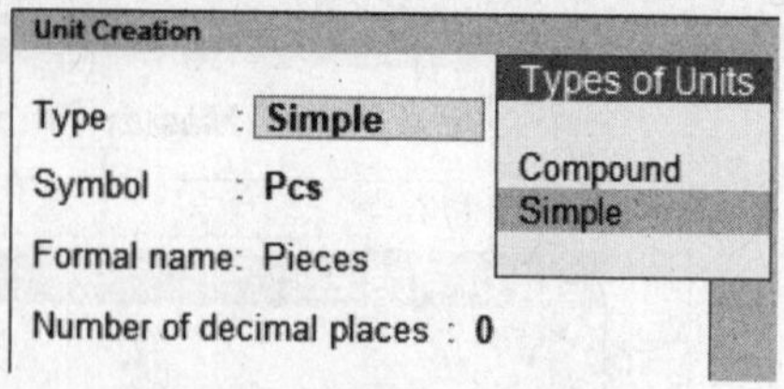

F-3B: Unit (UoM) Creation

UoM create करने के लिए Masters Creation Menu से *Unit* Select करे (F-2A)। Unit creation screen में F12 से Configuration set कर, Symbol में Unit का छोटा नाम type करे। Formal Name में पूरा नाम type करे. Voucher में अगर Unit Quantity fraction में entry करना हो तो Decimal places में सोच समझकर value type करे (Voucher entry के बाद Decimal value को change नहीं कर सकते)।

04 Stock Group

Creation of *Stock Group* is optional. Stock Group is required to organise Inventory in better way.

At Masters creation Menu (GoT>Create-F-2A), select *Stock Group* to get *Stock Group* Creation Screen (F-4B). Click F12:Configure button to get *Stock Group* Configuration screen and set the options (F-4A). Enter the following Particulars (F-4B):

- **Stock Group Name**: Enter Name of Stock Group
- **Parent Stock Group**: At *Under* field, select the parent Stock Group for the Stock Group being created (select *Primary* to create top level Group). The first Stock Group created must be placed under *Primary*.
- **Stock Group Quantity**: At Should *Quantities of Items be Added?*, set *Yes* to get Total Stock Quantity of the child Stock Items under the Stock Group (if all child Stock Items are measured in same UoM), else set *No* (Stock Group Quantity is not computed).

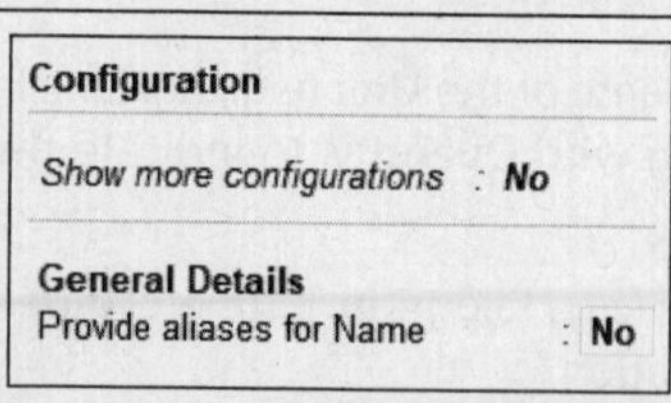

F-4A: Stock Group Configuration

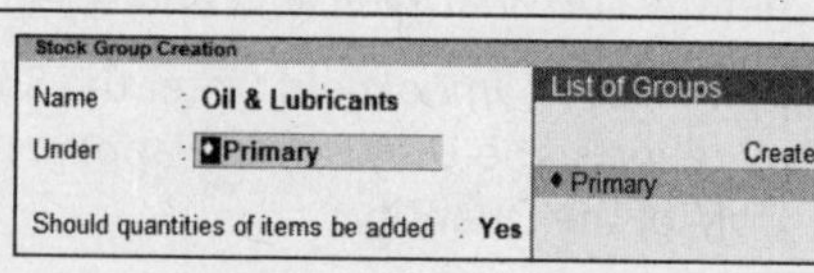

F-4B: Stock Group creation

Stock Group Create करने के लिए, Masters Creation Menu (F-2A) से Unit select करें। *Stock Group* field में Stock Group Name entry करें (F-4B)। *Under* field में Parent (मूल) Stock Group select करें (या *Primary* select करो)।

05 Multiple Godowns

Godowns (Warehouse) are location of materials storage. Tally automatically creates a Godown called *Main Location* (F-5A) To store Stock Items at different locations, create Godown.

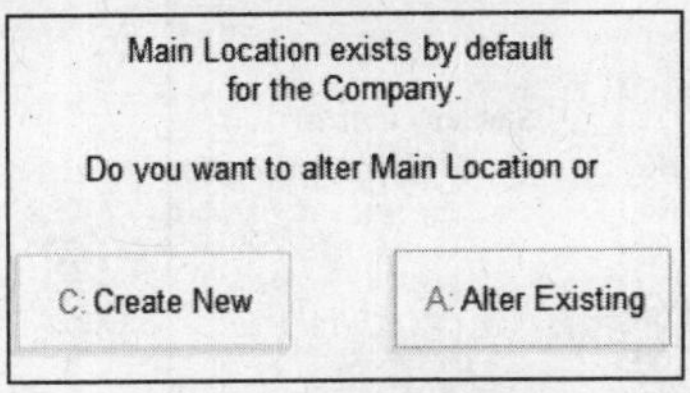

F-5A: Godown creation message

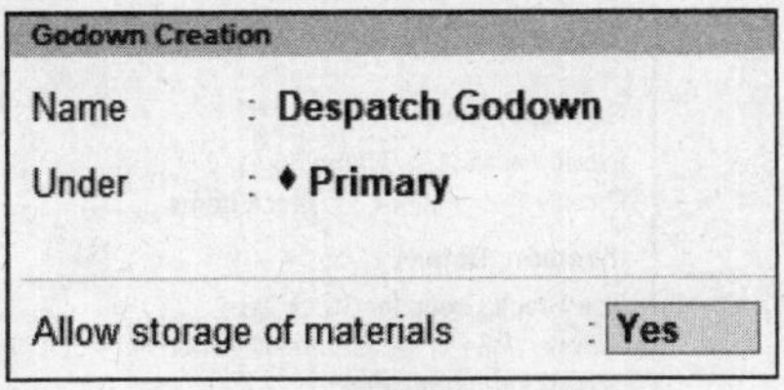

F-5B: Godown creation

Creation of Godown Master: At Masters Creation Menu (*GoT>Create*), select *Godown (F-2A)*. A message appears about existence of auto created default *Main Location* (F-5A). To change the name of Main Location, click *A:Alter Existing* and change the Name. Click *Create New* (F-5A) to get Godown Creation screen (F-5B). Click F12:Configure button and set the Configuration Options (F-5C). At Godown Creation screen (F-5B), enter the following particulars :

- **Godown Name**: At *Name*, enter Name of the Godown.
- **Parent Godown**: At *Under*, select the Parent Godown (select *Primary* to create a top level Godown and the first Godown). Like Stock Groups, Godowns may also be organized into various levels.
- **Allow Storage of Materials**: If you have set *Yes* at *Allow Storage of Materials* at Configuration (F-5C), then set the option at Godown entry screen also (F-5B)

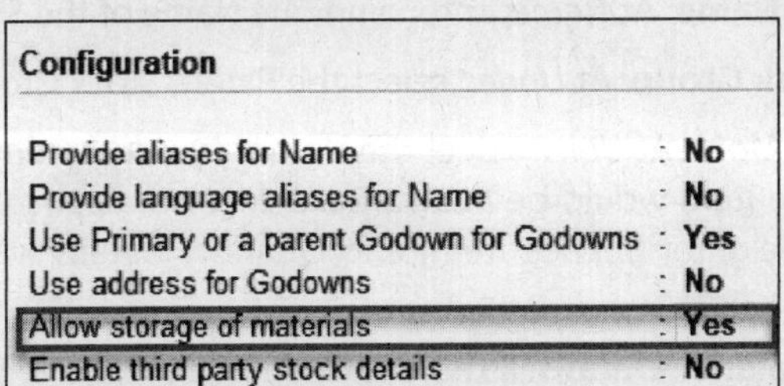

F-5C: Godown Entry Configuration

Godown Create करने के लिए, *Masters Creation* Menu (F-2A) से *Godowns* select करें। Name field में Stock Godown Name entry करें (F-5A)। *Under* field में Parent (मूल) Godown select करें (या *Primary* select करें)।

06 Stock Item

Create a Stock Item for each Inventory Item that you want to keep separate transaction & stock account.

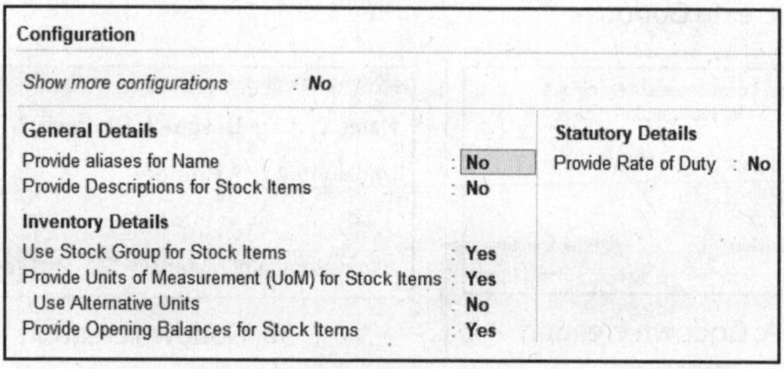

F-6A: Stock Item Configuration

At *Masters creation* Menu (GoT>Create), select *Stock Item* (F-2A) to get Stock Item Creation screen (F-6B). Click F12:Configure to get Stock Item Configuration screen and set the options (F-6A). Now enter the following particulars.

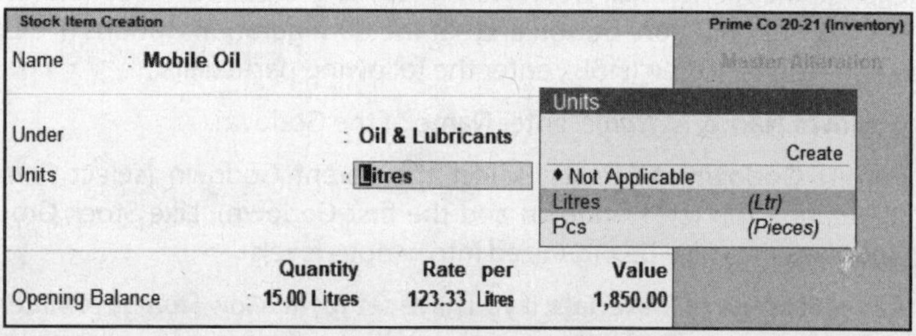

F-6B: Stock Item Cretaion

- **Stock Item Name**: At *Name*, enter a unique Name of the Stock Item.
- **Parent Stock Group**: At *Under*, select the Parent Stock Group
- **Stock Item UoM**: At *Units*, select the Unit of Measurement (from pop-up) in which the Item would be measured. Select *Not Applicable* if no UoM is applicable (e.g, for Service Item) and Quantity details will not be maintained for such Item.
- **Opening Balance Details**: If there is Opening Stock as at *Books Beginning From* date, at *Opening Balance* fields, enter Opening Stock Quantity details as follows:

- **Opening Stock Quantity**: At *Quantity*, enter the Opening Stock Quantity as on *Books beginning from date.*
- **Opening Stock Rate**: At *Rate*, enter the Opening Stock Rate (if you do not know the Rate, leave it blank, enter the Opening Stock value, Tally will compute & fill up the Rate).
- **Opening Stock Value**: The Opening Stock value is computed from the Opening Stock Quantity & Opening Stock Rate as entered and displayed at Value field. However, you may change the Amount. The Rate will get changed accordingly.

Stock Item Create करने के लिए, *Masters Creation* Menu (F-2A) से *Stock Item* select करे। Stock Item creation screen में Name field में Stock Item Name entry करे (F-6B)। *Under* field में Parent (मूल) Stock Group select करे (या *Primary* select करे)। Units field में UoM select करे। *Opening Balance* field में Opening Stock (अगर हो तो) details entry करे। F12 से Configuration set करे।

Godown Details entry of Opening Stock: After creation of new Godowns, during creation / alteration of Stock Item Master (F-6B), as explained, at entry of Opening Stock details, you get a screen to enter Godwnwise break up of Opening Stock (F-6C). Enter the Quantity, Rate & Value of Opening Stock lying in each Godown.

Allocations of : **Mobile Oil**
for: **15.00 Litres**

Godown	Quantity	Rate	per	Amount
Despatch Godown	10.00 Litres	125.00	Litres	1,250.00
Main Location	**5.00 Litres**	**120.00**	Litres	**600.00**
	15.00 Litres			1,850.00

F-6C: Godown Details of Opening Stock

Godown का Opening Stock (अगर हो तो) details भी entry करे (F-6C)।

07 Alteration / Deletion of Inventory Masters

To Alter / Delete Inventory Masters as discussed above, select *GoT> Alter* to get List of Masters (F-2A) and then select the Master. The Masters list will be displayed. Now select the Master record to get the Alteration screen

- **Master Alteration**: To Alter the Master record, edit the data in the respective field and save (as explained during Entry).

- **Master Deletion**: To Delete the Master record, press Alt+D. A message Delete Yes / No appears. Type Y to Delete. The master will be Deleted (you cannot get back!)

Restriction in Deletion of Inventory Masters: In following cases, the Inventory Master Record cannot be Deleted.

- **Stock Group**: The *Stock Group* would not be deleted if it is parent of any Stock Group or Stock Item.
- **Godown**: The *Godown* cannot be deleted if it has been referred in any Voucher
- **UoM**: The *UoM* cannot be deleted if it has been referred in any Stock Item.
- **Stock Item**: The *Stock Item* cannot be deleted if it has been referred in any Voucher.

Stock Group / Stock Item Alteration के लिए, GoT>Alter> Stock Group, या GoT>Alter> Stock Item select कर list of Master (F-2A) से Master record select करें। Alter करने के लिए field में data change करें। Delete करने के लिए Alt+D press करें। Stock Group/ Stock Item के Parent Group (*Under* field) में entry किया हुआ Stock Group Master Delete नहीं कर सकते। Voucher में entry किया हुआ Stock Item Master / Godown भी Delete नहीं कर सकते।

08 Inventory Masters Lists

Master lists shows the list of respective Master records entered. It is useful to view/verify the Masters data and Edit mistakes instantly while viewing.

- **Display of Inventory Master list** : Select *GoT>Chart of Accounts* to get *List of Masters.* Now select the respective Master to get Masters records. In list of Stock Items, using F5 toggle button you may view alphabetical list of Stock Items or in hierarchical order of Stock Group/ Stock Item.
- **Alteration / Deletion of Masters**: While viewing the Master record as explained above, you may also instantly Alter/ Delete the Master record as explained above.

GoT>Chart of Accounts में Unit/ Stock Group/ Stock Item option select कर Master List पाए। Master List से Master select कर उसकी details view / edit कर सकते हैं या Master record Delete भी कर सकते हैं।

09 Inventory Masters - Key Points

- F11 से *Maintain Inventory* में *Yes* set कर Inventory system activate करें।

- Unit (UoM) और Stock Item Master create करना अनिवार्य है। जरूरत हो तो Stock Group और Godown Master भी create करे।
- Stock Item Master create करते वक्त Opening Stock details entry करे, या Stock Item Alteration से Opening Stock details entry करे। Multiple Godown create किये हो तो Godownwise Opening Stock Details entry करे।
- Stock Item list में Opening Stock print नहीं होता। Opening Stock entry के बाद, Stock Item Master check करने के लिए Stock Statement में (जैसे बाद में समझाए हैं) Opening Stock details print करे। अगर multiple godwon create किया हो तो Godown details के साथ Opening Stock Print करे। Stock Statement check करे. Stock Item Alteration से गलतियां सुधारे।
- Chart of Accounts में सिर्फ Master के Alias मिलता है, बाकी कोई info नहीं मिलता।

Invoicing 02-02

We have explained Accounting Vouchers in Accounts section. Now we discuss about Accounting Vouchers like Sales, Purchase, Debit Note, Credit Note with Inventory details.

01 Inventory linking in Ledger Accounts

Ledger Account Creation / Alteration has been explained in Accounts section. Some additional details are to be set up for Inventory linked Ledger Accounts (like Sales, Purchase, Sales Return & Purchase Return), to link with Inventory system.

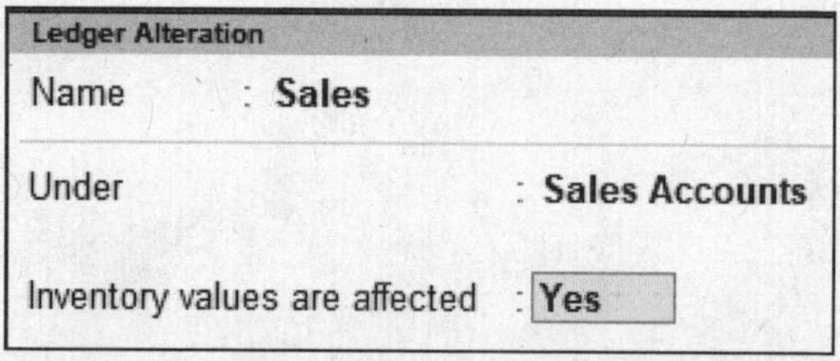

F-1A: Inventory Linked Ledger Account creation

At Ledger Creation (GoT>Create>Ledger) / Alteration (GoT>Alter>Ledger) screen, set *Yes* at *Inventory Values are affected* (F-1A), to enable Inventory details entry for such ledger accounts in Voucher. Click *F12:Configure* and set *Yes* at *Use Inventory Allocations for Ledgers* (F-1B).

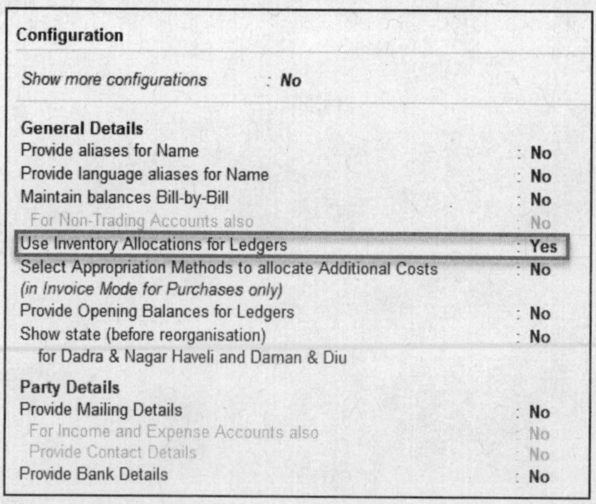

F-1B: Inventory Linked Ledger Configuration

Sales / Purchase Ledger Accounts के Configuration में *Inventory Values are Affected* में *Yes* set करे (F-1A)। Configuration में *Use Inventory Allocation for Ledger* में *Yes* set करे (F-1B)।

02 Party Ledger Accounts set up for Invoicing

Party Ledger Accounts (Customer / Supplier) has been explained in Accounts Receivables / Payables Chapter (§03/01-12). To enter additional info for Invoicing, at *Ledger Creation* (*GoT>Create>Ledger*) / *Alteration* (*GoT>Alter>Ledger*) screen (F-2A), click *F12:Configure* and set the relevant options (F-2B). At Party Ledger Account Creation / Alteration screen (F-2B), enter the respective details. Click *I:More Details* button and enter the desired additional details (F-2C).

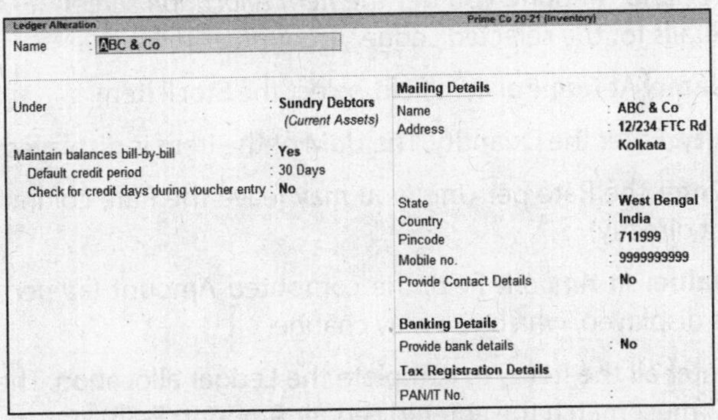

F-2A: Party Ledger Account Creation / Alteration

Party Ledger Accounts के Configuration (F-2B) में Mailing Details, Contact Details, Bank Details बगैरह के option set कर Ledger Accounts में उनकी details entry करे (F-2A / F-2C), जो पहले ही Accounts Receivables / Payables Chapter (§03/01-12) में बताया गया है।

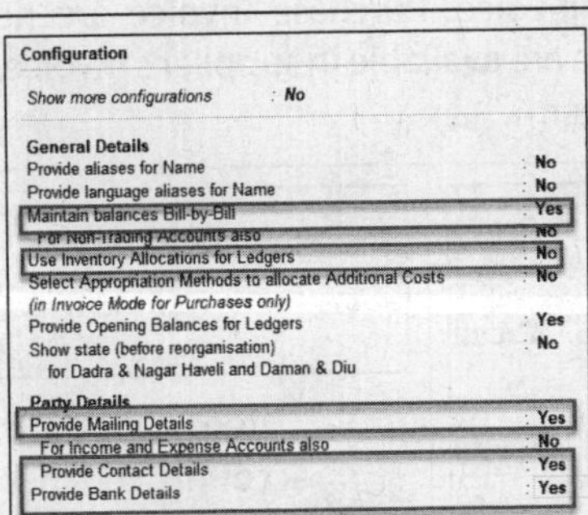

F-2B: Configuration set up for Party Ledger Accounts

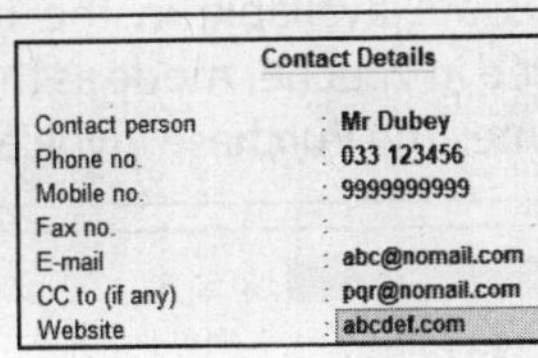

F-2C: Contact Details of Party

03 Inventory Details Entry in Accounts Voucher

Entry of Accounts Voucher (GoT>Voucher) like Sales (F8), Purchase (F9), Debit Note (Alt+F5), Credit Note (Alt+F6) have been explained earlier in Journal Book chapter (01-07). At Voucher entry screen (GoT>Voucher), click *H:Change Mode* (or press Ctrl+H) and select *As Voucher* from the list (F-3A). At first ledger Account, select the Party Account and Amount as explained earlier (F-3B).

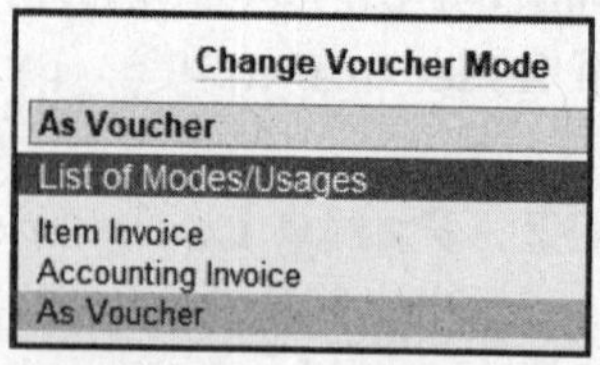

F-3A: Voucher Mode selection

Next, on entry of Inventory Linked Ledger Account (like Purchase, Sale Ledger Account etc), and Amount, you get the *Item Allocation* screen (F-3C) to enter the Item Details for the selected Ledger account, as follows:

- **Item Name**: At *Name of Item* field, select the Stock Item
- **Quantity**: Enter the Quantity. The UoM of the Item is displayed at *Per* field
- **Rate**: Enter the Rate per Unit (you may leave the Rate column and enter amount directly)
- **Item Value**: At *Amount* field, the computed Amount (as per Quantity & Rate) is displayed, which you may change.

This way, enter all the Items to complete the Ledger allocation. The total Item Value (F-3C) must match the entered Ledger Amount (F-3B).

After entry of Inventory Linked Ledger Accounts (F-3B) and the Inventory details (F-3C), you may enter other Ledger Accounts(if any), in the main voucher screen (F-3B). When the total of Debits equals to total of Credits, the ledger entries are terminated. Enter Voucher Narration and save the voucher (F-3B).

Manually created Sales Invoice are normally entered in Voucher mode as all details are available in the manual invoice. Purchase Invoice are normally entered in Voucher mode as the details are available in supplier's Invoice, which becomes the Purchase Invoice for Buyer.

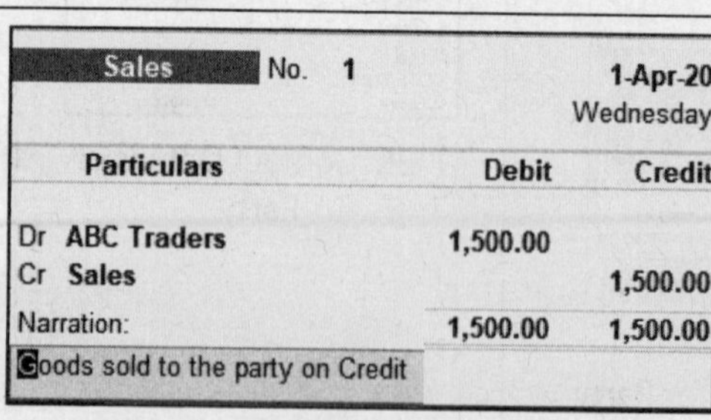

F- 3B: Sales Voucher entry As Voucher

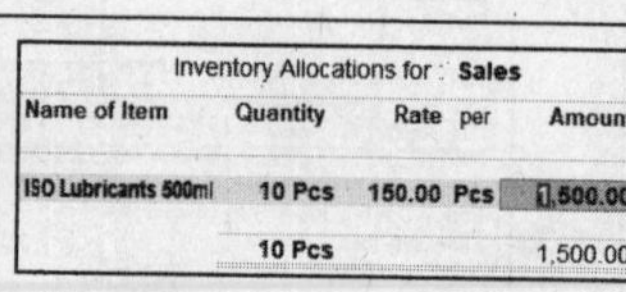

F-3C Item Allocation in Accounts Voucher

Account Voucher entry में *H:Change Mode* (F-3A) से *Account Voucher* select कर Voucher Entry में (F-3B) Sales / Purchase Ledger और Amount entry के बाद Inventory Allocation screen में Item details entry करे (F-3C)। Single Mode Voucher entry के लिए Voucher Mode में Accounting Invoice (F-3A) select कर Header में Party (Customer/ Supplier) ledger select करे। Details section में Sales / Purchase Ledger Account select कर Item details entry करे। फिर दूसरे ledger account की entry करे।

04 Invoicing

In Inventory Voucher Entry in Voucher form, explained as above, accounting details are entered first and then Inventory allocation of the ledger account is entered (useful for entry of manually created Invoice). Now, we discuss Invoice Entry (Item Invoice Mode), useful for on-line Invoice entry (F-4C). Stock Item details (Item, Rate, Quantity etc) are entered (F-4C/F-4B). The computation of Invoice for each Item, automatically gets done during entry (F-4B) (manual computation not needed).

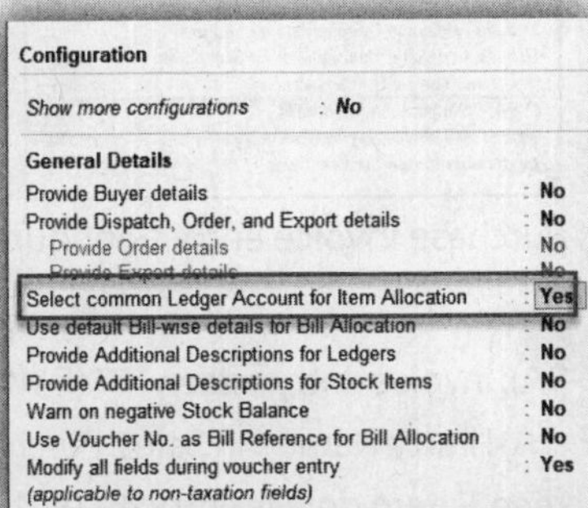

F-4A: Invoice Entry Configuration

Sales Invoice Entry: At Sales Voucher entry screen (F-4C), as explained above, click *H:Change Mode* (or press Ctrl+H) and select *Item Invoice* (F-3A) to get Invoice entry screen (F-4C).

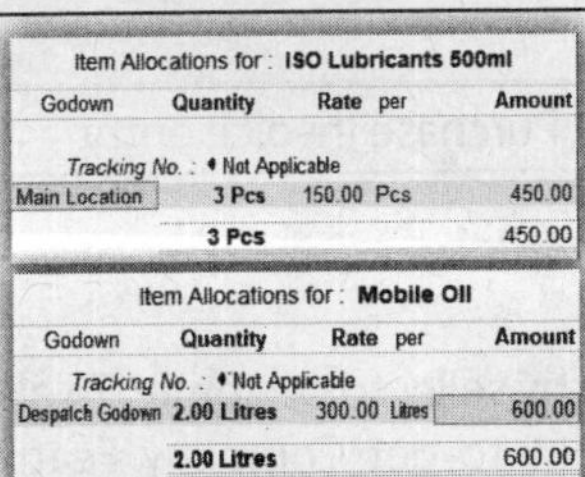

F-4B: Invoice Item Details entry

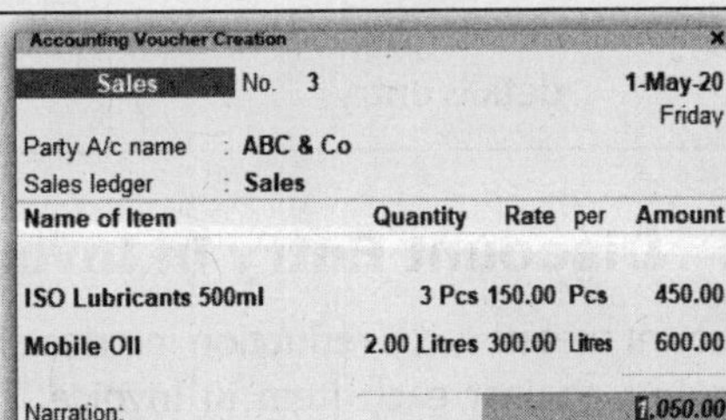

F-4C:Invoice Entry

At the header, select Party Ledger Account (F-4C). Next select Sales (for sales Invoice) / Purchase (for Purchase Invoice) Ledger Account (F-4C). Next, enter

Item Details as explained in Voucher entry with Inventory details (F-4B/ F-4C). To terminate Items entry, press <enter> at *Name of Item*.

Next enter other ledger accounts (Ledger Account, Amount), if any. Net Invoice value (Total Item Value and Other Ledger Accounts) is shown. Type *Yes* at Accept Yes / No to save the Invoice (F-4C)

Purchase Invoice entry: In the same way, enter Purchase Invoice (F-5C) with Item details (F-5B). For Purchase Invoice entry, to enter the supplier Invoice reference also (F-5C), at Purchase Invoice Entry Configuration (click F12) set Yes at *Provide Supplier Invoice Details* (F-5A), In Invoice entry screen, enter Supplier Invoice Number and Invoice Date for reference (F-5C).

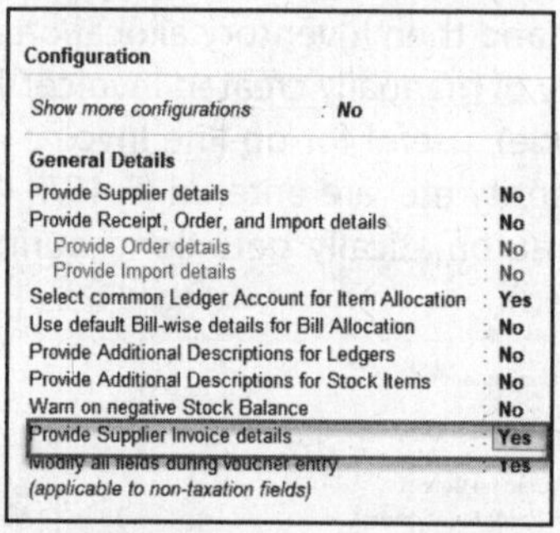

F-5A: Purchase Invoice entry Configuration

Sales / Purchase Invoice entry के लिए, Voucher entry screen में Ctrl+H press कर *Item Invoice* select कर (F-3A); Invoice entry screen पाए (F-4C/ F-5C) I Configuration option set करे (F-4A / F-5A) I Party Name और Sale / Purchase Account select करने के बाद Item allocation screen में Item details entry करे (F-4B / F-5B) I

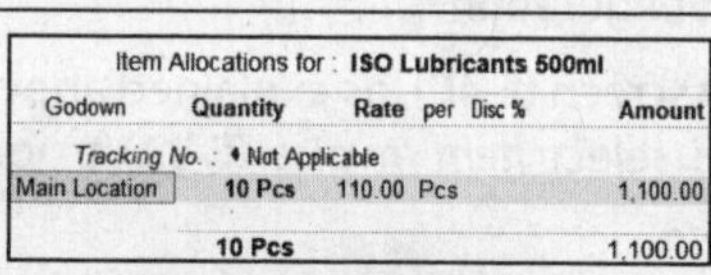

F-5B: Purchase Invoice Item details entry

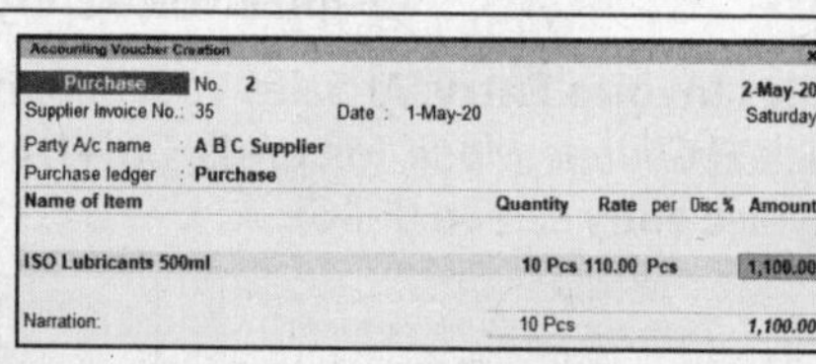

F-5C: Purchase Invoice entry

05 Discount Entry in Invoice

Discount means some reduction in price offered by seller to customer. To allow Discount against each Item in Invoice, click F11 to get Company Features (F-6A). Under *Inventory* section, set *Yes* at *Use Discount Column in Invoices.* Consequently, you get Discount column during Invoice entry (F-6B).

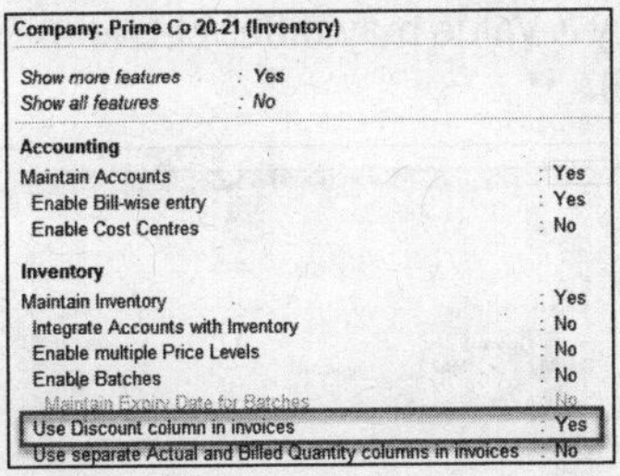

F-6A: Company Features set up

At Item allocation screen (F-6C), enter Discount Rate (in %) at *Discount* column against the respective Item. The computed Net Amount (Product value less Discount) is displayed at Amount column.

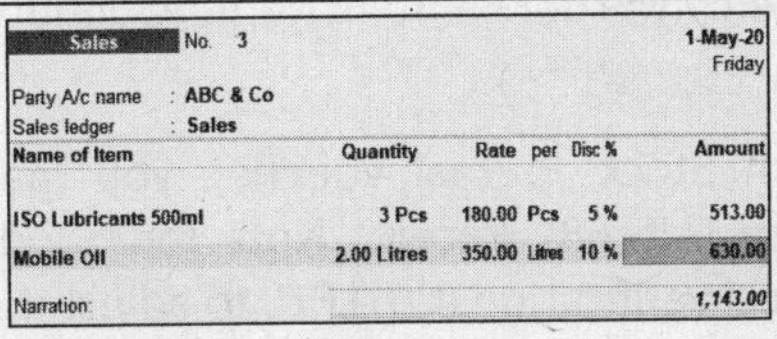

F-6B: Invoice Entry (with Discount)

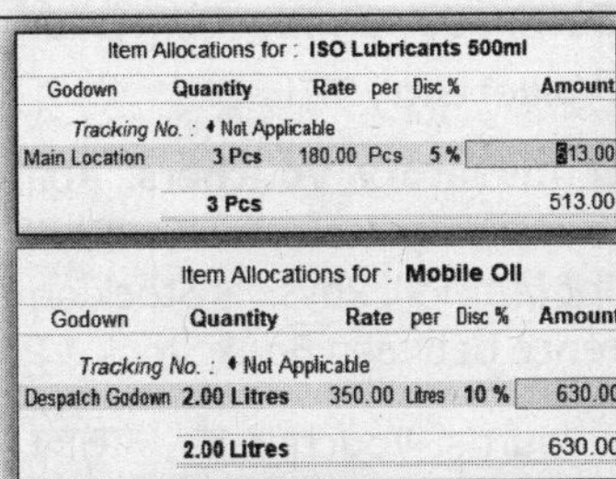

F-6C: Item Discount Entry in Invoice

Invoice में Discount entry करने के लिए F11 पर Click कर Use Discount Column in Invoices में Yes set करे। अब Invoice entry screen में Discount column मिलेगा (F-6B/F-6C)। उसमें Discount % entry करे. Discount के बाद का Net Amount Display होगा।

06 Stock Journal Voucher

Stock Journal Voucher is used to make internal Stock Adjustment (e.g., shortage, wastage, excess or any other increase or decrease in stock), stock transfers, etc.

At Voucher entry screen, click Alt+F7 to get to get Stock Journal Voucher entry screen (F-7A). Enter the Voucher Date.

At left part, enter the Source (Consumption: i.e Items OUT, e.g for Shortages found, Transfer Out, etc) Item details (Item name, Quantity, Rate & Amount). Similarly, at Right part, enter the Destination (Production) Item details.

Apart from Stock adjustment, Stock Journal Voucher is also used for Manufacturing, Assembling, Disassembling etc, in which Items consumed are entered in Source (Consumption) section, and Items Produced are entered in Destination (Production) side.

The quantity as entered for the Item in Source column is reduced from Stock, and the quantity as entered for the Item in Destination column is added in

Stock. The Item, Quantity & Value may differ between Source (Consumption) & Destination (Production).

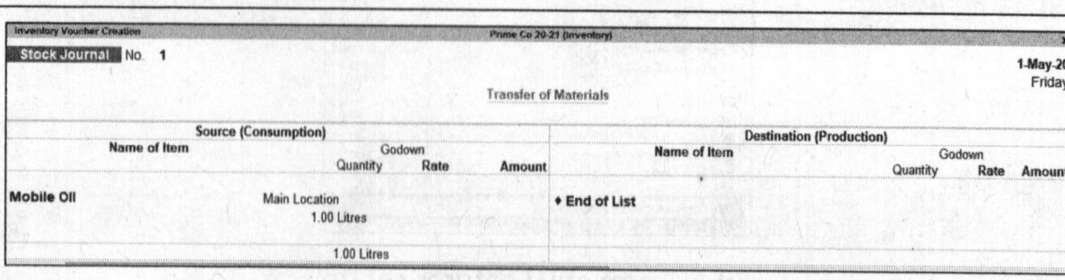

F- 7A: Stock Journal Voucher (for adjustment of Stock)

Stock Adjustment के लिए *GoT>Voucher* select कर Alt+F7 click कर Stock Journal Voucher entry करे। Left side Source (Consumption) column में Item Out और Right side Destination (Production) column में Item In का details (Item Name, Quantity, Rate, Value) entry करे।

Other Inventory Vouchers: Apart from Stock Journal Voucher, you may create Delivery Note for Goods Delivery (Alt+F8), Receipt Note for Goods Receipt (Alt+F9), Physical Stock on physical verification (Ctrl+F7), to adjust the difference between Book Stock & Physical Stock.

Stock Journal Voucher के अलावा, *GoT>Voucher* select कर, Alt+F8 से Goods Delivery के लिए Delivery Note और Goods Receipt के लिए Alt+F9 से Receipt Note भी इसी तरह entry करे। इसके अलावा Book Stock और Physical Stock adjust करने के लिए Ctrl+F7 से Physical Stock Voucher entry करे।

07 Invoice Printing

Voucher printing options and steps are explained in Accounts section. Here we explain additional steps related to Invoice Printing. After Sales Invoice entry, you may immediately print Invoice, or print in a separate session after Invoice Entry.

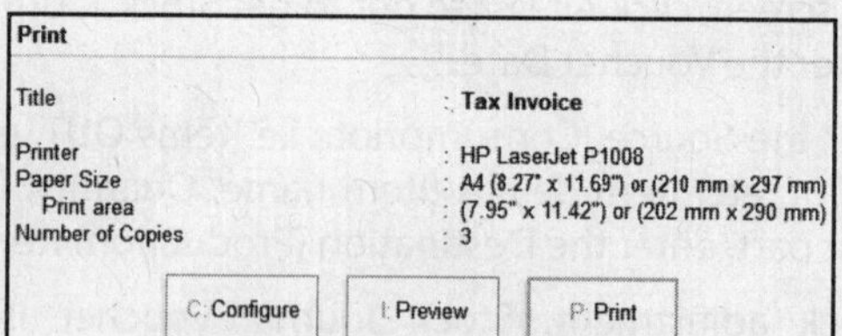

F-8A: Invoice Printing

At Invoice *Entry / Alteration* screen (F-4C / F-6B), press Ctl+*P* to get Invoice Printing screen (F-8A). At Invoice Printing screen, Click C:Configure (or Type C) and change Configuration options as desired (8B-1 to 8B-3), setting *Copies* option (F-8C)

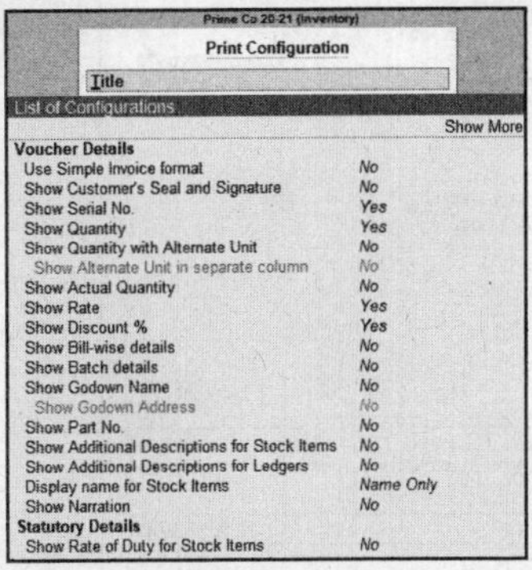

F-8B1:Invoice Printing Configuration Part-1

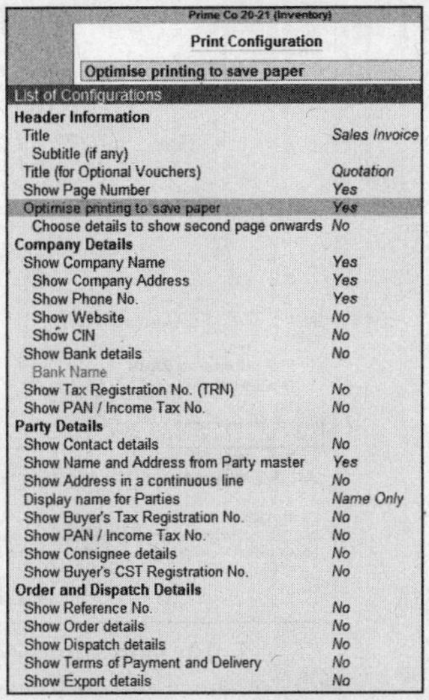

F-8B2: Invoice Printing Configuration Part-2

Click I:Preview (or Type I) to preview the Invoice before printing (F-8A), Click P:Print (or Type P) to print the Invoice on Printer in desired Format (F-9A/ F-9B).

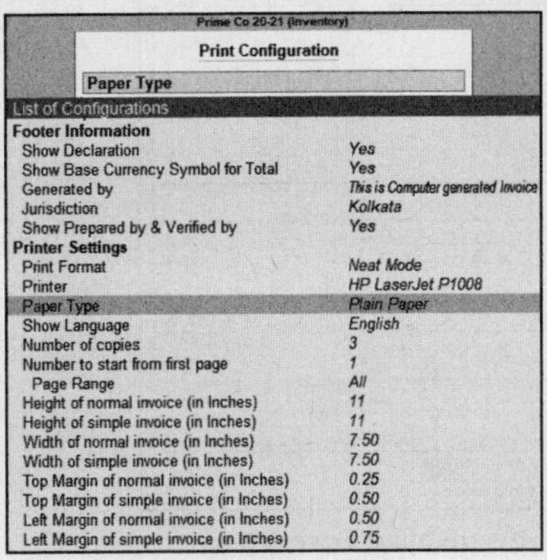

F-8B3: Invoice Printing Configuration Part-3

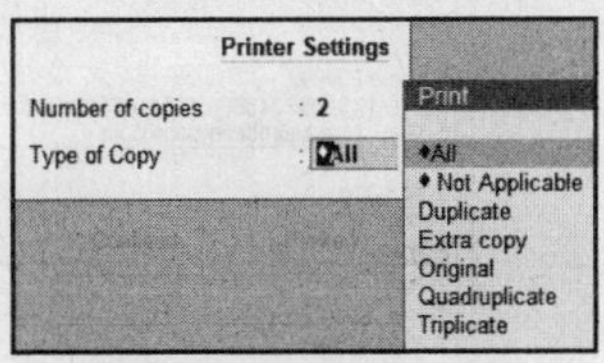

F-8C: Copies option set up

Sales Invoice issued by Seller to Buyer becomes Purchase Invoice for the Buyer. So, Purchase Invoice is normally not printed by Buyer. However, Buyer may print in its own Format for internal use, in the same way as Sales Invoice. Debit Note & Credit Notes are also printed in same way.

SUBJECT TO KOLKATA JURISDICTION
(Original)

Invoice No. **3** Dated **1-May-20**

Prime Co 20-21 (Inventory)
12 B B Rd
Akrur Mansion
12th Floor
Kolkata 709999
Contact : 03312345678,1234567890
E-Mail : nomail@nocompany.com

INVOICE

Party : **ABC & Co**
12/234 FTC Rd
Kolkata

Sl No.	Description of Goods	Quantity	Rate	per	Disc. %	Amount
1	**ISO Lubricants 500ml**	**3 Pcs**	180.00	Pcs	5 %	**513.00**
2	**Mobile Oil**	**2.00 Litres**	350.00	Litres	10 %	**630.00**
	Total					**₹ 1,143.00**

Amount Chargeable (in words) *E. & O.E*
INR One Thousand One Hundred Forty Three Only

Declaration
We declare that this invoice shows the actual price of the goods described and that all particulars are true and correct.

for Prime Co 20-21 (Inventory)

Prepared by Verified by Authorised Signatory

This is Computer generated Invoice

F-9A: Sales Invoice in Print (in Simple Format)

Sales Invoice entry में Ctrl+P click कर C:Configuration से Invoice Printing option set कर *P:Print* button से Invoice print करे। Seller से मिला हुआ Invoice buyer के लिए Purchase Invoice बन जाता है. इसलिए Buyer Purchase Invoice print करते हैं।

INVOICE *(Original)*

Prime Co 20-21 (Inventory)
12 B B Rd
Akrur Mansion
12th Floor
Kolkata 709999
Contact : 03312345678,1234567890
E-Mail : nomail@nocompany.com

Invoice No. **3** | Dated **1-May-20**

Buyer (Bill to)
ABC & Co
12/234 FTC Rd
Kolkata

Sl No.	Description of Goods	Quantity	Rate	per	Disc. %	Amount
1	**ISO Lubricants 500ml**	**3 Pcs**	180.00	Pcs	5 %	**513.00**
2	**Mobile Oil**	**2.00 Litres**	350.00	Litres	10 %	**630.00**
	Total					**₹ 1,143.00**

Amount Chargeable (in words) E. & O.E
INR One Thousand One Hundred Forty Three Only

Declaration
We declare that this invoice shows the actual price of the goods described and that all particulars are true and correct.

for Prime Co 20-21 (Inventory)

Prepared by Verified by Authorised Signatory

SUBJECT TO KOLKATA JURISDICTION

This is Computer generated Invoice

F-9B: Sales Invoice in Print (in Neat Format)

08 Inventory Masters - Key Points

- Invoice Entry / Alteration screen (F-4C / F-6B) screen में Ctrl+P से C:Configuration button से Configuration set कर (8B1 to 8B3) से P:Print button Printer में Invoice Print करे।

- Voucher entry screen में H:Change Mode (Ctrl+H) से As Voucher select कर Voucher mode में entry करे, Accounting Invoice select कर Accounting Invoice mode में entry करे, Item Invoice select कर Invoice mode में entry करे।
- Voucher / Invoice printing के लिए Voucher / Invoice entry screen में Ctrl+P से Printing screen में C:Configure button से Configuration set कर P:Print button से Voucher / Invoice Print करे।

Inventory Reports 02-03

01 Accounts Reports with Inventory Details

After entry of Vouchers / Invoices with Inventory Details, at the respective Accounts Report like Cash / Bank Book, Ledger, etc, explained earlier.

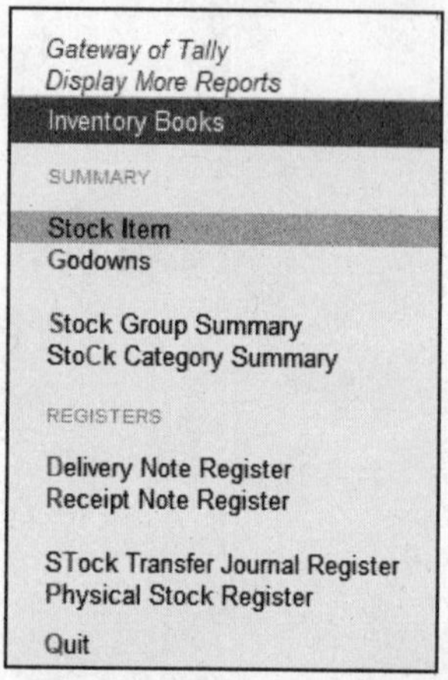

F-1A: Inventory Books menu

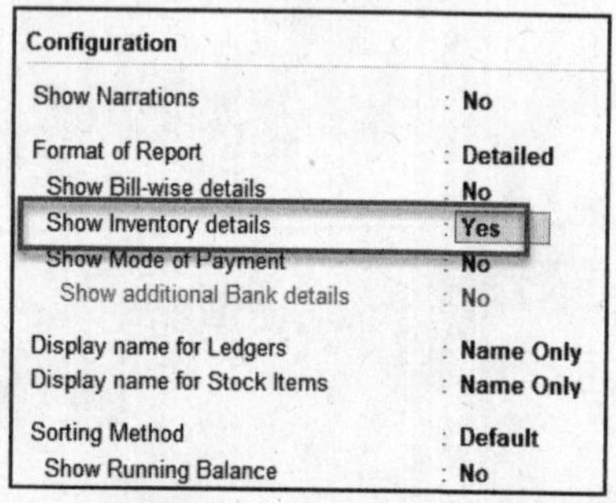

F-1B: Configuration set up for Inventory Details in Accounts Books

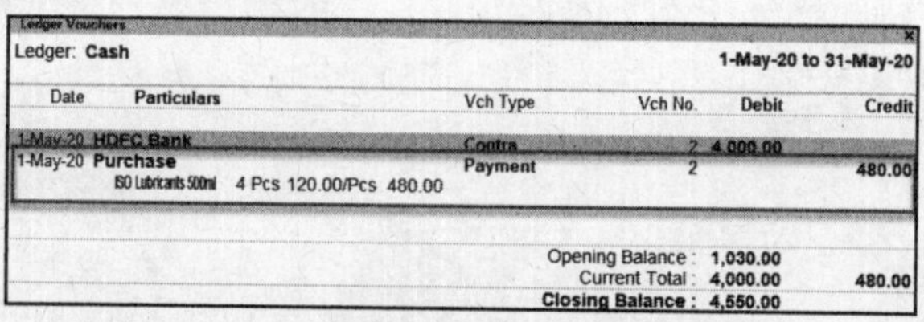

F-2A: Cash Book with Inventory Details

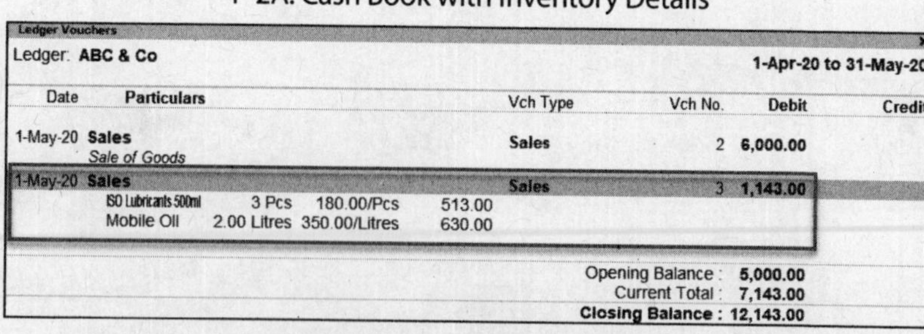

F-2B: Ledger Book with Inventory Details

To view Accounts Reports with Inventory details, click *F12:Configure* at the respective Report display screen and set *Yes* at *Show Inventory Details* (F-1B). This way, Inventory details may be printed even in Account Books like Cash Book, Bank Book, Journal Books, Ledger Book, where applicable (F-2A / F-2B), apart from Sales / Purchase Registers (F-3A/ F-3B) and Debit / Credit Note Registers.

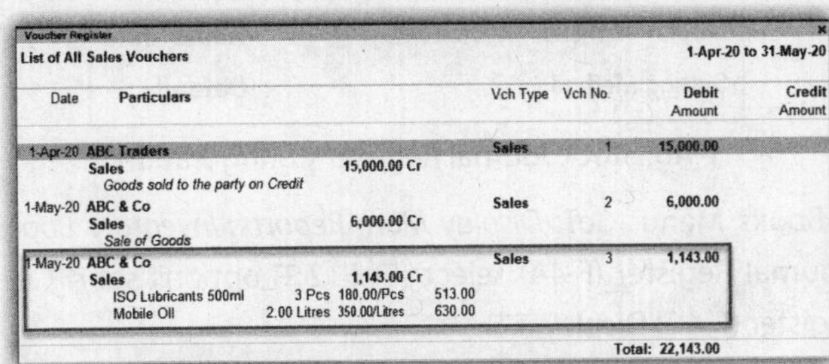

Voucher Register

List of All Sales Vouchers — 1-Apr-20 to 31-May-20

Date	Particulars				Vch Type	Vch No.	Debit Amount	Credit Amount
1-Apr-20	ABC Traders				Sales	1	15,000.00	
	Sales		15,000.00 Cr					
	Goods sold to the party on Credit							
1-May-20	ABC & Co				Sales	2	6,000.00	
	Sales		6,000.00 Cr					
	Sale of Goods							
1-May-20	ABC & Co				Sales	3	1,143.00	
	Sales		1,143.00 Cr					
	ISO Lubricants 500ml	3 Pcs	180.00/Pcs	513.00				
	Mobile Oil	2.00 Litres	350.00/Litres	630.00				
						Total:	22,143.00	

F-3A: Sales Register with Inventory Details

Select *GoT>Display More Reports>Inventory Books* to get Inventory Books menu to get various Inventory Reports, as explained next.

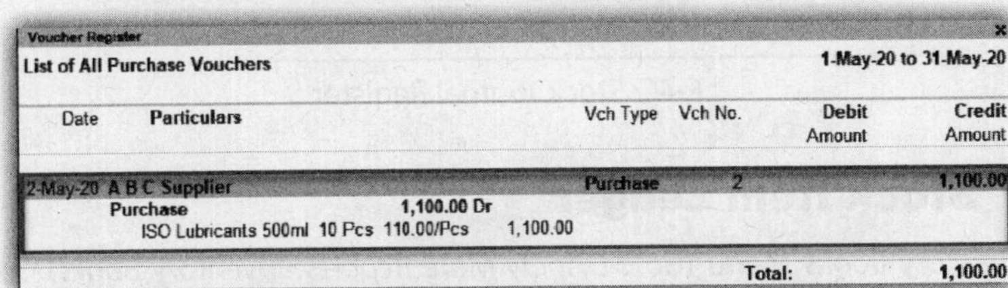

Voucher Register

List of All Purchase Vouchers — 1-May-20 to 31-May-20

Date	Particulars				Vch Type	Vch No.	Debit Amount	Credit Amount
2-May-20	A B C Supplier				Purchase	2		1,100.00
	Purchase		1,100.00 Dr					
	ISO Lubricants 500ml	10 Pcs	110.00/Pcs	1,100.00				
							Total:	1,100.00

F-3B: Purchase Register with Inventory Details

Voucher में Item details entry के बाद Accounts Report के Configuration option में Show Inventory Details option में Yes set कर (F-1A) Accounts report में Item details print कर सकते हैं (F-2A / F-2B, F-3A/ F-3B)।

GoT>Display More Reports>Inventory Books से Inventory Books menu (F-1A) में Stock Items related Reports के options मिलेंगे।

GoT>Display More Reports>Inventory Books select कर Inventory Books menu से Inventory Reports मिलेंगे।

02 Stock Journal Register

At Inventory Books Menu (*GoT>Display More Reports>Inventory Books*), select *Stock Transfer Journal Register* (F-1A). At Stock Journal Register (F-4C), Click F12: Configure, set the options (F-4B) to get Stock Journal Register (F-4C)

Configuration	
Show Narrations	: **No**
Format of Report	: **Detailed**
Show Inventory details	: **Yes**
Show Descriptions for Stock Items	: **No**
Display name for Stock Items	: **Name Only**
Sorting Method	: **Default**

F-4B: Stock Journal Register Configuration

Inventory Books Menu (*GoT>Display More Reports>Inventory Books)* में Stock Transfer Journal Register (F-4A) select कर F12 से options set कर (F-4B) Stock Journal Register (F-4C) Display करे।

Voucher Register

List of All Stock Journal Vouchers — **1-Apr-20 to 31-May-20**

Date	Particulars		Vch Type	Vch No.	Inwards Quantity	Outwards Quantity
1-May-20	**Mobile Oil**		Stock Journal	1		**1.00 Litres**
	ISO Lubricants 500ml	(-)1 Pcs				

F-4C: Stock Journal Register

03 Stock Item Ledger

At *Inventory Books* Menu (*GoT>Display More Reports>Inventory Books)*, select *Stock Item* (F-1A) and then select a Stock Item to get Monthly Break Up of the Stock Item. Select a Month. Click *F2 : Period* button and set the period to get Stock Item Ledger (F-5B).

Stock Item Vouchers — Prime Co 20-21 (Inventory)

Stock Item : **ISO Lubricants 500ml** — **1-May-20 to 31-May-20**

Stock details for: **All Types**

Date	Particulars		Vch Type	Vch No.	Inwards Quantity	Inwards Rate	Inwards Value	Outwards Quantity	Outwards Rate	Outwards Value	Closing Quantity	Closing Rate	Closing Value
1-May-20	**Opening Balance**				12 Pcs	120.00	**1,440.00**				12 Pcs	120.00	**1,440.00**
1-May-20	**(as per details)**		**Sales**	3				3 Pcs	171.00	**513.00**			
	ISO Lubricants 500ml	**513.00 Cr**											
	Mobile Oil	**630.00 Cr**											
1-May-20	**(as per details)**		**Stock Journal**	1				1 Pcs					
	Mobile Oil	**(-)1.00 Litres**											
	ISO Lubricants 500ml	**(-)1 Pcs**											
	Loss on Spllage, breakage tc												
1-May-20	**(as per details)**		**Payment**	2	4 Pcs	120.00	**480.00**				12 Pcs	117.25	**1,407.00**
	ISO Lubricants 500ml	**480.00 Dr**											
	Cash purchase of materials												
2-May-20	**(as per details)**		**Purchase**	2	10 Pcs	110.00	**1,100.00**				22 Pcs	113.95	**2,507.00**
	ISO Lubricants 500ml	**1,100.00 Dr**											
	Totals as per 'Transaction' values :				26 Pcs	116.15	**3,020.00**	4 Pcs	128.25	**513.00**	22 Pcs	113.95	**2,507.00**
	Totals as per 'Default' valuation :				26 Pcs	116.15	**3,020.00**	4 Pcs	128.25	**513.00**	22 Pcs	116.15	**2,555.38**

F-5B: Stock1 Item Ledger

Click F12:Configure button and set the options(F-5A). Click B:Basis of Valuation button and set the Valuation Method (F-6B) / Godown Types (F-6A) / Voucher Types (F-6C) from the list.

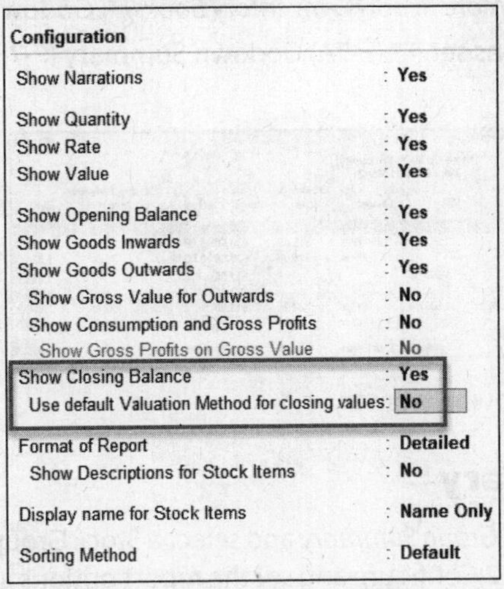

F-5A: Stock Item Ledger Configuration

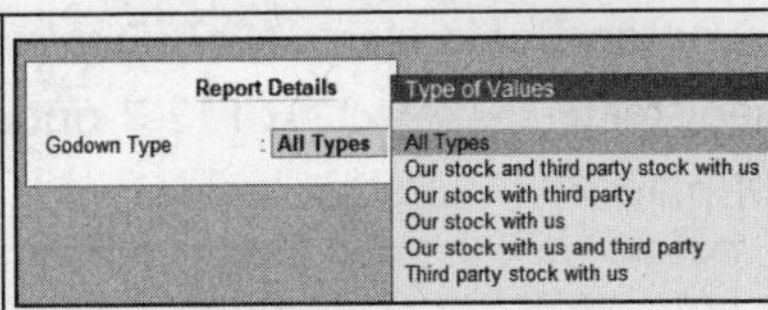

F-6A: Godown Type selection

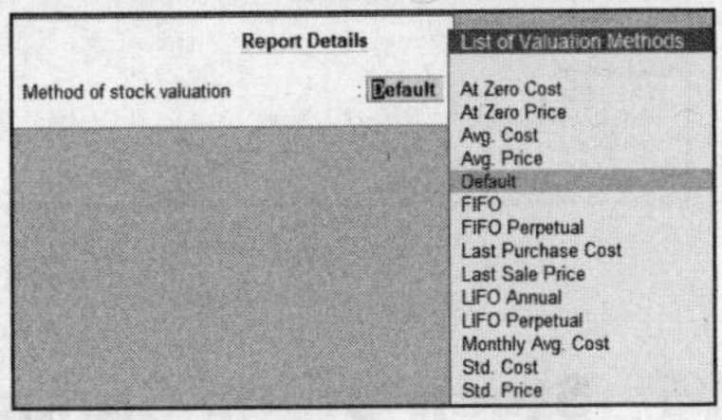

F-6B: Valuation Method selection

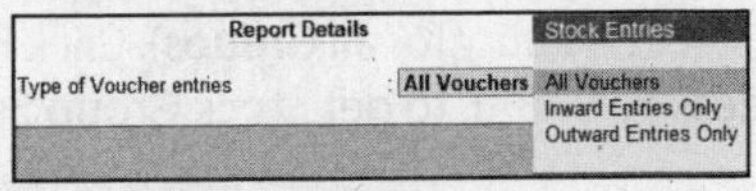

F-6C: Voucher Entries Selection from *B:Basis of Value* button

Inventory Books Menu (*GoT>Display More Reports>Inventory Books)* में Stock Item Ledger (F-1A) select कर F12 से options set कर (F-5A) Stock Item Ledger (F-5B) Display करें।

04 Godown Register

At *Inventory Books* Menu (*GoT>Display More Reports>Inventory Books)*, select *Godowns* (F-1A) and then select a Godown (or select Primary to get Report of all Godowns). Click *F2 : Period* and set the period to get Godown Summary (F-7B). Click F12:Configure and set the options as desired (F-7A).

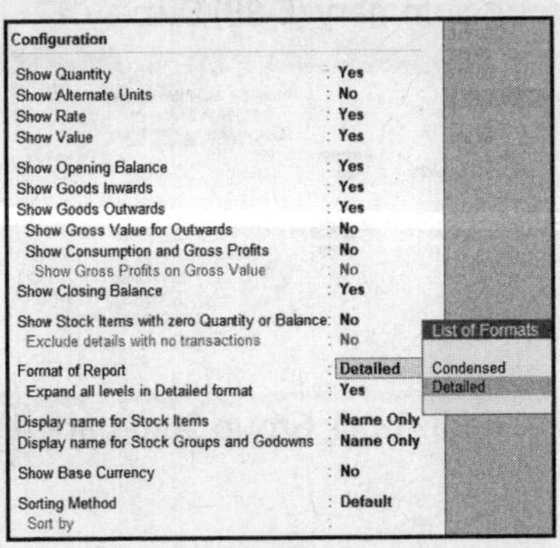

F-7A: Godown Register Configuration

Inventory Books Menu (*GoT>Display More Reports>Inventory Books)* में Godown Register (F-1A) select कर F12 से options set कर (F-7A) Godown Summary (F-7B) Display करे।

Godown Summary — Primo 20-21 (Inventory)

Prime Co 20-21 (Inventory)
1-Apr-20 to 31-Mar-21

Particulars	Opening Balance			Inwards			Outwards			Closing Balance		
	Quantity	Rate	Value	Quantity	Rate	Value	Quantity	Rate	Value	Quantity	Rate	Value
Despatch Godown	10.00 Litres	125.00	1,250.00				2.00 Litres	315.00	630.00	8.00 Litres	125.00	1,000.00
Oil & Lubricants	10.00 Litres	125.00	1,250.00				2.00 Litres	315.00	630.00	8.00 Litres	125.00	1,000.00
Mobile Oil	10.00 Litres	125.00	1,250.00				2.00 Litres	315.00	630.00	8.00 Litres	125.00	1,000.00
Main Location			2,040.00			1,580.00			513.00			3,035.38
Oil & Lubricants			2,040.00			1,580.00			513.00			3,035.38
ISO Lubricants 500ml	12 Pcs	120.00	1,440.00	14 Pcs	112.86	1,580.00	4 Pcs	128.25	513.00	22 Pcs	116.15	2,555.38
Mobile Oil	5.00 Litres	120.00	600.00				1.00 Litres			4.00 Litres	120.00	480.00
Grand Total	10.00 Litres		3,290.00			1,580.00	2.00 Litres		1,143.00	8.00 Litres		4,035.38

F-7B: Godown Summary

05 Stock Group Summary

At *Inventory Books* Menu (F-4A), select *Group Summary* and select a Stock Group (select *Primary* for all Groups). Click F12:Configure and set the report options as desired (F-8A), to get Stock Group Summary (F-8B).

Configuration

Show Quantity	: Yes
Show Alternate Units	: No
Show Rate	: Yes
Show Value	: Yes
Show Opening Balance	: Yes
Show Goods Inwards	: Yes
Show Goods Outwards	: Yes
Show Gross Value for Outwards	: No
Show Consumption and Gross Profits	: No
Show Gross Profits on Gross Value	: No
Show Closing Balance	: Yes
Show Stock Items with zero Quantity or Balance	: No
Exclude details with no transactions	: No
Type of Grouping	: Stock Group-wise (Method of Info.: Stock Group-wise / Stock Item-wise)
Format of Report	: Detailed
Expand all levels in Detailed format	: Yes
Display name for Stock Items	: Name Only
Display name for Stock Groups	: Name Only
Show Base Currency	: No
Sorting Method	: Default
Sort by	Closing Balance

F-8A: Stock Group Summary Configuration

Inventory Books Menu में Stock Group Summary (F-4A) select कर F12 से options set कर (F-8A) Stock Group Summary (F-8B) Display करे।

Stock Summary — Prime Co 20-21 (Inventory)

Prime Co 20-21 (Inventory)
1-Apr-20 to 31-Mar-21
Stock details for : All Types

Particulars	Opening Balance			Inwards			Outwards			Closing Balance		
	Quantity	Rate	Value	Quantity	Rate	Value	Quantity	Rate	Value	Quantity	Rate	Value
ISO Lubricants 500ml	12 Pcs	120.00	1,440.00	14 Pcs	112.86	1,580.00	4 Pcs	128.25	513.00	22 Pcs	116.15	2,555.38
Main Location	12 Pcs	120.00	1,440.00	14 Pcs	112.86	1,580.00	4 Pcs	128.25	513.00	22 Pcs	116.15	2,555.38
Mobile Oil	15.00 Litres	123.33	1,850.00				3.00 Litres	210.00	630.00	12.00 Litres	123.33	1,480.00
Despatch Godown	10.00 Litres	125.00	1,250.00				2.00 Litres	315.00	630.00	8.00 Litres	125.00	1,000.00
Main Location	5.00 Litres	120.00	600.00				1.00 Litres			4.00 Litres	120.00	480.00
Grand Total			3,290.00	14 Pcs		1,580.00			1,143.00			4,035.38

F-8B: Stock Group Summary

06 Inventory Reports - Key Points

- GoT>Display More Report>Account Books से Cash / Bank Book, Ledger, Journal, Sales Register, Purchase Register, Debit Note Register, Credit Note Register select कर, F12 से Configuration में Show Inventory Details में Yes set कर Accounts Books में Inventory Details Display / Print करें।
- GoT> Display More Report>Statement of Inventory>Movement Analysis menu से Stock Group Analysis और Stock Item Analysis Display / Print करें।
- GoT>Stock Summary से Stock Group और Stock Item के summary Display / Print करें।
- GoT> Display More Report>Inventory Books menu से Stock Group और Godown के Inventory Report print करें।
- GoT> Display More Report>Inventory Books menu से Stock Journal और Physical Stock Voucher Register print करें।

Point of Sale 02-04

PoS (*Point-of-Sale*) is a retail counter outlet, like a checkout counter in a shop, or any other point of Cash sales. The seller prints the Sales Invoice, handing over the Invoice to the customer, and the customer makes full payment thereof, over the counter.

Retail Sales Counter में, जहाँ sale करते ही full payment मिल जाता है, वहाँ Quick Invoicing के लिए PoS System उपयोग किया जाता है।

01 PoS Voucher Type creation

In Tally Prime, Point of Sales (PoS) is Sales Voucher Type. Select *GoT>Create>Voucher Type* to create PoS Voucher type (F1A).

At *Voucher Type creation* screen, at the *Left Part*, set the options as follows (F- 1A):

- **Voucher Type Name**: At *Name*, enter the Voucher Type Name.
- **Voucher Type**: At *Type of Voucher*, select *Sales* as PoS is a type of Sales Voucher.
- **Abbreviation***:* At *Abbr*, enter short name (Abbreviation) of the Voucher Type. This is printed in all Books of Accounts, for the Voucher Type.
- **Method of Numbering**: At *Method of Numbering* field, select *Automatic.* The voucher numbers will be automatically posted serially as per Date.
- **Mode**: At *Use Advance Configuration,* set *No.*
- **Common Narration**: At *Use Common Narration***,** set *No* (In PoS, normally no Narration is entered for faster entry).
- **Ledger Narration**: At the field *Narration for each entry***,** set *No* (In PoS, normally no Ledger narration is entered for faster entry).

Under the *Printing* section at the *Right Part*, set the Printing options as follows:

- **On-line Printing**: At *Print after Saving*, set *Yes* to directly print the PoS Invoice immediately on entry.
- **Use for PoS Invoicing**: Set *Yes* to define it as PoS Type Voucher, to inherit special characteristics of PoS voucher.
- **Print Message 1 & Print Message 2***:* Enter the messages texts that you like to print at the bottom of each Invoice.
- **Default Print Title**: Enter the Title of the Document to be printed.

Declaration: At *Set Alter Declaration* (F-1A), set Yes to enter Declaration for PoS Voucher, else set No.

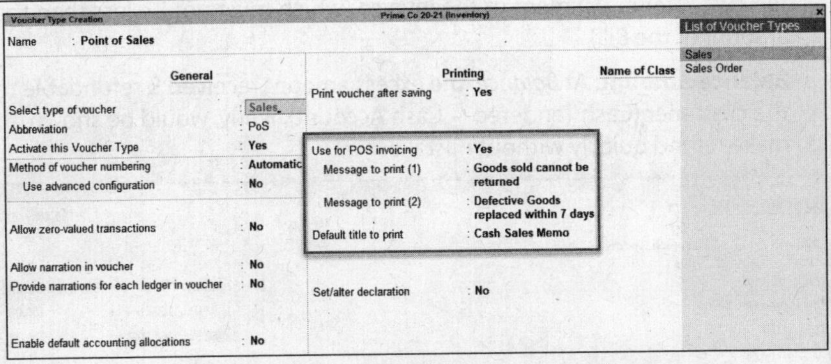

F-1A: Point of Sales Voucher Type creation

PoS Voucher Type Create करने के लिए *GoT>Create>Voucher Type* select करे. Voucher Type creation में *Select Type of Voucher* में *Sales* select करे (F-1A). *Use for PoS Invoicing* में *Yes* set करे और बाकी options अपने अनुसार set करे।

02 PoS Invoice Entry

Sales Voucher entry have been explained earlier. To create *PoS Sales Invoice* (F-2A), click *F8:Sales* and then select PoS Voucher Type from the Voucher Type list (F-2A).

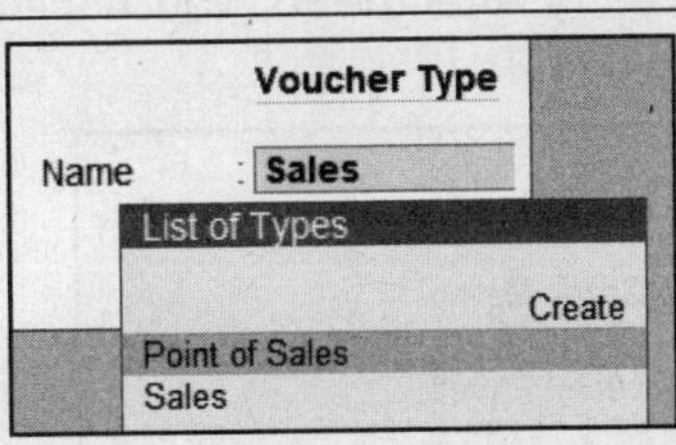

F-2A: PoS Voucher Type Selection

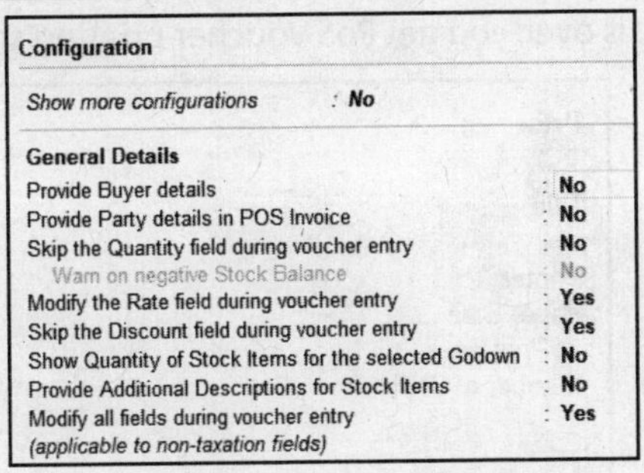

F-3A: PoS Voucher Entry Configuration

At Voucher entry screen, click F8:Sales and select PoS Voucher type from list (F-2A) to get PoS Voucher Entry screen (F-3B). Click F12:Configure and set the PoS Voucher entry configuration options (F-3A). As full payment is received immediately on sale, in PoS Voucher, no need to select any Party Ledger Account (F-3B). Enter the Item details like Sales Voucher entry explained earlier, then enter Payment details as follows :

- **Cash Ledger Account**: At *Cash*, select the Cash Ledger Account from list.
- **Tendered Amount**: At *Cash Tendered*, enter the amount Tendered by the customer in payment of the Invoice (which must not be less than the amount of the Bill)
- **Balance Amount**: At *Balance,* the excess amount received & refundable to the customer (Cash Tendered – Cash Account), if any, would be shown, to make refund quickly without mistake.

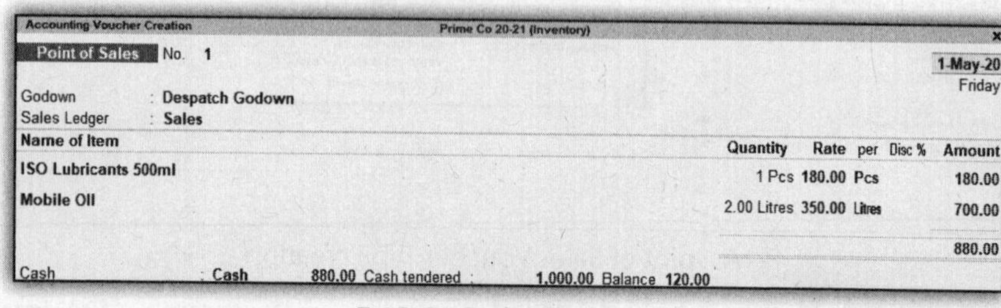

F-3B: PoS Voucher Entry

GoT>Voucher में F8:Sales से PoS Voucher select कर PoS Voucher entry screen पाए (F-3B)। चूँकि Sale करते वक्त पूरा Payment मिल जाता है, इसलिए Customer Ledger select करने की जरूरत नहीं। Sales Ledger select करे, फिर Item details select करे. फिर Payment details entry करे।

03 PoS Invoice Printing

Normally PoS Invoice is printed on line during entry. After the PoS voucher entry is over, you get PoS Voucher printing screen (F-4A).

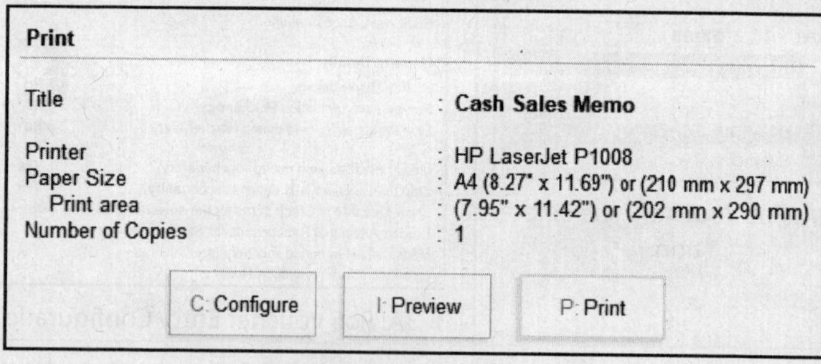

F-4A: PoS Printing

At PoS Voucher printing screen (F-4A), Click (C:Configure) to set Configuration option (F-4B) / (I:Preview) to Preview the Invoice / (P:Print) the PoS Invoice on Printer (F-5A), as explained earlier.

Prime Co 20-21 (Inventory)

Print Configuration

Title

List of Configurations

Show More

Voucher Details	
Show Serial No.	Yes
Show Stock Item Name in a single line	Yes
Show Units with Quantity	Yes
Show Rate	Yes
Show Units with Rate	No
Show Discount %	No
Show Discount Amount	Yes
Show Part No.	No
Show Additional Descriptions for Stock Items	No
Display name for Stock Items	Name Only
Show Narration	No
Statutory Details	
Header Information	
Title	Cash Sales Memo
Subtitle (if any)	
Show Time	No
Company Details	
Show Company Name	Yes
Show Company Address	Yes
Party Details	
Show Name and Address from Party master	No
Footer Information	
Show Card/Cheque No.	No
Show complete Card No.	No
Show Base Currency Symbol for Total	No
Printer Settings	
Printer	HP LaserJet P1008
Number of copies	1

F-4B: PoS Printing Configuration

Prime Co 20-21 (Inventory)
12 B B Rd
Akrur Mansion
12th Floor
Kolkata 709999
Contact : 03312345678,1234567890
E-Mail : nomail@nocompany.com

Cash Sales Memo

Bill No. : 1
Date : 1-5-2020

Sl	Description	Qty	Rate	Disc.Amt	Amount
1	ISO Lubricants 500ml	1 Pcs	180.00	0	180.00
2	Mobile Oil	2.00 Litres	350.00	0	700.00
	Total				880.00

Cash	:	880.00
Cash Tendered	:	*1000.00*
Balance	:	*120.00*
Total Paid		880.00

We declare that this invoice shows the actual price of the goods described and that all particulars are true and correct.

Goods sold cannot be returned
Defective Goods replaced within 7 days bewteen 3pm to 8pm

F-5A: PoS Invoice in print

PoS Voucher entry करने पर Ctrl+P से PoS Printing screen पाए (F-4A). F12:Configure से Printing Configuration set करे (F-4B). P:Print button से PoS Invoice print करे (F-5A)।

04 PoS Register

Select *GoT>Display More Reports> Account Books>PoS Register* to get *PoS Register* (F-6B), showing list of PoS Vouchers. Click F12:Configure and set the Display configuration options (F-6A). To Print PoS Register, press Ctrl+P and click the button to Configure (*C:Configure)*, Preview (*I:Preview)*, Print on Printer (*P:Print*) the PoS Register.

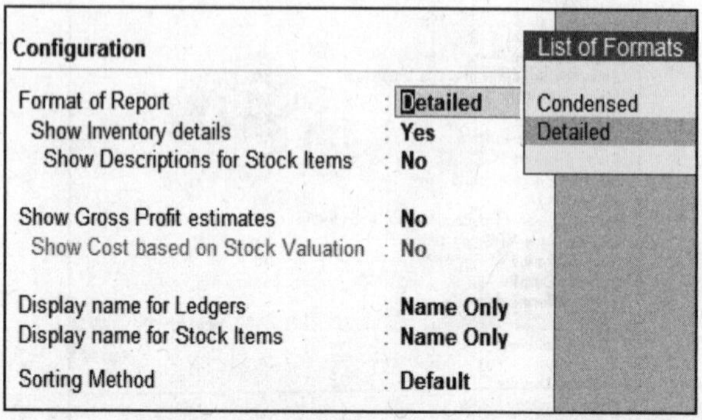

F-6A: PoS Register Display Configuration

GoT>Display More Reports> Account Books>PoS Register select कर PoS Register (F-6B) display और Print करे।

POS Register

List of All POS Vouchers — **For 1-May-20**

Date	Vch Type	Vch No.	Gift Vouchers	Credit/Debit Card Pymt	Cheque	Cash	Total
1-May-20	Point of Sales	1				880.00	880.00

F-6B: PoS Register Display

05 Point of Sale - Key Points

- Voucher Type creation screen से Sales Voucher Type से PoS Voucher Type create करे।
- PoS Voucher entry करने के लिए Voucher Entry screen में F8 click कर फिर Sales Voucher Type list से Pos Voucher select करे।
- PoS Counter में Sale करते वक्त ही full payment मिलता है, इसलिए PoS Voucher में कोई Party Ledger entry नहीं होता।
- एक PoS Bill का Payment Multiple Mode में Payment हो सकता है, जैसे Cash, Cheque, Reward Point, Discount coupon बगैरह।
- Tally Prime का PoS system बहुत ही Basic है. इसमें Free items, promotional scheme, Reward Points बगैरह का features नहीं है।
- Simple Accounting System के लिए PoS Voucher से retail Cash sales entry करे, Credit sales Invoice entry से करे।

PART 3

Basic Tax Accounting

Almost all organisations are to comply with statutory requirements to Charge Tax in Invoices, Deduct tax for some specified payments, as per law, Print Challans to deposit such Tax with Government and submit Statutory Returns. Tax Accounting section covers the aspects of Tax Accounting, describing the steps of Company & Masters Set Up, Tax charging in Invoice, Tax Deduction from Payments, Tax Challans Printing, Tax Reports printing.

Goods & Services Tax (GST) describes Company Set Up, GST Rates Set Up, Tax Ledger, Party Ledger, Invoicing, Input Tax adjustment, Tax payment, Challans, Statutory Returns Printing.

Tax Deducted at Source (TDS) describes Company Set Up, creation & set up for Ledger Accounts related with TDS transactions, Vouchers with TDS transactions, Tax Deposit with Government, Tax Challan & TDS Statutory Reports.

कानून के अनुसार organisation की Tax charge करने और Government को Tax जमा करने की जिम्मेदारी होती है। इस अध्याय में Tax संबंधित कार्य और हिसाब, government account में Tax जमा और Statutory Tax Return printing के बारे में समझाया है।

Goods & Services Tax (GST) में GST संबंधित Company Set Up, GST Rates Set Up, Tax Ledger, Party Ledger, Invoicing, Input Tax adjustment, Tax payment, Challans, Statutory Returns Printing के बारे में समझाया है।

Tax Deducted at Source (TDS) में TDS संबंधित Company Set Up, Ledger Accounts creation, Vouchers, Tax Deposit, Tax Challan Printing और TDS Statutory Reports Printing के बारे में समझाया है।

GST Masters 03-01

Goods & Service Tax (GST)

So far, we have explained the operational details of Accounting with Tally, for organisations to which GST is not applicable. Now, we discuss about the additional aspects related to GST, for organisation registered under GST, without repeating the common points already discussed in earlier chapters.

01 GST Activation for the Company

At K:Compnay tab, click *F11*. At Company Features screen (F-1A). Under *Taxation* section, at *Enable Goods & Services Tax (GST)*, set Yes.

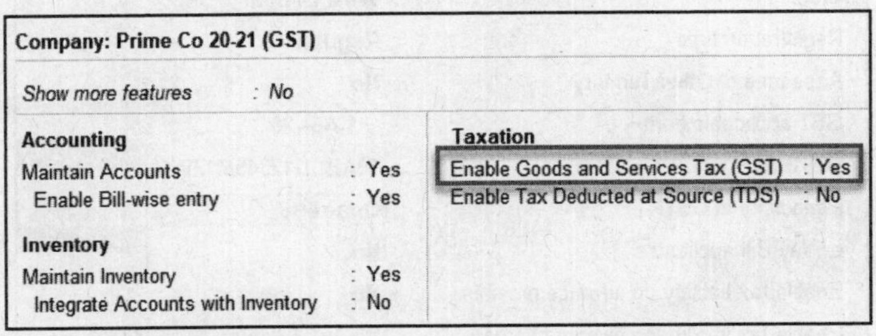

F-1A: Company Features GST activation

At *GST Details* screen, set as follows (F-1B):

- **State**: Select the State / UT, from the *List of States* in which the company is registered with GST
- **Registration Type**: Select *Regular* (registered as Regular Dealer), select *Composition* (registered as Composition Dealer).
- **Assessee of Other Territory**: Set *Yes* if the business unit is located in Exclusive Economic Zone (other territory), else set *No.*
- **GSTIN/UIN**: Correctly enter the complete 15 digit State /UT GSTIN allotted.
- **Applicable From**: Enter the date of applicability of GST (e.g 1 July 2017).
- **Periodicity of GSTR-1**: Select *Monthly / Quarterly* as applicable for the organisation.
- **E-way Bills details**: Set *No / Yes* as per e-way Bills applicability for the organisation (and then enter the e-way Bill related details)

- **Tax Liability for Advance Receipt**: At *Tax Liability for Advance Receipt*, set Yea / *No*, as per applicability of Tax liability for the organisation
- **Tax Liability on Reverse Charge**: At *Enable Tax Liability on Reverse Charge*, set *Yes / No as per* applicability of Reverse Charge for Purchase from Unregistered Dealer.
- **Activate GST Rate Details**: At *Set / Alter GST Rate Details* set *No* (set the Tax Rates at Item Master explained later).
- **Activate GST Classification**: At *Enable GST Classification* set *No* to keep things simpler.
- **LUT / Bond Details**: Set *Yes* (applicable for certain Importers / Exporters only), else set *No*

GST Details

State	: **West Bengal**
Registration type	: **Regular**
Assessee of Other Territory	: **No**
GST applicable from	: **1-Apr-20**
GSTIN/UIN	: **19ABCD12345M1ZW**
Periodicity of GSTR1	: **Quarterly**
e-Way Bill applicable	: **No**
Enable tax liability on advance receipts	: **No**
Enable tax liability on reverse charge *(Purchase from unregistered dealer)*	: **No**
Set/alter GST rate details	: **No**
Enable GST Classifications	: **No**
Provide LUT/Bond details	: **No**

Periodicity
Monthly
Quarterly

F-1B: Company GST details entry

GST Activate करने के लिए, F11 click कर Company Features में Taxation section में *Enable Goods & Services Tax (GST)* में Yes set कर (F-1A), Company GST details screen (F-1B) में option set करें।

02 Unit Quantity Code (UQC) set up in Unit of Measure (UoM)

We have explained UoM Master in Inventory section. At *GoT>Create* or *GoT>Alter* select *Unit*. At *UoM Master creation/ Alteration* (F-2A), at Unit Quantity Code (UQC) select the UQC from the list (F-2A).

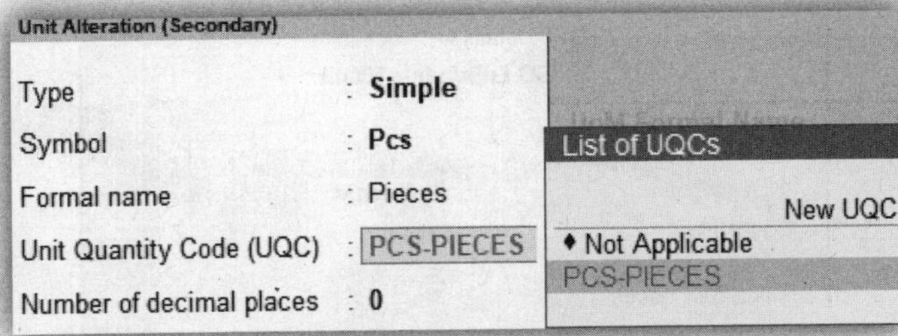

F-2A: UQc set up in UoM Master

GoT> Create या GoT>Alter से Unit select कर Unit of Measurement (UoM) Master के Unit Quantity Code (UQC) field में list से UQC select करे (F-2A)।

03 Stock Item GST Set Up

We have already explained Stock Item entry in Inventory System. Here we explain GST related additional details entry.

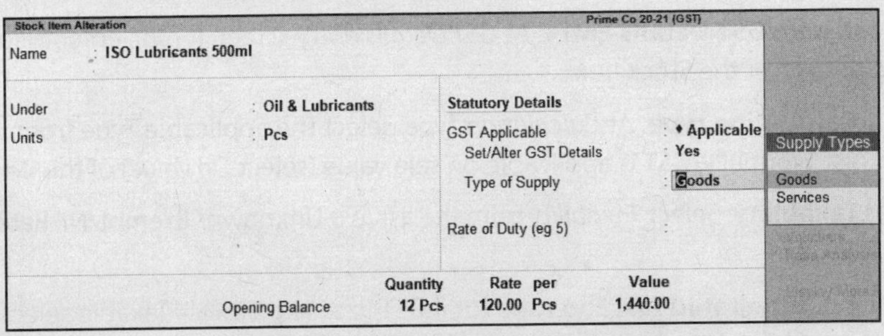

F-3A: Stock Item creation / alteration

Stock Item GST Applicability set up : Select *GoT>Create* or *GoT>Alter* and select *Stock Item* to get *Stock Item Creation / Alteration* screen (F-3A). Under *Statutory Details* section (F-3A), set as follows:

- **GST Applicable**: Select *Applicable* for Items to which GST is applicable, *Not Applicable* for Non-GST Items.
- **GST Rate Details**: Having set *Yes* at the above option, at *Set / Alter GST* details, set *Yes* to get *GST Details* screen to enter GST details for the Stock Item, as described next (F-3B).
- **Type of Supply**: Select Goods / Service as applicable from *Supply Type* list (F-3A)

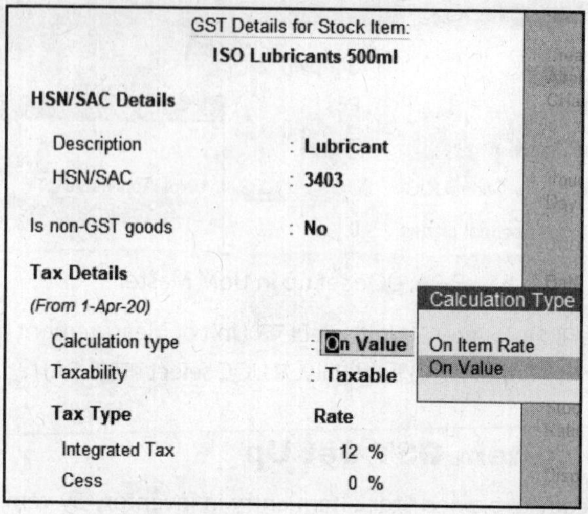

F-3B: Stock Item GST Details set up

Stock Item GST Details Entry: At *GST Details* entry screen (F-3B), enter following details for the Stock Item:

- **Calculation type**: At *Calculation Type*, select the applicable Type from the list. Normally, GST is applicable on sale value (select *On value*) of the Item.
- **Taxability**: Select *Taxability* from the list (e.g Unknown/ Exempt/Nil Rated/ *Taxable*)
  - **Integrated Tax**: Enter the total GST Rate (e.g 12%), if Taxable selected at Taxability.
  - **Cess**: Enter Cess Rate if applicable for the Item, otherwise leave zero (Cess is charged in some Items like Pan Masala, Tobacco Products, Aerated Water, Motor Car, etc).

Stock Item में GST details set up करने के लिए Stock Item Master के Statutory Details section में *GST Applicable* में *Applicable* select करे (F-3A)। *Set / Alter GST details* (F-3A) में Yes select करे और Stock Item GST details entry करे (F-3B)।

Multiple Stock Item GST details set up: To set up GST details of multiple Stock Items in one screen, select *GoT>Display More Reports>GST Reports>GST Rate Set Up.* Select Stock Group to get the list of Stock Items (F-4B). Click *F12:-Configure* and set the options (F-4A). At GST Rate Update screen (F-4B), select the Stock Item and set the unfilled values. This is useful when Rate of any Item / Item Group changes, as all details (like HSN, calculation Type etc) cannot be set from Update screen.

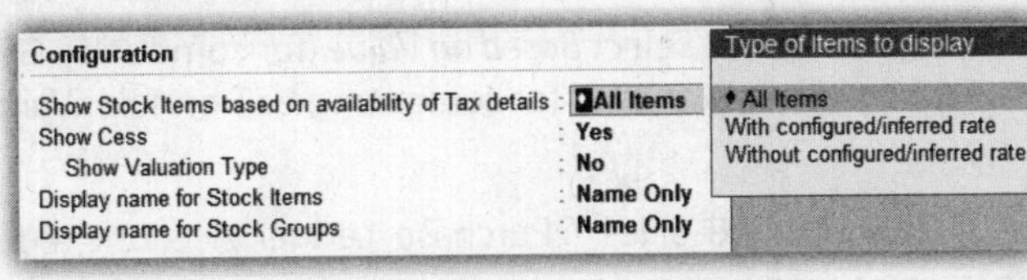

F-4A: GST Rate Update Configuration

कई Stock Items के GST Details को एक साथ set करने के लिए GoT>Display More Reports>GST Reports>GST Rate Set Up select कर. Item select करे और Item की GST Details set करे (F-4B)।

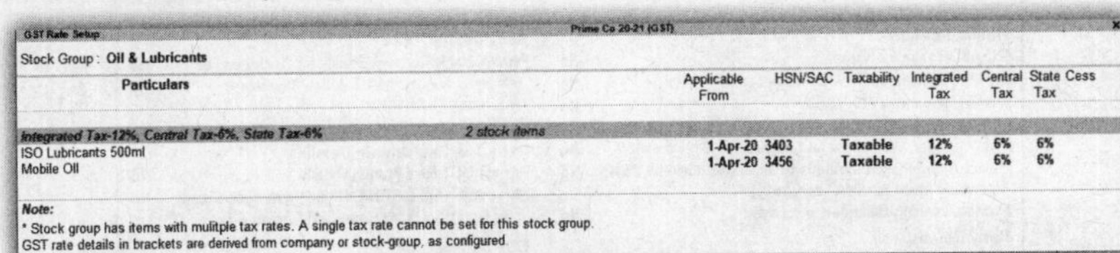

F-4B: GST Rate Update

04 Sales / Purchase Ledger Account GST set up

We have already explained Inventory set up for Inventory linked ledger Account (Sales / Purchase). We now explain the additional steps of GST details set up for such Ledger Accounts.

At *GoT>Create>Ledger* or *GoT>Alter>Ledger* and select Sales / Purchase Ledger to get Ledger Account Creation / Alteration screen (F-5A).

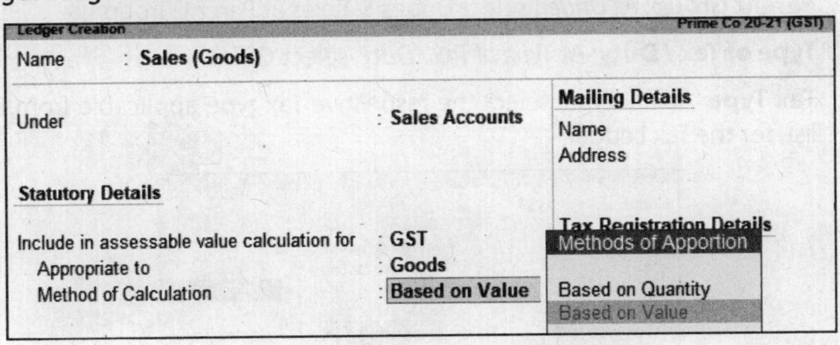

F-5A: GST set up in Sales / Purchase Ledger

At Ledger Creation / Alteration screen, under *Statutory Information* section, set as follows (F-5A):

- **GST Applicability**: At *Include in Assessable Value*, select, select *GST* from the list.
- **Appropriate to**: Select Goods / Services (so you should create separate Ledgers for Goods Sale and Services Sale).

– **Method of Calculation**: Select *Based on Value* (for computing GST on Sale Value as %) / *Based on Quantity* (for computing GST on sales Value on Sale Quantity).

GoT>Create या GoT>Alter से Sales / Purchase Ledger Account (F-5A) में GST details (F-5B/F-5C) set करें।

05 GST Ledger Accounts Creation

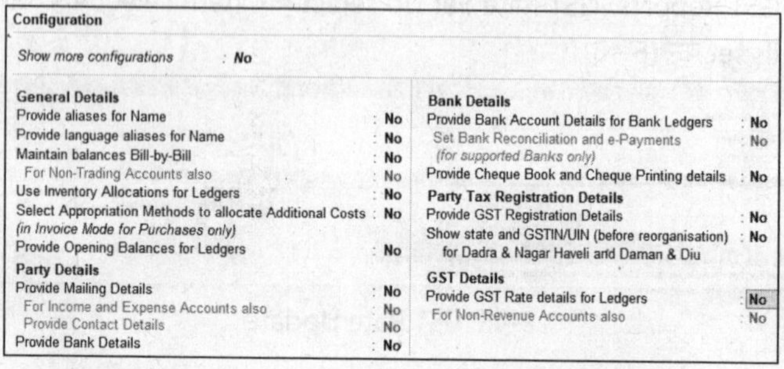

F-6A: GST Ledger Account Configuration

Ledger Account creation has been explained in Accounts section. Select *GoT>Create>Ledger* to create Ledgers for Central Tax (CGST: F-6C), State / UT Tax (SGST/UTGST:F-6D), Integrated Tax (IGST:F-6B) Ledgers**.** At Ledger Account Creation screen (F-6B to F-6D), enter as follows:

– **Tax Ledger Account Name**: At *Name*, enter the Tax Ledger Name

– **Parent Group**: At *Under*, select Duties & Taxes at Parent Group

– **Type of Tax / Duty**: At *Type of Tax / Duty*, select GST

– **Tax Type**: At *Tax Type*, select the respective Tax type applicable from the list, for the Tax Ledger

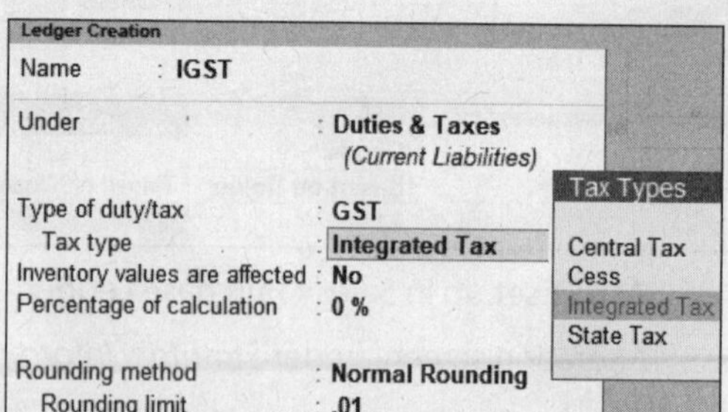

F-6B: IGST Ledger Account creation

This way, create a Tax Ledger for each Tax component of GST (IGST, CGST, SGST/UTGST). For Cess Ledger, select further select the *Valuation Type* from the list (F-6E).

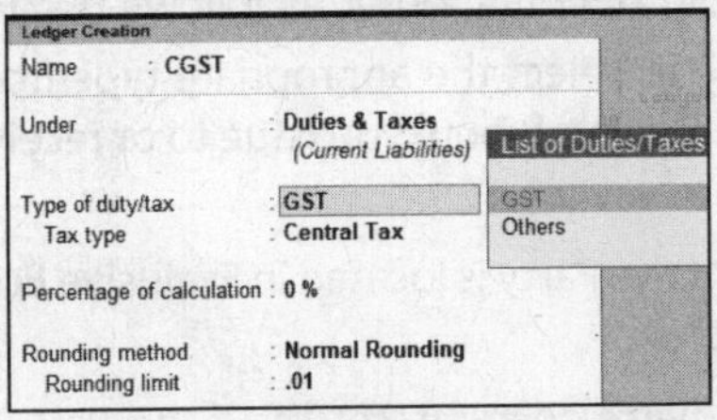

F-6C: CGST Ledger Account

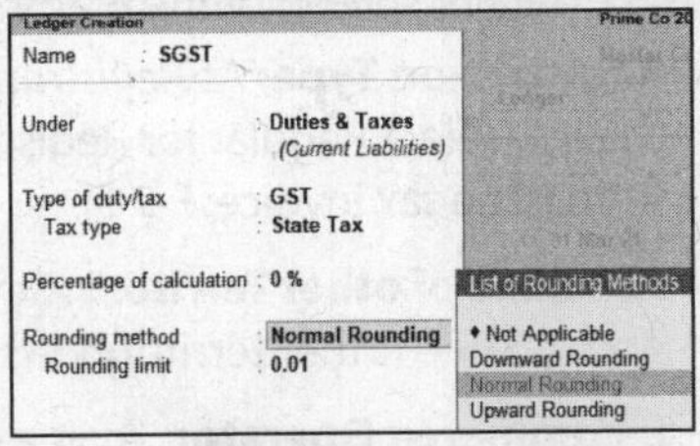

F-6D: SGST Tax Ledger Account

GST Ledger (IGST, CGST, SGST/UTGST Ledger) create करने के लिए GoT>Create> Ledger select करे और Ledger Account create करे (F-6B to F-6D)। Type of Duty / Tax में GST select करे और Tax Type select करे। अगर Cess applicable हो तो इस तरह Cess Account (F-6E) भी create करे।

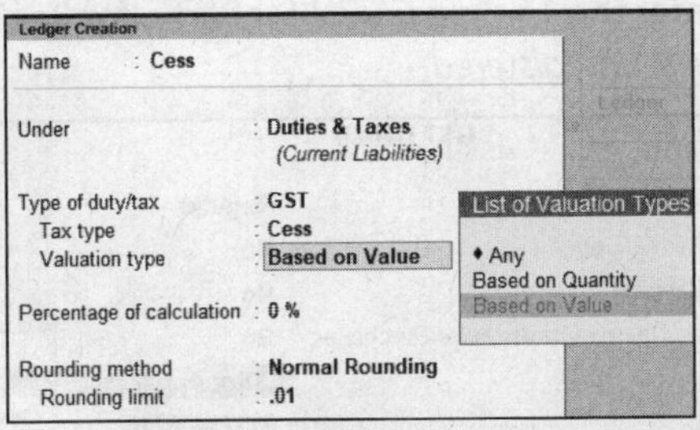

F-6E: Cess Ledger Account

06 Party Ledger Accounts GST set up

Ledger Account Creation / Alteration has been explained in Accounts section. Here we explain GST related additional details entry in Party (Customer / Supplier) Ledger Accounts. At Ledger Account Creation (GoT>Create>Ledger) / Alteration (GoT>Alter>Ledger), Click *I:More Details* and select *GST Registration Details* (F-7A) to enter *GST Details* (F-7B) of the Party.

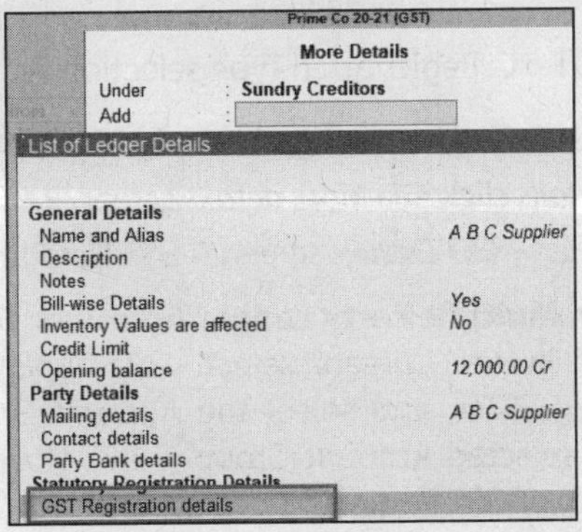

F-7A: Party Ledger GST Details activation

At *GST details* screen of the Party Ledger Account, enter as follows (F-7B):

- **Registration Type**: At *Registration Type*, select the appropriate type from the list (select Regular for Registered Dealers whom you issue to or receive from issue tax invoice: F-7C).
- **Assessee of other Territory**: Set *Yes* if the Party is located in Exclusive Economic Zone (other territory), else set *No.*
- **E-commerce Operator**: At *Is e-commerce operator*, set Yes if the Party is e-commerce operator, otherwise set No.
- **Deemed Exporter**: Set *Yes* if the Party is deemed Exporter, otherwise select *No.*
- **Party Type**: Select Party Type form the Party Type list (F-14C) (select *Not Applicable* for Parties other than Deemed Exporter/Embassy / SEZ)
- **GSTN / UIN**: Enter the 15 digit GSTIN for Party (for Registration Type other than *Consumer* & *Unregistered*)

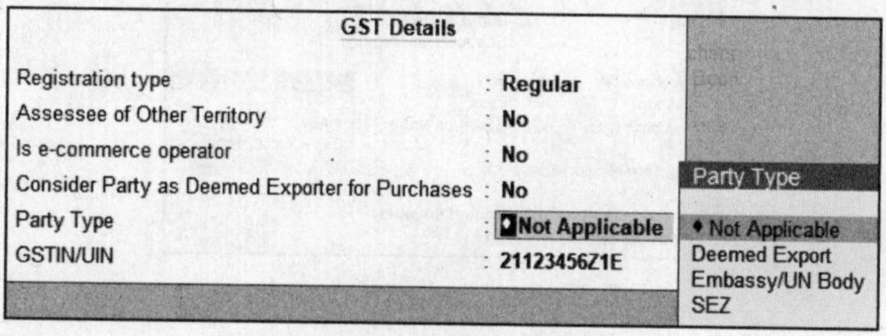

F-7B: Party Ledger GST Details entry

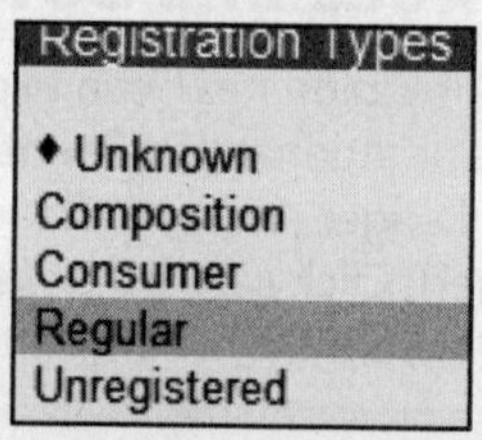

F-7C: Registration Type selection list

GoT>Create>Ledger / GoT>Alter>Ledger) से Party (Customer / Supplier) Ledger Account में *I:More details* click करें। *More details* screen में *GST Registration details* select करें (F-7A) और Party *GST Details* screen में GST Details entry करें (F-7B)।

GST Details entry in Multiple Party Ledger Accounts: To update GST details for multiple Parties in one screen, select *GoT>Display More Reports>GST Reports>Update Party GSTIN*, and select the Account Group to get the list Ledger Accounts of selected Account Group (F-8B). Now enter data in blank fields (or modify data) of GST Particulars of the Parties.

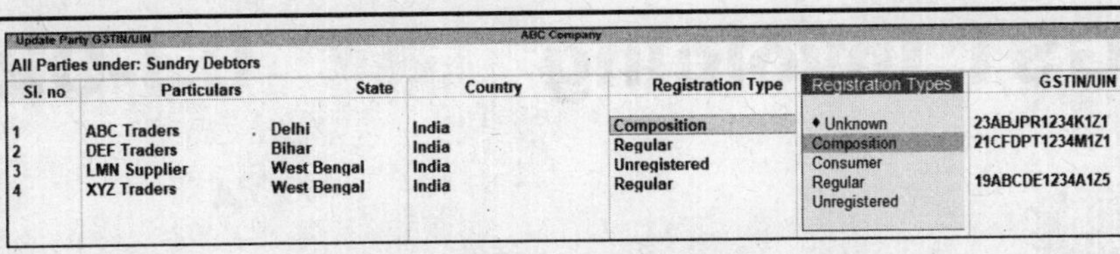

F-8B: Multi Party GSTN / UIN Updation screen

कई Party (Customer / Supplier) Ledger के GST Details एक साथ set करने के लिए GoT>Display More Reports>GST Reports>Update Party GSTIN select करे. Party select करे और Party की GST Details set करे (F-8B)।

05 GST Masters - Key Points

- F11 से Company Features में Enable Goods & Services में Yes set कर Company के लिए GST activate करे और Company GST details entry करे।
- Company Features में Set Alter GST details में No set करे। GST details (GST Rates etc) सिर्फ Stock Item में ही set करे, Stock Group, या कोई भी Ledger Account में GST Details activate न करे।
- Unit (UoM) Master में हर UoM record में UQC set करे।
- हर Stock Item में GST details entry करे।
- Sale / Purchase ledger Account में GST related details entry करे।
- GST Ledger Accounts create करे।
- Party Ledger Account में GST details entry करे।

GST Invoicing 03-02

We have explained Invoicing without GST. Here we discuss about additional details in respect of GST entry in Invoice and Invoice Printing with GST details.

01 GST Sales Invoice Entry

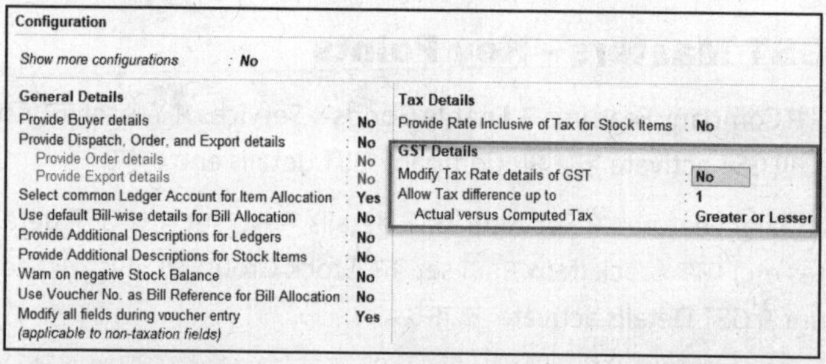

F-1A: GST Details Configuration set up in Invoice

We have described Sales, Purchase, Debit Note & Credit Note creation / alteration (GoT>Voucher) in Inventory chapter (02-02). GST set up at Company Features (F11), various Masters and Accounting Vouchers have also been explained in previous chapter (03-01). Now we explain additional details in respect of entry of GST details in Invoice.

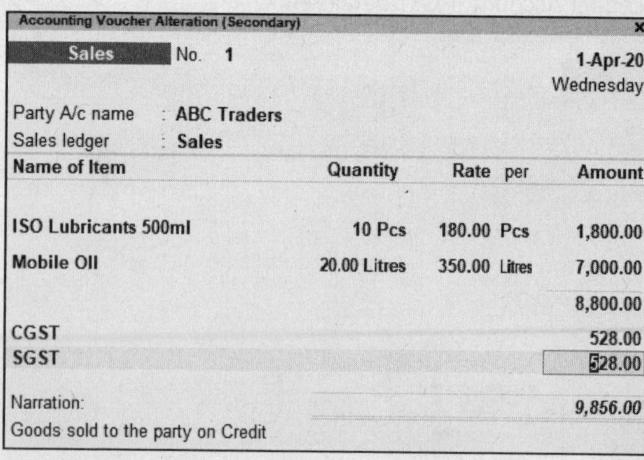

F-1B: GST Sales Invoice entry

At *Sales Voucher* entry screen (*GoT>Voucher*) in *Item Invoice* mode (F-1B), Click *F12:Configure*. At Configuration screen (F-1A), under *GST Details*, set the options as desired (F-1A). At, Invoice entry screen (F-1B), set the following additional details related to GST.

– **Tax Classification set up**: On selection of Sales / Purchase Ledger Account, at Tax Classification Details screen, select the Classification from *Nature of Transaction* list (F-1C).

– **Tax Ledger selection**: After entry of Item details, select the appropriate GST Ledger Account (CGST and SGST for Intra Sate (within Sate), IGST for Inter Sate (outside state) Sales). The computed Tax Amount in respect of the Tax Ledger Account will be automatically carried at Amount column. Now enter other ledger account and amount, if any.

– **Tax Analysis**: Click I:More Details button and select *Tax Analysis*. Press Alt+F5 to get Detailed *GST-Tax Analysis* (F-1D) showing HSN Code, Taxable Amount and Tax Component (CGST/SGST) in respect of each Item for review and verification.

Tax Classification selection

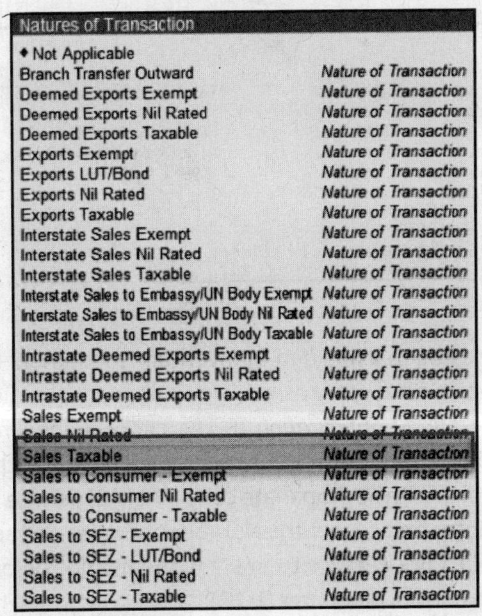

F-1C: Tax Classification List

GST - Tax Analysis

Particulars		Taxable Value	Tax rate	Duty/Tax Value
Sales Taxable		**8,800.00**		**1,056.00**
ISO Lubricants 500ml (3403)		*1,800.00*		*216.00*
Item Value (Sales Value 1,800.00)	*1,800.00*			
Central Tax			*6%*	*108.00*
State Tax			*6%*	*108.00*
Mobile Oil (3456)		*7,000.00*		*840.00*
Item Value (Sales Value 7,000.00)	*7,000.00*			
Central Tax			*6%*	*420.00*
State Tax			*6%*	*420.00*
** Value overridden by user*				
			Total	**1,056.00**

F-1D: Invoice GST Analysis

In the same way, you may enter GST details in Purchase Invoice entry.

GST Sales Invoice entry करने के लिए GoT>Voucher में F8:Sales Invoice entry screen में *F12:Configure* click कर GST Details section में GST संबंधित options set कर ले (F-1A)। Invoice entry screen में (F-1B), Sales Ledger entry के बाद, *Tax Classification* select करे (F-1C)। GST Ledger account select करे। Invoice में GST Amount automatic compute होगा (F-1B)। Alt+F5 click कर GST Analysis में GST details check कर ले (F-1D)। इस तरह Purchase Voucher में भी GST details entry करे।

02 GST Invoice Printing

Print

Title	: **Tax Invoice**
Printer	: HP LaserJet P1008
Paper Size	: A4 (8.27" x 11.69") or (210 mm x 297 mm)
Print area	: (7.95" x 11.42") or (202 mm x 290 mm)
Number of Copies	: 3

C: Configure | I: Preview | P: Print

F-2A: GST Invoice Printing

Invoice Printing has been explained in Inventory section (02-02). To instantly print the GST Invoice after entry as explained above, at Invoice entry screen, press Ctrl+P. At *Printing Configuration* (F-2A), click *C:Configure* to set Invoice Prining Configuration options (F- 2B), as explained in earlier chapters. To print multiple copy Invoice with appropariate copy labels, at Invoice Printing Configuration, under Printer section, set the Number of Copies and select the approprate option (F-2C). Click *I:Peview* to preview the Invoice before prining, Click *P:Print* to print the Invoice on Printer (F-2D).

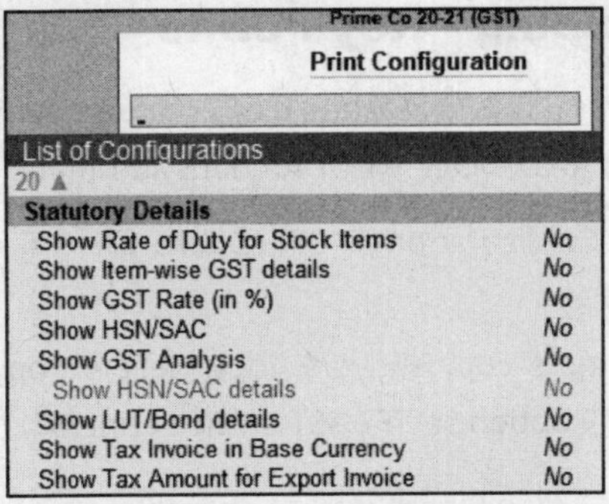

F-2B: Invoice Printing GST Details Configuration

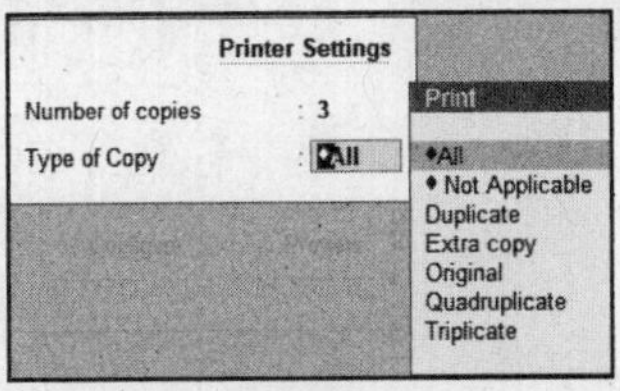

F-2C: Multiple Invoice Copy Print option

GST Invoice print करने के लिए Invoice entry screen (F-1B) में Ctrl+P से Invoice Printing screen (F-2A) में C:Configure button से Invoice Printing GST Details Configuration option set करे (F-2B)। Number of Copies option set kare (F-2C) और P:Print button (F-2A) से Printer में Invoice print करे (F-2D)।

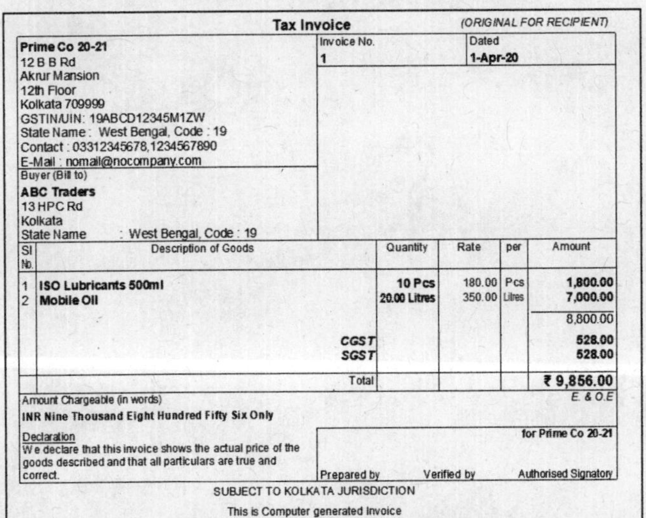

Tax Invoice (ORIGINAL FOR RECIPIENT)

Prime Co 20-21
12 B B Rd
Akrur Mansion
12th Floor
Kolkata 709999
GSTIN/UIN: 19ABCD12345M1ZW
State Name : West Bengal, Code : 19
Contact : 03312345678,1234567890
E-Mail : nomail@nocompany.com

Invoice No. **1** | Dated **1-Apr-20**

Buyer (Bill to)
ABC Traders
13 HPC Rd
Kolkata
State Name : West Bengal, Code : 19

Sl No.	Description of Goods	Quantity	Rate	per	Amount
1	**ISO Lubricants 500ml**	**10 Pcs**	180.00	Pcs	**1,800.00**
2	**Mobile Oil**	**20.00 Litres**	350.00	Litres	**7,000.00**
					8,800.00
	CGST				**528.00**
	SGST				**528.00**
	Total				**₹ 9,856.00**

E. & O.E

Amount Chargeable (in words)
INR Nine Thousand Eight Hundred Fifty Six Only

Declaration
We declare that this invoice shows the actual price of the goods described and that all particulars are true and correct.

for Prime Co 20-21

Prepared by Verified by Authorised Signatory

SUBJECT TO KOLKATA JURISDICTION

This is Computer generated Invoice

F-2D: GST Invoice in Print

03 GST Invoicing - Key Points

- Company Features और सभी Masters में GST features set करने के बाद Invoice में GST details entry करें। Invoice में GST Amount automatic compute होता है।
- Invoice Printing Configuration में GST details print के options set करे और Invoice print करें।
- GST Invoice multiple copy (Buyers Copy, Sellers Copy, Transporter Copy, बगैरह) print के लिए option set कर GST Invoice print करें।

GST Reports 03-03

After Voucher entries like Sales, Purchase, Debit / Credit Notes, Advance, Refunds, Reverse Charge Adjustments, etc, you may view /print the GST Statutory Reports for filing through GSTN Portal.

01 GST Reports Menu

All GST related Reports are available at GST Menu. Select *GoT>Display More Reports>GST Reports* to get *GST Reports Menu* (F-1A).

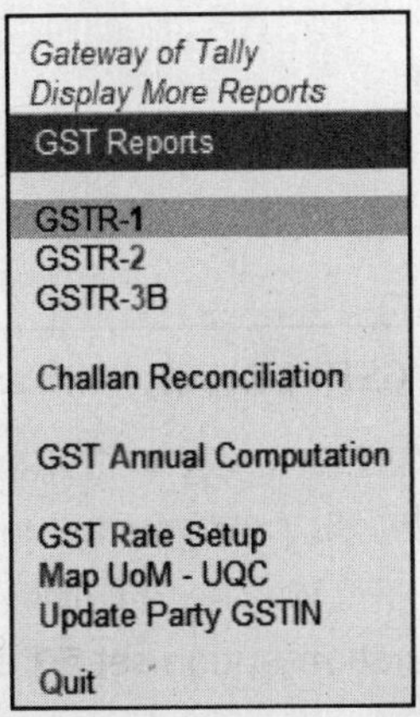

F-1A: GSTR Reports menu

GST Reports Menu के लिए *GoT>Display More Reports>GST Reports* select करे (F-1A)।

02 GSTR-1

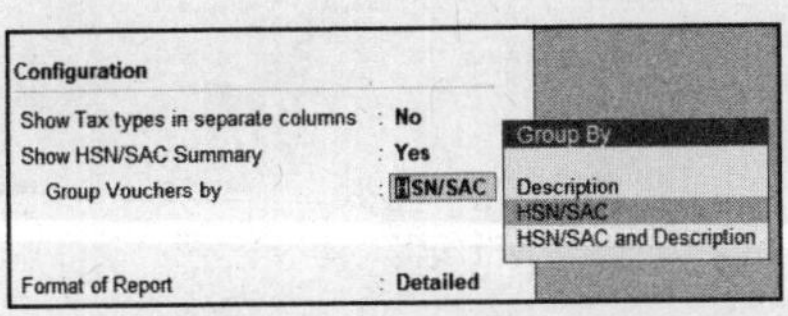

F-2A: GSTR-1 Report Configuration

At GST Reports menu (F-1A), select GSTR-1. At GSTR-1 Display (F-2B), at the report header, the statistic of Vouchers, separately for Clean Accepted Vouchers, Incomplete Vouchers (GST related details not completely available) and Irrelevant Vouchers (Vouchers not related with GST) are displayed. The figure such Incomplete Vouchers are not included in the Report Table. So, such Incomplete vouchers must be corrected properly. To rectify the Mismatch / Incomplete Vouchers, drill down through the relevant line in the header. The list of offended vouchers will be listed showing the reason/nature of mismatch / errors. These Vouchers then must be edited resolving all errors. Click *F12:Configure* and set the GSTR-1 Configuration options (F-2A) and view the corrected report (F-2C).

GSTR-1 — Prime Co 20-21 (GST)

GSTIN : 19ABCD12345M1ZW — 1-Apr-20 to 31-Dec-20

Particulars		Voucher Count
Total Vouchers		15
Included in Return		1
Included in HSN/SAC Summary	*0*	
Incomplete Information in HSN/SAC Summary (Corrections needed)	*1*	
Not relevant in this Return		10
Uncertain Transactions (Corrections needed)		4

Sl No.	Particulars	Voucher Count	Taxable Amount	Tax Amount	Invoice Amount
1	B2B Invoices - 4A, 4B, 4C, 6B, 6C				
	Taxable Sales				
	Reverse charge supplies				
2	B2C(Large) Invoices - 5A, 5B				
3	B2C(Small) Invoices - 7				
4	Credit/Debit Notes(Registered) - 9B				
5	Credit/Debit Notes(Unregistered) - 9B				
6	Exports Invoices - 6A				
7	Tax Liability(Advances received) - 11A(1), 11A(2)				
8	Adjustment of Advances - 11B(1), 11B(2)				
9	Nil Rated Invoices - 8A, 8B, 8C, 8D	1	500.00		500.00
	Total	1	500.00		500.00
	HSN/SAC Summary - 12				
	Document Summary - 13				

Note: Voucher count and values are not provided for HSN/SAC Summary and Document Summary. Drill down for details.

F-2B: GSTR-1 Report (with errors)

GST Reports Menu (F-1A) में GSTR-1 select कर GSTR-1 Report पाए (F-2B)। अगर कोई Voucher में कोई असंगति रह गयी हो तो वह Voucher report में मान्य नहीं होंगे. Report Header में drill down कर ऐसे गलत Voucher की गलती सुधारे। Report screen में F12:-Configure से Report Configuration option set कर (F-2A) संशोधित GSTR-1 (F-2C) Display / Print करे।

GSTR-1 — Prime Co 20-21 (GST)

GSTIN : 19ABCD12345M1ZW — 1-a-20 to 31-Dec-20

Particulars		Voucher Count
Total Vouchers		17
Included in Return		6
Included in HSN/SAC Summary	*6*	
Incomplete Information in HSN/SAC Summary (Corrections needed)	*0*	
Not relevant in this Return		11
Uncertain Transactions (Corrections needed)		0

Sl No.	Particulars	Voucher Count	Taxable Amount	Integrated Tax Amount	Central Tax Amount	State Tax Amount	Cess Amount	Tax Amount	Invoice Amount
1	B2B Invoices - 4A, 4B, 4C, 6B, 6C	3	6,815.00		267.78	267.78		535.56	7,350.56
	Taxable Sales		*6,815.00*		*267.78*	*267.78*		*535.56*	*7,350.56*
	Reverse charge supplies								
2	B2C(Large) Invoices - 5A, 5B								
3	B2C(Small) Invoices - 7	3	10,180.00		610.80	610.80		1,221.60	11,401.60
4	Credit/Debit Notes(Registered) - 9B								
5	Credit/Debit Notes(Unregistered) - 9B								
6	Exports Invoices - 6A								
7	Tax Liability(Advances received) - 11A(1), 11A(2)								
8	Adjustment of Advances - 11B(1), 11B(2)								
9	Nil Rated Invoices - 8A, 8B, 8C, 8D								
	Total	6	16,995.00		878.58	878.58		1,757.16	18,752.16
	HSN/SAC Summary - 12								
	Document Summary - 13								

Note: Voucher count and values are not provided for HSN/SAC Summarynd Document Summary. Drill down for details.

F-2C: GSTR-1 (Corrected)

03 GSTR-2

At GST Reports menu (F-1A), select GSTR-2. Like GSTR-1, resolve all the errors. Click F12:Configure and set the options (F-3A) to view corrected GSTR-2 Report (F-3B).

Configuration		List of Formats
Show Tax types in separate columns	: No	
Ignore differences in value up to	: 1	
Show Tax details of	: Both	
Show HSN/SAC Summary	: Yes	
Group Vouchers by	: HSN/SAC	
Format of Report	: Detailed	Condensed Detailed

F-3A: GSTR-2 Configuration

GST Reports Menu (F-1A) में GSTR-2 select कर GSTR-2 Report पाए (F-3B)। बताये गए तरीके से गलत/असंगत Voucher की गलती सुधारे. GSTR-2 Report screen में F12:Configure से Report Configuration option set कर (F-3A) संशोधित GSTR-2 (F-3B) Display / Print करे।

GSTR-2   Prime Co 20-21 (GST)

GSTIN/UIN : 19ABCD12345M1ZW   1-Apr-20 to 31-Mar-21

Particulars		Voucher Count
Total Vouchers		18
Included in Return		4
Invoices ready for returns	1	
Invoices with mismatch in information	3	
Uncertain Transactions (Corrections needed)		1
Not relevant in this Return		13
Incomplete Information in HSN/SAC Summary (Corrections needed)		0

Particulars	Voucher Count	Taxable Amount	Tax Amount				Input Tax Credit				Reconciliation Status
			Integrated Tax Amount	Central Tax Amount	State Tax Amount	Cess Amount	Integrated Tax Amount	Central Tax Amount	State Tax Amount	Cess Amount	
To be reconciled with the GST portal											
B2B Invoices - 3, 4A	2	24,242.50	746.70	595.20	595.20		746.70	595.20	595.20		
Taxable Purchases		*24,242.50*	*746.70*	*595.20*	*595.20*		*746.70*	*595.20*	*595.20*		
Reverse charge supplies											
Credit/Debit Notes Regular - 6C	1	200.00		12.00	12.00			12.00	12.00		
To be uploaded on the GST portal											
B2BUR Invoices - 4B											
Import of Services - 4C											
Import of Goods - 5											
Credit/Debit Notes Unregistered - 6C											
Nil Rated Invoices - 7 - (Summary)	1	480.00									
Composition											
Exempt		*480.00*									
Nil Rated											
Non GST											
Advance Paid -10A - (Summary)											
Adjustment of Advance - 10B - (Summary)											
Total Inward Supplies		**24,922.50**	**746.70**	**607.20**	**607.20**		**746.70**	**607.20**	**607.20**		
ITC Reversal/Reclaim - 11 - (Summary)											
Total No. of Invoices	4										

F-3B: GSTR-2 Return

04 GSTR-3B

At GST Reports menu (F-1A), select GSTR-3B. Like GSTR-1 & 2, resolve errors (if any). Click F12:Configure, and set the Configuration options (F-4A) to get the corrected GSTR-3 Report (F-4B).

Configuration		List of Formats
Show Tax types in separate columns	: Yes	
Format of Report	: Detailed	Condensed Detailed

F-4A: GSTR-3B Report Configuration

GST Reports Menu (F-1A) में GSTR-3B select कर GSTR-3B Report पाए (F-4B). गलत/

असंगत Voucher की गलती सुधारे। GSTR-4B Report screen में F12:Configure से Report Configuration option set कर (F-4A) संशोधित GSTR-2 (F-4B) Display / Print करे।

GSTR-3B — Prime Co 20-21 (GST)

GSTIN : 19ABCD12345M1ZW — 1-Apr-20 to 31-Mar-21

Particulars		Voucher Count
Total Vouchers		**18**
Included in Return		11
Participating in return tables	*11*	
No direct implication in return tables	*0*	
Not relevant in this Return		7
Uncertain Transactions (Corrections needed)		0

Table No.	Particulars	Taxable Amount	Integrated Tax Amount	Central Tax Amount	State Tax Amount	Cess Amount	Tax Amount
3.1	**Outward supplies and inward supplies liable to reverse charge**	16,995.00		878.58	878.58		1,757.16
3.2	**Of the supplies shown in 3.1 (a) above, details of inter-state supplies made to unregistered persons, composition taxable persons and UIN holders**						
4	**Eligible ITC**		2,426.70	607.20	607.20		3,641.10
A	ITC Available (whether in full or part)						
	(1) Import of goods						
	(2) Import of services						
	(3) Inward supplies liable to reverse charge (other than 1 & 2 above)						
	(4) Inward supplies from ISD						
	(5) All other ITC		2,426.70	607.20	607.20		3,641.10
B	ITC Reversed						
	(1) As per rules 42 & 43 of CGST Rules						
	(2) Others						
C	Net ITC Available (A) - (B)		2,426.70	607.20	607.20		3,641.10
D	Ineligible ITC						
	(1) As per section 17(5)						
	(2) Others						

Note: Amount is not shown for Input Credit to be Booked. Drill down for values.

F-4B: GSTR-3B Report

05 GST Annual Computation

At GST Reports Menu (F-1A), select *GST Annual Computation* to get the GST Annual Report for the entire Financial Year (F-5A).

GST Annual Computation — Prime Co 20-21 (GST)

GSTIN : 19ABCD12345M1ZW — 1-Apr-20 to 31-Mar-21

Particulars		Voucher Count
Total Vouchers		**18**
Included in Report		11
Included in HSN/SAC Summary	*10*	
Incomplete Information in HSN/SAC Summary (Corrections needed)	*1*	
Not relevant for this Report		7
Uncertain Transactions (Corrections needed)		0

Particulars	Taxable Amount	Integrated Tax Amount	Central Tax Amount	State Tax Amount	Cess Amount	Tax Amount
Liability						
Outward and Inward Supplies on Which Tax is Payable (Including Advances)	16,995.00		878.58	878.58		1,757.16
B2C supplies to unregistered persons	10,180.00		610.80	610.80		1,221.60
B2B supplies to registered persons including credit/debit note	6,815.00		267.78	267.78		535.56
B2B supplies to registered persons	*6,815.00*		*267.78*	*267.78*		*535.56*
Credit notes issued to registered persons						
Debit notes issued to registered persons						
Exports with payment of tax including credit/debit note						
Exports with payment of tax						
Credit notes issued for export on payment of tax						
Debit note issued for export on payment of tax						
SEZ supplies with payment of tax including credit/debit note						
SEZ supplies with payment of tax						
Credit notes issued to SEZs on payment of tax						
Debit notes issued to SEZs on payment of tax						
Deemed exports including credit/debit note						
Deemed exports						
Credit notes issued for deemed exports						
Debit notes issued for deemed exports						
Advances on which tax has been paid but invoice has not been issued						
Inward supplies on which tax is to be paid based on reverse charge						
Outward Supplies on Which Tax is not Payable						
Exports without payment of tax including credit/debit note						
Exports without payment of tax						
Credit notes issued for exports without payment of tax						
Debit notes issued for exports without payment of tax						
SEZ supplies without payment of tax including credit/debit note						
SEZ supplies without payment of tax						
Credit notes issued to SEZs without payment of tax						
Debit notes issued to SEZs without payment of tax						
Outward supplies subject to reverse charge including credit/debit note						
Outward supplies subject to reverse charge						
Credit notes issued based on reverse charge						
Debit notes issued based on reverse charge						
Exempted supplies including credit/debit note						
Exempted supplies						
Credit notes issued for exempted supplies						
Debit notes issued for exempted supplies						
Nil rated supplies including credit/debit note						
Nil rated supplies						
Credit notes issued for nil rated supplies						
Debit notes issued for nil rated supplies						

Particulars						
Non-GST supplies including credit/debit note						
Non-GST supplies						
Credit notes issued for non-GST supplies						
Debit notes issued for non-GST supplies						
Total Liability	**16,995.00**		**878.58**	**878.58**		**1,757.16**
Input Tax Credit						
Input Tax Credit		**2,426.70**	**607.20**	**607.20**		**3,641.10**
Import of goods (including supplies from SEZs)						
Import of goods - Inputs						
Import of goods - Capital Goods						
Import of goods from SEZ - Inputs						
Import of goods from SEZ - Capital Goods						
Import of services (excluding inward supplies from SEZs)						
Inward supplies liable to reverse charge						
Inward supplies from ISD						
All other ITC		2,426.70	607.20	607.20		3,641.10
All other ITC - Inputs		*746.70*	*607.20*	*607.20*		*1,961.10*
All other ITC - Capital Goods		*1,680.00*				*1,680.00*
All other ITC - Services						
Amount of ITC reclaimed						
ITC Reversal and Ineligible ITC Declared						
Non-payment of consideration to supplier (Rule 37)						
ISD credit note received (Rule 39)						
Excess ITC claimed, exempt & non-business supplies (Rule 42)						
Capital goods being used for exempted supplies (Rule 43)						
Ineligible credit (Section 17(5))						
Other reversals						
Input Tax Credit After Reversal & Ineligible ITC		**2,426.70**	**607.20**	**607.20**		**3,641.10**
HSN/SAC Summary						
Summary of Outward Supplies						
Summary of Inward Supplies						

F-5A: GST Annual Computation

GST Reports Menu (F-1A) में *GST Annual Computation* select कर GSTR-3B Report पाए. F12 से Configuration option set कर *GST Annual Computation* पाए (F-4B)।

06 GST Reports - Key Points

- GoT>Display More Reports>GST Reports से GSTR Report Menu पाए। GST registered dealer को GSTR-1, GSTR-3B और Annual Report (GSTR-9 / GSTR-9A) submit करना है।
- GSTR-1 Outwards Supply (यानि Sales) का Monthly / Quarterly Report है।
- GSTR-2 Inwards Supply का report है, जिसे GSTR-1 के बाद Inwards / Outwards matching कर submit करना है.
- GSTR-3B report GSTR-1, GSTR-2A से reconcile कर submit करना है।
- GSTR Annual Report पूरे साल का Sale, Purchase, Input Tax Credit और Tax Liability का संक्षिप्त विवरण (summarised statement) है, जिसे अगले 31 Dec तक submit करना है।

Tax Deducted at Source (TDS) 03-04

Tax Deducted at Source (TDS)

Certain payments are subjected to Income Tax Deduction at source (TDS). Such TDS will be deducted at time of payment or credit, whichever is earlier. Here we describe TDS by Deductor, for such specified payments made (other than Salary).

Income Tax rules के अनुसार Payment देनेवाला, कुछ खास nature के payments से TDS घटाकर Balance payment करता है और TDS government में deposit करता है।

01 TDS Activation for the Company

At Company Features (F11), under Taxation section, at *Enable Tax Deducted at Source*, set *Yes* (F-1A). At *Company TDS Deductor Details* screen (F-1B), enter the Company TDS Details. At *Set Alter details of person responsible* set *Yes* and enter Person Responsible Details (F-1C).

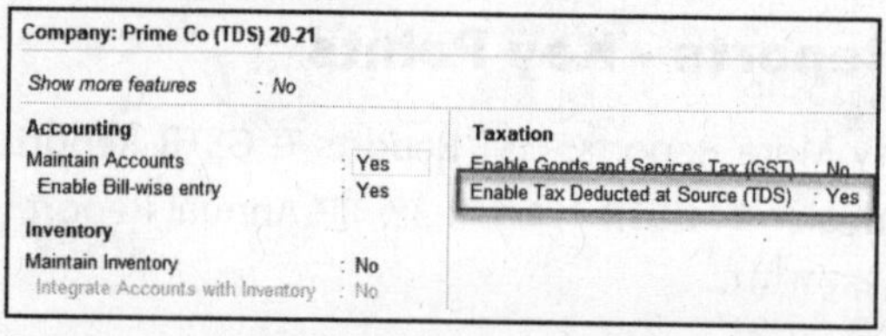

F-1A: Company Features TDS Activation

F11 click कर Company Features के Taxation section में *Enable Tax Deducted at Source* में *Yes* set करे (F-1A)। *Company TDS Deductor Details* में Company के TDS related details entry करे (F-1B)। *Set Alter details of person responsible* में Yes set कर (F-1B) Person Responsible की details entry करे (F-1C)।

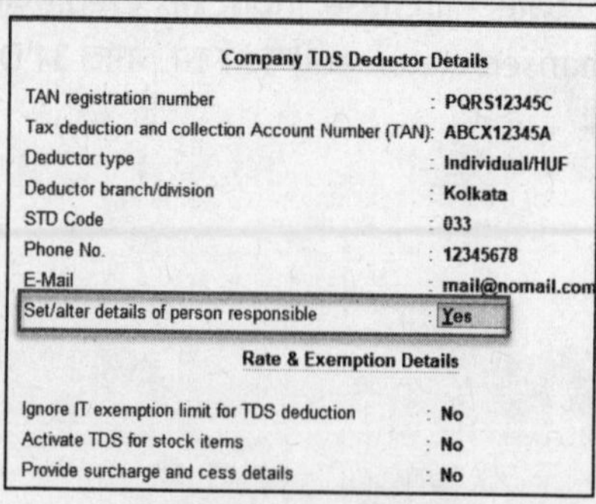

F-1B: Company TDS Deductor Details

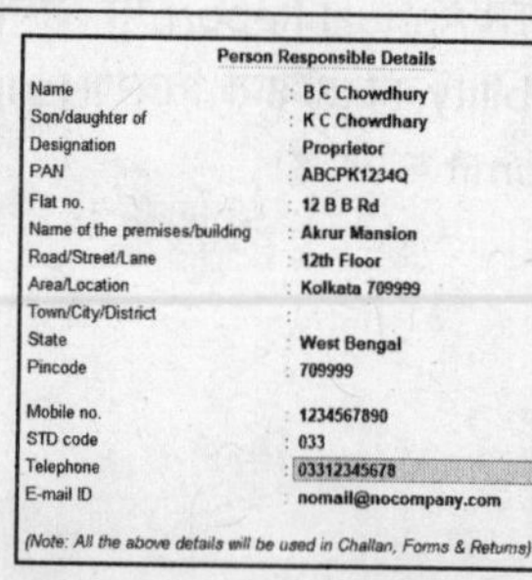

F-1C: Person Responsible details

02 TDS Deductible Payments

First create the *Nature of Payments* for which TDS is deducted by the Company. Select *GoT>Create>TDS Nature of Payment* to get *TDS Nature of Payment Creation* screen (F-2B). At *Name*, select the TDS Nature of Payment from List (Click *H:Helper/ Manual* toggle or press *Alt+H*, and enter the Nature of Payment in Manual Mode if the list does not appear), and relevant details. Click *F12:Configure* to set the Configuration options (F-2A).

Configuration	
Allow single bill value	: Yes
Allow Transporter Category	: No
Allow Software Royalty	: No
Allow relaxation in rate for Non-Residents	: No
Allow tax rate without PAN	: Yes

F-2A: TDS Nature of Payment Entry Configuration

TDS Nature of Payment Creation	
Name	: **Interest Other Than Interest on Securities**
Section	: **194A**
Payment code	: **94A**
Remittance code	:
Value limit for a single bill	: **5,000.00**
Rate for individuals/HUF	
With PAN	: **10 %**
Without PAN	: **20 %**
Rate for other deductee types	
With PAN	: **10 %**
Without PAN	: **20 %**
Threshold/exemption limit	: **25,000.00**
Accept ?	**Yes** or **No**

F-2B: TDS Nature of Payment Entry

GoT>Create>TDS Nature of Payment select कर *TDS Nature of Payment Creation* screen में TDS nature of payments Master की entry करे (F-2B)। Name field में list से TDS nature of Payment select करे। (Selection List नहीं मिले तो *H:Helper* button click करे और Name manually entry करे)। फिर बाकी info भी entry करे (F-2B) और *Yes* type करे save करें।

03 TDS Ledger Account

Ledger Account creation has been explained earlier. Select *GoT>Create>Ledger* to create TDS Ledger Account and enter the following details (F-3B).

- **Name**: Enter the TDS Ledger Account Name.
- **Parent Group**: At *Under*, select *Duties & Taxes*
- **TDS Type**: Select *TDS* from the list

Nature of Payment: Select Any (to maintain common TDS Ledger for all Nature of Payment) or select the Nature of Payment related to the TDS Account.

Click F12:Configure to set up Configuration options (F-3A).

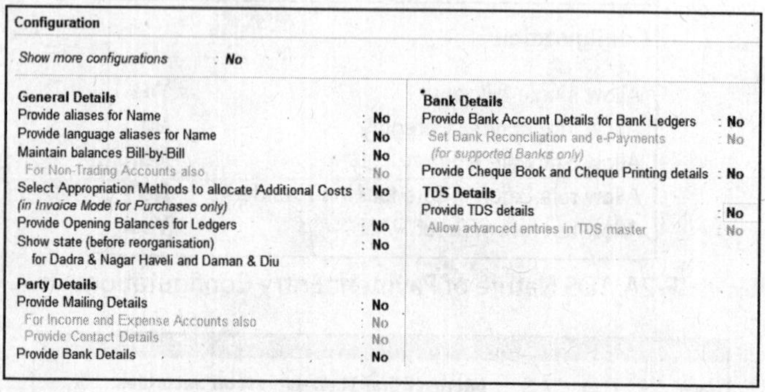

F-3A: TDS Ledger Account Configuration

GoT>Create>Ledger select करे, F12 से Configuration options set करें, Ledger creation screen में, TDS Ledger account details entry कर TDS Ledger Account create करें।

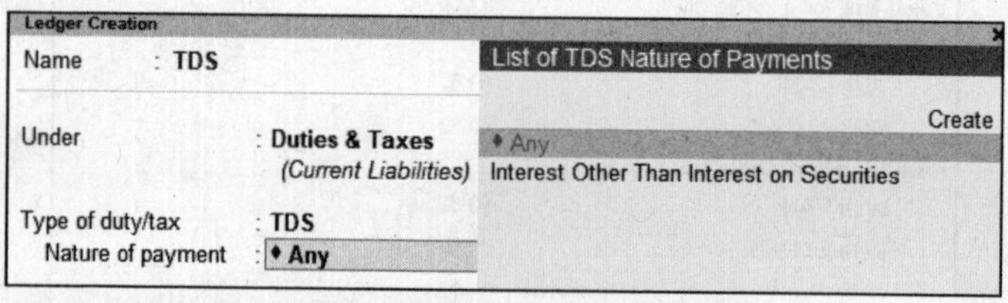

F-3B: TDS Ledger Account creation

04 TDS Nature of Payment

Ledger Creation / Alteration has been explained earlier. We describe additional details set up for TDS Deductee Ledger Account. Select GoT>Create > Ledger At Deductee Ledger Creation (F-4B), click *F12:Configure*. At Ledger Configuration, set Yes at *Provide TDS details* (F-4A) and then enter the TDS details for the Deductee Ledger Account (F-4B) at *Statutory Details* section of the TDS Deductee Ledger creation / alteration screen (F-4B).

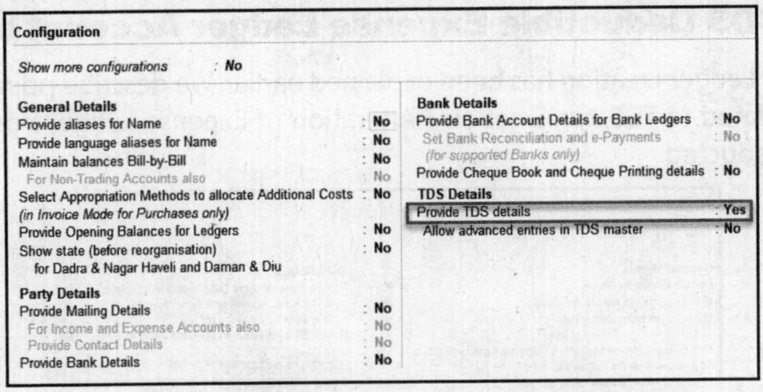

F-4A: Deductee Ledger Configuration

At *Is TDS Deductible?* set *Yes* and enter following details (F-4B):

- **TDS Nature**: At *Treat TDS as Expenses*, set *No* (where TDS Amount is deducted from the amount Payable to the Party. So, TDS is not company's expenses)
- **Organisation Type**: At *Deductee Type*, select the *Deductee Type* from the list, according to the nature of constitution of the Party.
- **TDS Voucher**: At *Deduct TDS in same Voucher*, set *Yes* if TDS is deducted in same Voucher

At Right part, under Tax Registration details, enter Address & PAN Details (PAN is mandatory). Set *Yes* at *Provide PAN details* (F-4B) and enter *Effective Date* and *Name of Deductee* as per I Tax records (F-4C).

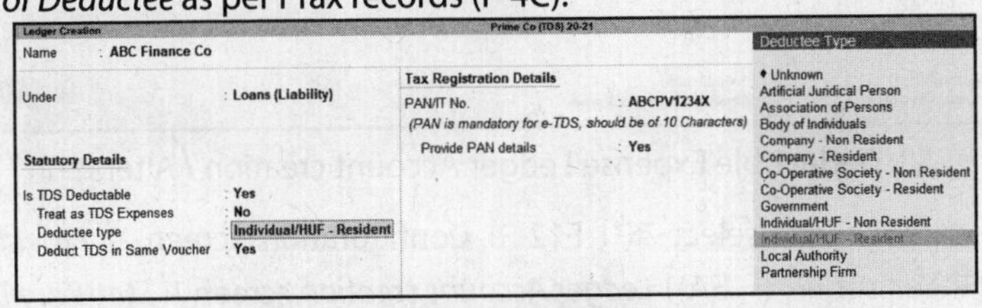

F-4B: Deductee TDS details set up

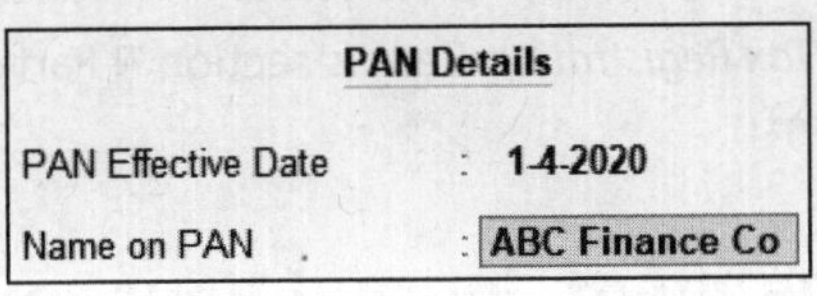

F-4C: Deductee PAN details

GoT>Create>Ledger select करें। F12 से Configuration screen में *Provide TDS Details* में Yes set करें। *Ledger Account creation* screen में *Statutory Details* section में *Is TDS Deductible?* में set Yes कर TDS related details entry करें। *Tax Registration Details* section में Party के Income Tax PAN संबंधित details entry करें।

05 TDS Deductible Expense Ledger Account set up

Expense Ledger creation has been explained earlier. We describe points exclusively related to TDS, for Creation / Alteration of Expense Ledger from which TDS is deducted.

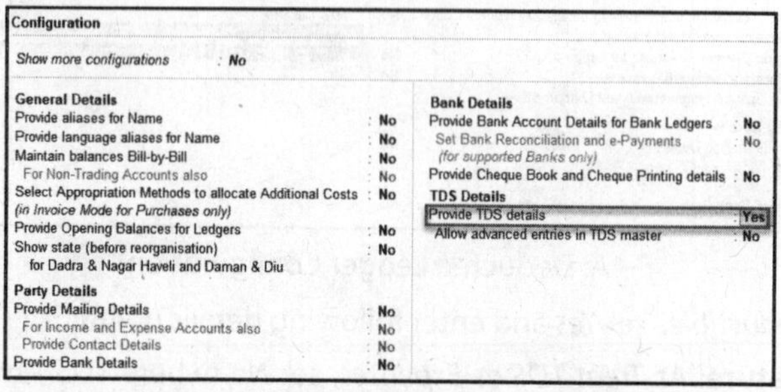

F-5A: Ledger Account Configuration

Select GoT>Create>Ledger. At Expense Ledger Account creation / Alteration (F-5B), click *F12:Configure*. At Ledger Account Configuration (F-5A), Under *TDS details* section, at *Provide TDFS Details*, set Yes (F-5A). At Ledger Account creation / Alteration (F-5B), under *Statutory Details*, at *Is TDS Applicable*, select *Applicable*. At *Nature of Payment*, select the Nature of Payment from the list.

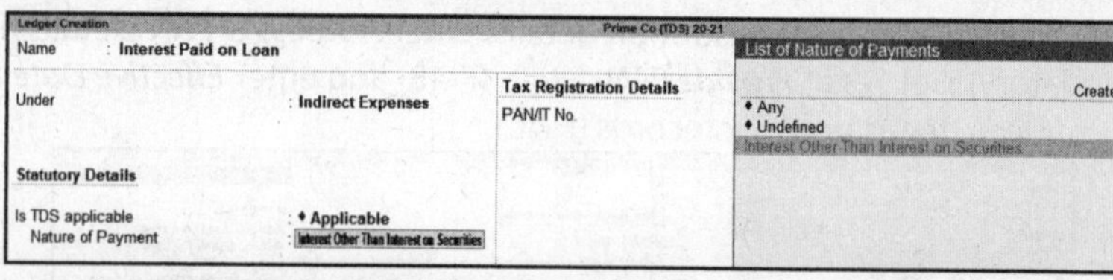

F-5B: Deductible Expense Ledger Account creation / Alteration

GoT>Create>Ledger select करें। F12 से Configuration screen में *Provide TDS Details* में Yes set करें (F-5A)। *Ledger Account creation* screen में *Statutory Details* section में *Is TDS Deductible?* में *Applicable* select कर Nature of Payment me List से select करें (F-5B)। *Tax Registration Details* section में Party के Income Tax PAN संबंधित details entry करें।

06 TDS Adjustment Journal Voucher

Select GoT>Voucher, Click F7 and create a Journal Voucher (F-6B) to book the expense and adjust the TDS linking with the Deductee Account. At Journal Voucher creation screen (F-6B), click F12:Configure and set the TDS related options (F-6A).

Configuration

Show more configurations : **No**

General Details		**Bank Details**	
Use Cr/Dr instead of To/By during voucher entry	: **Yes**	Use default Bank Allocations	: **No**
Preallocate bills for Payment/Receipt/Journal Vouchers	: **No**	Use Auto Cheque Numbering	: **No**
Use default Bill-wise details for Bill Allocation	: **No**	Select Cheque Range	: **No**
Show Inventory details	: **No**	Print Cheque after saving Voucher	: **No**
Show list of Bills for selection	: **No**	Show Cheque details before printing	: **No**
Show Final Balances for each Bill	: No	**TDS Details**	
Show Bill-wise Details	: **No**	Modify Tax details for TDS	: **Yes**
Show Bill-wise details in multiple lines	: No	Show TDS Bill Allocations	: **Yes**
		Show Tax Analysis details for TDS	: **Yes**

F-6A: Voucher Configuration

At Journal Voucher screen (F-6B), first enter details of TDS deductible expenses ledger account and select the TDS Nature of Payment from the list (F-6C). Next, select TDS Ledger Account and enter the amount of TDS deducted. Next, select the Deductee Ledger Account. The details of TDS are auto carried and shown at TDS Nature of Payment Details (F-6D) for information. In the main voucher screen (F-6B), enter the Voucher Narration and save the Voucher.

Accounting Voucher Creation

Journal No. 1 — 1-Aug-20 Saturday

Particulars	Debit	Credit
Dr **Interest Paid on Loan**	10,000.00	
Cr **TDS**		1,000.00
Cr **ABC Finance Co**		9,000.00
Narration:	10,000.00	10,000.00

TDS Adjustment on Interest payment

F-6B: TDS Adjustment Journal Voucher

TDS Nature of Payment Details

Nature of Payment

Interest Other Than Interest on Securities

F-6C: TDS Nature of Payment selection

TDS Nature of Payment Details

Type of Ref	Name				Nature of Payment	Assessable Amount	TDS	Payable Amount
New Ref	Jrnl / 1 / 13				Interest Other Than Interest on Securities	10,000.00 Cr	1,000.00 Cr	9,000.00 Cr
	Income Tax	*10 %*	*On*	*10,000.00 Cr*	*1,000.00 Cr*			
	Surcharge	*0 %*	*On*	*1,000.00 Cr*				
	Education Cess	*0 %*	*On*	*1,000.00 Cr*				
	Secondary Education Cess	*0 %*	*On*	*1,000.00 Cr*				
	Total					10,000.00 Cr		9,000.00 Cr

F-6D: TDS Nature of Payment details

TDS deduction के लिए Journal Voucher से Dedcutee का account से TDS adjust किया जाता है। GoT>Voucher में F8:Journal Voucher entry screen में F12 से TDS related Configuration options set करें (F-6A)। Journal Voucher में TDS DEdcutible expenses ledger और Amount entry कर (F-6B) TDS nature of payment Details screen में list से Nature of Payment select करें (F-6C)। TDS Ledger select कर TDS deduction amount entry करने से (F-6C) TDS details auto carried हो जाएगा (F-6D). Voucher Narration entry कर (F-6B) Voucher save करें।

07 TDS Deposit to Government

Select GoT>Voucher. Click F5:Payment to create a Payment Voucher for Deposit of TDS to Government (F-7B). At *Payment Voucher* entry screen (F-7B), click F12:Configure and set the TDS related options (F-6A).

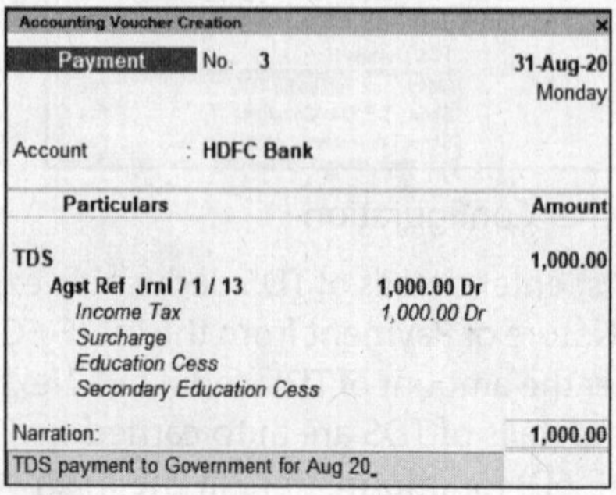

F-7A: TDS Payment Voucher

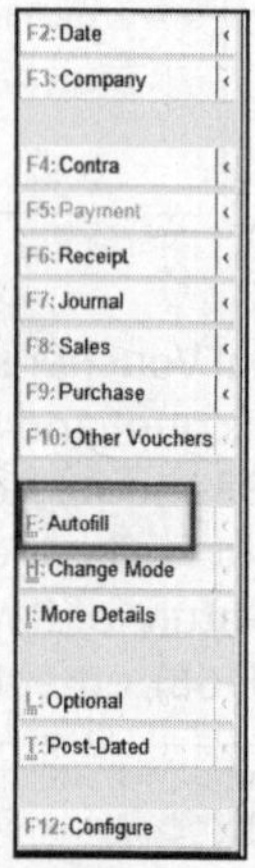

F-7B: Buttons

At Payment Voucher screen (F-7A), click *E:Autofill* (Ctrl+F) button (F-7B) to get Autofill screen (F-7D). At *Type of Transaction*, select Stat Payment. Fill up TFDS related details. Select the Bank Account. At Main Voucher screen (F-7A), enter the TDS ledger account and amount. At *TDS Nature of Payment* screen, select the pending TDS reference (F-7C). At Payment Voucher (F-7B) the details would be carried. Enter Voucher Narration (F-7B) and save the Voucher.

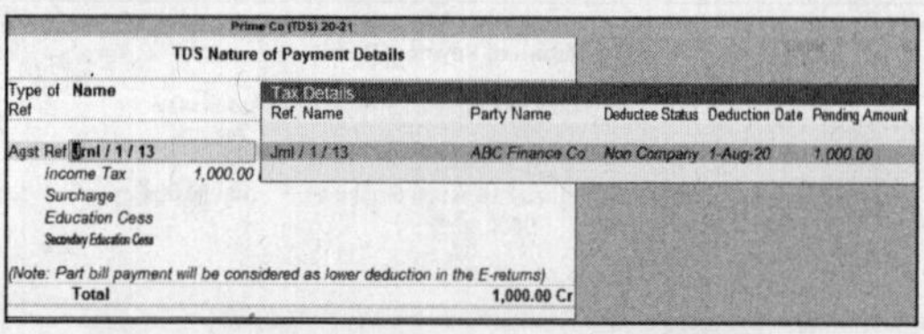

F-7C: TDS payment details

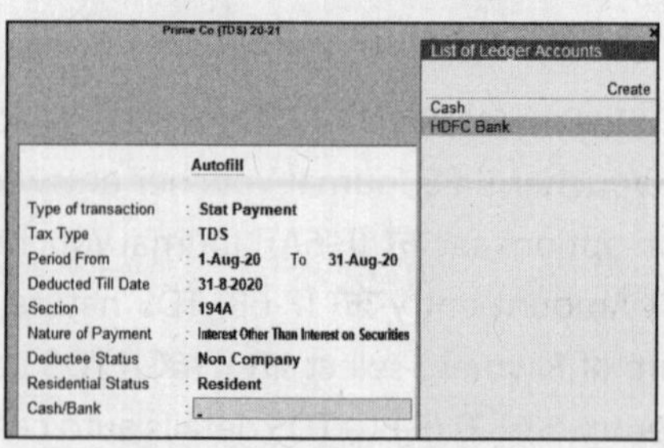

F-7D: TDS Stat Auto fill

TDS Deposit के लिए GoT>Voucher में F5 से Payment Voucher select कर F12 से Voucher Configuration option set करे (F-7A)। Voucher entry screen में F:Autofill button click कर Autofill screen में Details entry करे और Bank Account select करे (F-7D)। Payment Voucher screen में TDS account select कर TDS Nature of Payment में TDS Deduction का Reference select करे (F-7C)। सारे details Payment Voucher में carry हो जायेगा (F-7B)। Voucher Narration entry करे और Payment Voucher save करे (F-7B)।

08 TDS Deposit Challan Printing

On entry of Payment Voucher for deposit of TDS as explained above, at Payment Voucher entry screen (F-7A), click *P:Print* button to get the *Payment Voucher Printing* screen (F-8A). Click *C:Configure* button and set *Yes* at *Print as TDS Challan* option (F-8A). Click P:Print button to print the challan (F-9A) on printer.

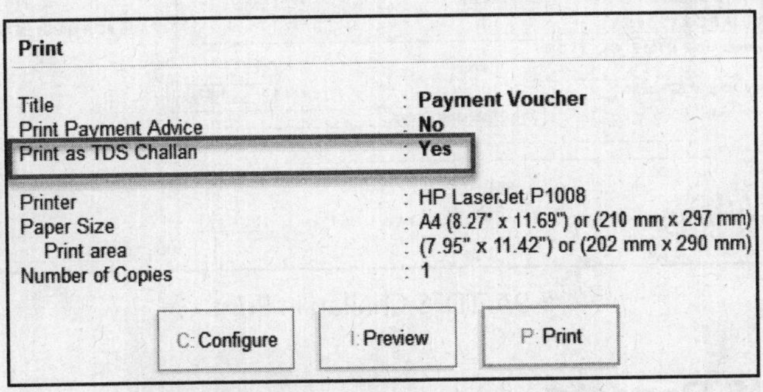

F-8A: TDS Challan Printing

TDS Deposit के Payment Voucher entry कर (F-7B), Ctl+P button click कर, Printing screen में Print as TDS Challan में Yes set कर P:Print button click करे (F-8A) और TDS Tax challan (F-9A) printer से print करे।

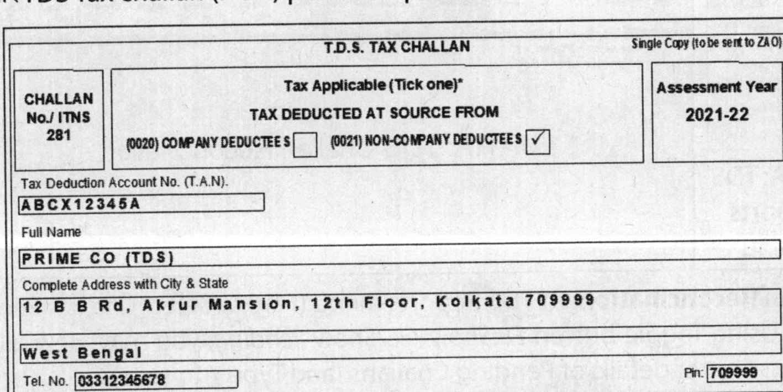

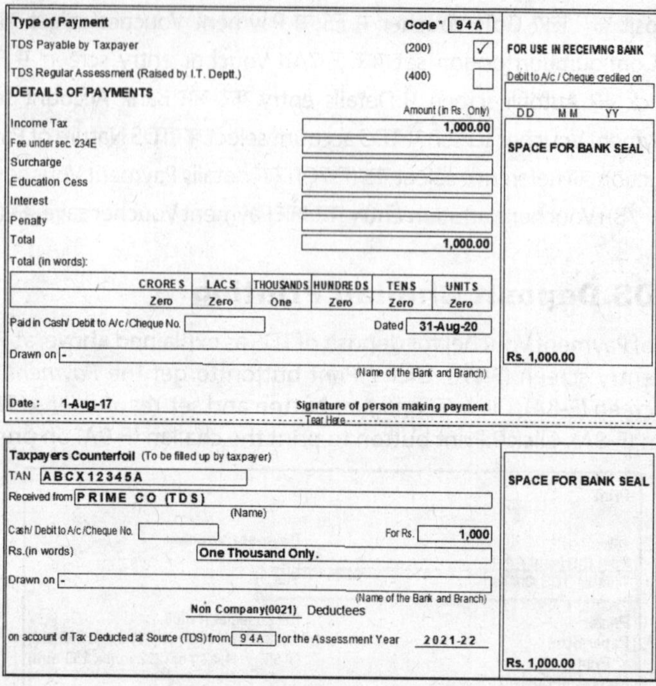

Type of Payment Code* 94A

TDS Payable by Taxpayer (200) ✓

TDS Regular Assessment (Raised by I.T. Deptt.) (400)

FOR USE IN RECEIVING BANK

Debit to A/c / Cheque credited on

DD MM YY

DETAILS OF PAYMENTS Amount (in Rs. Only)

Income Tax	1,000.00
Fee under sec 234E	
Surcharge	
Education Cess	
Interest	
Penalty	
Total	1,000.00

SPACE FOR BANK SEAL

Total (in words):

CRORES	LACS	THOUSANDS	HUNDREDS	TENS	UNITS
Zero	Zero	One	Zero	Zero	Zero

Paid in Cash/ Debit to A/c /Cheque No. Dated 31-Aug-20

Drawn on - Rs. 1,000.00

(Name of the Bank and Branch)

Date : 1-Aug-17 **Signature of person making payment**

Tear Here

Taxpayers Counterfoil (To be filled up by taxpayer)

TAN ABCX12345A

SPACE FOR BANK SEAL

Received from PRIME CO (TDS)

(Name)

Cash/ Debit to A/c /Cheque No. For Rs. 1,000

Rs.(in words) One Thousand Only.

Drawn on -

(Name of the Bank and Branch)

Non Company(0021) Deductees

on account of Tax Deducted at Source (TDS) from 94A for the Assessment Year 2021-22

Rs. 1,000.00

F-9A: TDFS Challan in Print

09 TDS Reports

Select *Display>Statutory Reports>TDS* Reports to get TDS Reports Menu (F-10A).

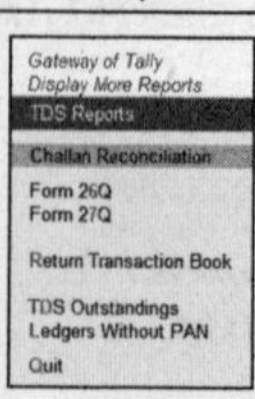

F-10A: TDS Reports Menu

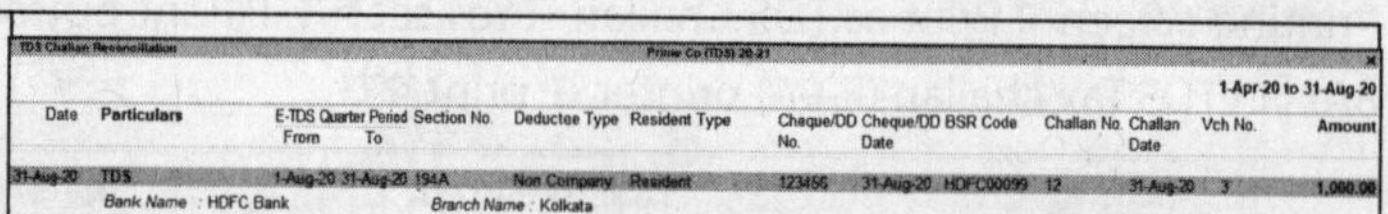

TDS Challan Reconciliation — Prime Co (TDS) 20-21 — 1-Apr-20 to 31-Aug-20

Date	Particulars	E-TDS Quarter Period From	To	Section No.	Deductee Type	Resident Type	Cheque/DD No.	Cheque/DD Date	BSR Code	Challan No.	Challan Date	Vch No.	Amount
31-Aug-20	TDS	1-Aug-20	31-Aug-20	194A	Non Company	Resident	123456	31-Aug-20	HDFC00099	12	31-Aug-20	3	1,000.00
	Bank Name : HDFC Bank			*Branch Name* : Kolkata									

F-11A: TDS Challan Reconciliation

Challan Reconciliation: At TDS Reports menu (F-10A), select *Challan Reconciliation*. Using Toggle button *F8:Show All /Show Pending*, you may view all paid Challans / enter details of Pending Challans (and Type Y to save).

– **Form 26Q**: Form 26Q is Quarterly Return of TDS in respect of all payments other than salaries. The top portion shows the statistics of vouchers from where you may drill down to view the related voucher list. At TDS Reports menu (F-10A), select Form 26Q to get the Form 26Q dully filled up, for the specified Period (F-12A).

– **Form 27Q**: At TDS Reports menu (F-10A), select Form 26Q to get the Form 26Q dully filled up, for the specified Period, in respect of payments to NRI, if any.

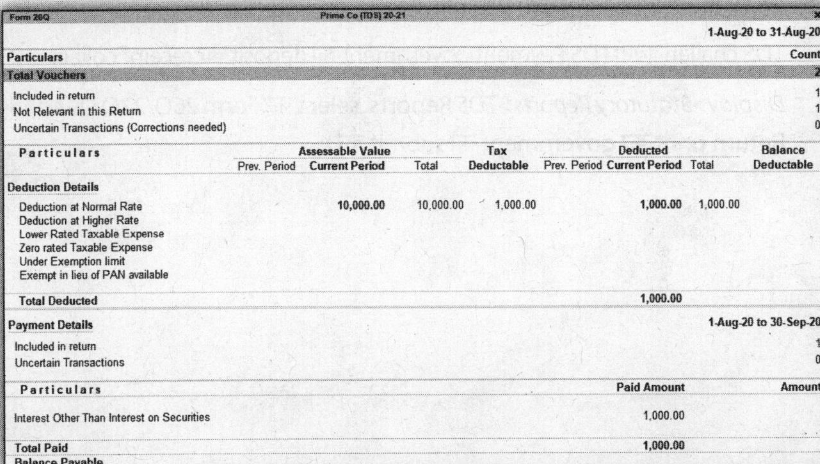

Form 26Q — Prime Co (TDS) 20-21

1-Aug-20 to 31-Aug-20

Particulars	Count
Total Vouchers	2
Included in return	1
Not Relevant in this Return	1
Uncertain Transactions (Corrections needed)	0

Particulars	Assessable Value Prev. Period	Assessable Value Current Period	Total	Tax Deductable	Deducted Prev. Period	Deducted Current Period	Total	Balance Deductable
Deduction Details								
Deduction at Normal Rate		10,000.00	10,000.00	1,000.00		1,000.00	1,000.00	
Deduction at Higher Rate								
Lower Rated Taxable Expense								
Zero rated Taxable Expense								
Under Exemption limit								
Exempt in lieu of PAN available								
Total Deducted						1,000.00		

Payment Details — 1-Aug-20 to 30-Sep-20

Particulars	Count
Included in return	1
Uncertain Transactions	0

Particulars	Paid Amount	Amount
Interest Other Than Interest on Securities	1,000.00	
Total Paid	1,000.00	
Balance Payable		

F-12A: TDS Return 26Q

– Display>Statutory Reports>TDS Reports select कर TDS Reports Menu (F-10A) पाए।

– TDS Reports Menu (F-10A) में *Challan Reconcilation* select कर TDS Deposit Challan की list पाए और Pending challans में challan details entry करे (F-11A)।

– TDS Reports Menu (F-10A) में Form 26Q select कर TDS Deposit का Quarterly Return पाए (F-12A)।

– TDS Reports Menu (F-10A) में Form 27Q select कर NRI के संबंधित TDS Deposit का Quarterly Return पाए।

10 Tax Deducted at Source (TDS) - Key Points

- F11 Company Features में Enable Tax Deducted at Source में Yes set कर Company me TDS activate करे।
- TDS Ledger Account create कर TDS details set करे। अगर कई तरह के Nature of Payments का TDS deduction हो तो हर nature of Payment के लिए अलग TDS ledger create करे, इससे reconciliation करना और TDS deposit करना आसान होगा।

- Party Ledger Account me TDS details set करे।
- TDS Deductible Expenses Ledger Account में TDS details set करे।
- TDS Deduction के Journal Voucher में TDS details entry करे।
- TDS deduction के बाद government में TDS deposit के लिए Payment Voucher entry करे और TDS challan print करे।
- TDS challan द्वारा TDS Payment government को deposit कर receipt collect करे।
- *Display>Statutory Reports>TDS* Reports select कर Form 26Q/27Q Quarterly Return print कर government को submit करे।

PART 4

Basic Payroll

Payroll Masters explains Activation & Set Up of Payroll Features for the Company, Pay Heads creation, Employee Masters and Employee Pay Structure set up.

Payroll Masters में Company के Payroll set up, हर तरह के Payroll Masters जैसे, Pay Heads, Employee Masters and Employee Pay Structure set up के बारे में समझाया है।

Payroll Vouchers explains Payroll Voucher Entry, Attendance / Production entry, Pay structure set up and computation of Pay.

Payroll Vouchers में Pay Voucher Entry, Employee के Pay structure set up, Payroll computation के बारे में समझाया है।

Payroll Reports explains printing of Pay Slip, Pay Sheet and other Pay Reports.

Payroll Reports में Payroll संबंधित सभी Reports जैसे Pay Slip, Pay Sheet बगैरह के बारे में समझाया है।

Payroll Masters 04-01

In this chapter, we explain activation of Payroll System, Master creation / set up for Payroll

01 Company Features Payroll set up

Click *F11* at K:Company Tab (or press F11 key). At Company Features screen (F-1A) at the top left, set Yes at *Show More features* and set Yes at *Show All Features* to get the Payroll set up options (otherwise Payroll options will not be shown in the screen). Under Payroll section, set Yes at *Maintain Payroll*, to activate Basic Payroll Features for the Company (F-1A).

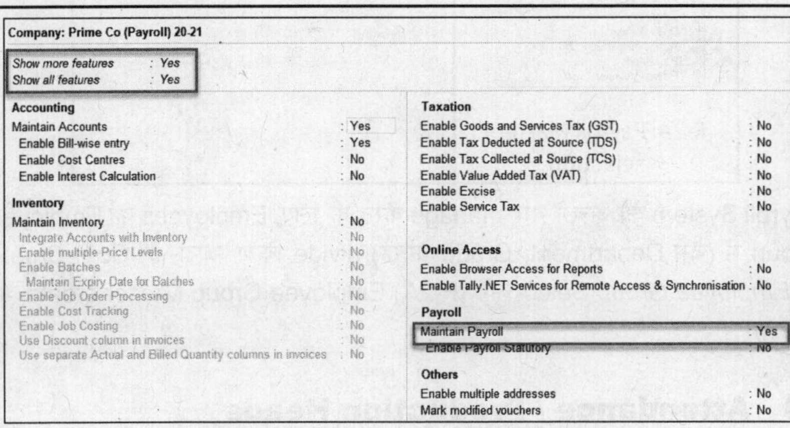

F-1A: Payroll Activation for the Company

Company में Payroll option activate करने के लिए K:Company tab से F11 click कर Company Features (F-1A) के top दोनों option *Show More Features* और *Show All Features* में Yes set कर Payroll section के *Maintain Payroll* में *Yes* set करे (F-1A)।

02 Employee Group Creation

For better management of Payroll System, Employees are normally grouped into Departments / Grades. Select *GoT*>Create> Employee *Group* from Masters List (F-2A). At *Employee Group* Master Creation / Alteration (F-3A), enter as follows:

- **Employee Group Name**: At *Name*, Enter Employee Group Name.
- **Parent Group**: At *Under*, select *Primary* or another Employee Group from the list of Groups. The first created Group must be placed under Primary.
- **Group Salary Structure**: At *Define Salary Details*, Set Yes to define Group salary structure applicable for all Employees of the group, else set No (to set up salary structure of individual employee at Employee Master).

If there are few Employees, All Employees may be placed under auto created *Primary* Group (no need to create Employee Group), to keep the system simple.

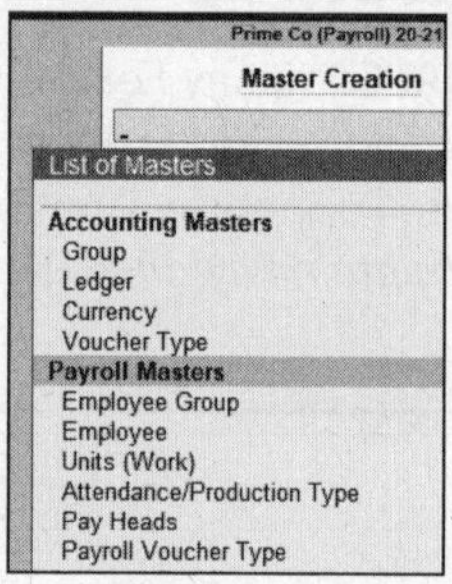

F-2A: Payroll Masters selection

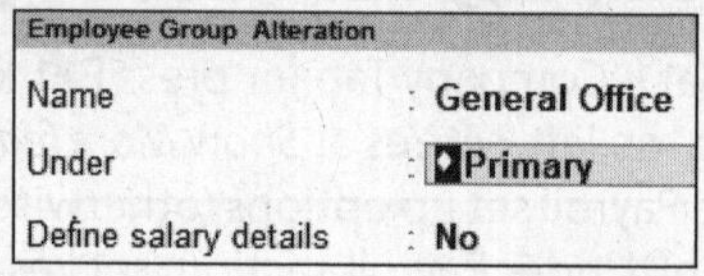

F-3A: Employee Group Creation

Payroll System को अच्छी तरह manage करने के लिए, Employees को Employee Group में (जैसे Department, Grade बगैरह) divide किया जाता है। *GoT>Create* से *Employee Group* Select कर (F-2A) Employee Group Master create करे (F-3A)।

03 Attendance / Production Heads

Attendance / Production Heads are created to maintain records for each type of Attendance (like Attendance, Medical Leave, Privilege Leave, Without Pay) etc, for Time based Salary computation and Production Heads (For Production based wages Computation). If Salary is manually computed and entered in Payroll Voucher, as explained in next chapter, there may not be any need to create Attendance / Production heads.

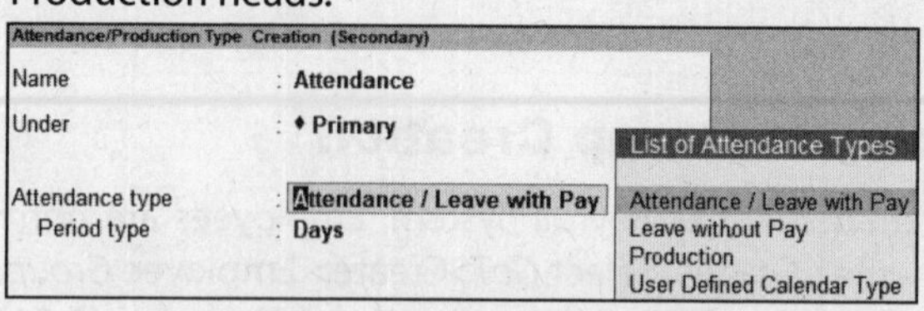

F-4A: Attendance Head creation

Select *GoT*>Create. Select *Attendance / Production Type* from Masters List (F-2A). At *Attendance / Production Type* creation screen (F-4A), enter as follows:

- **Name**: Enter Attendance / Production Head Name.
- **Parent Group**: At *Under* select Primary or another *Attendance / Production* Head. The first created Head must be placed under *Primary*.
- **Attendance Type**: Select the type from the list.
- **Period Type**: Days would normally be auto selected.

GoT>Create से Masters List (F-2A) से Attendance / Production Type select कर Attendance / Production head create करे (F-4A)।

04 Pay Head Creation

To create a Pay Head, select *GoT>Create*. Select *Pay Head* from *List of Masters* (F-2A). At Pay Head entry / Alteration screen, enter as follows (F-2B):

- **Pay Head Name**: At *Name*, enter the Name of Pay Head. A Ledger Account of this Name would be automatically created on saving the Pay Head.
- **Pay Head Type**: At *Income Type*, select the Pay Head Type from the list (F-2E).
  - **Income Type**: This field appears only when you select *Earnings from Employees* or *Reimbursement to Employees* (*Incomes* for Employee) at *Pay Head Type*. Select the *Income Type* from the list.
- **Account Group**: At *Under*, select the Parent Account Group for the Pay Head Ledger (or Create the desired Account Group).
  - **Pay Head Nature**: At *Affect Net Salary*, set *Yes* for Pay Heads which affect Net Pay in Pay Slip (like Basic, DA, I Tax, P tax, P F Deduction, ESI Deduction etc)
- **Pay Head Title**: At *Name to be displayed in Payslip*, write Brief Pay head name in to be printed in PaySlip / Pay Register
  - **Gratuity Includible**: At *Use for Calculation of Gratuity* (this appears only when you select Earnings for Employees at Pay Head Type (F-1B), set *Yes* for those Earnings Pay Heads which are included in Gratuity computation (such as Basic Salary, HRA, etc.), else set *No* for those Earnings Pay Heads which are NOT included in Gratuity computation (such as Overtime).
- **Calculation Type**: At *Calculation Type*, select the Calculation Type from Calculation Type list.
- **Attendance / Leave**: Depending on selection of Calculation Type, you may get further option like *Attendance / Leave with Pay*. Select accordingly from the list.

- **Calculation Period**: This option appears for Calculation Type *Flat Rate* or *Computed Value* (depending on selection of Calculation type, the next options vary). Select from the list.
- **Rounding Info**: At *Rounding Method*, select the *Rounding Method* and then select the Rounding Limit.

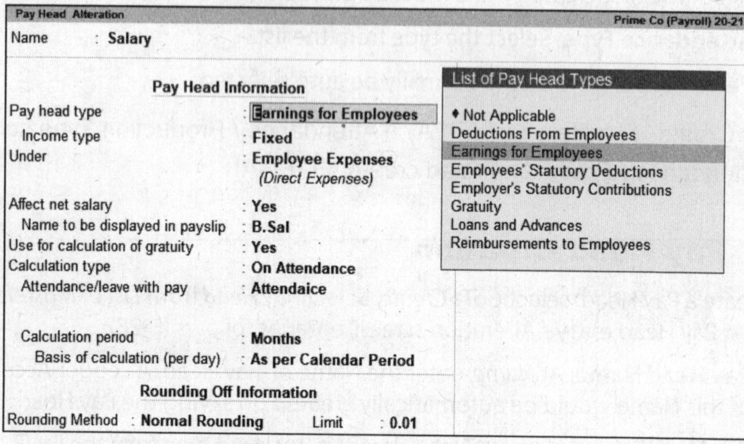

F-2B: Pay Head creation / Alteration

At Pay Head creation (F-2B), click F12 and set the configuration options (F-3A).

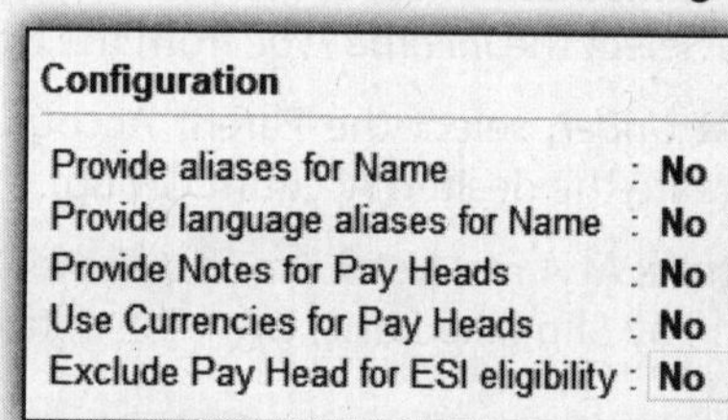

F-3A: Pay Head Configuration

GoT>Create से Payroll Masters section में Pay Heads select कर Configuration set कर (F-3A) Pay Heads (जैसे Basic Salary, DA, Overtime, Bonus) create करे (F-3B to F-3C)।

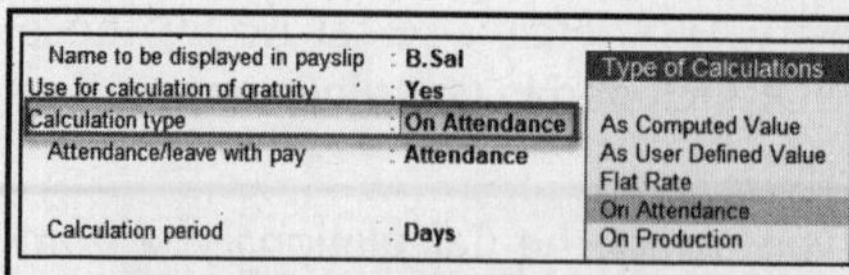

F-3B: Calculation Type List selection

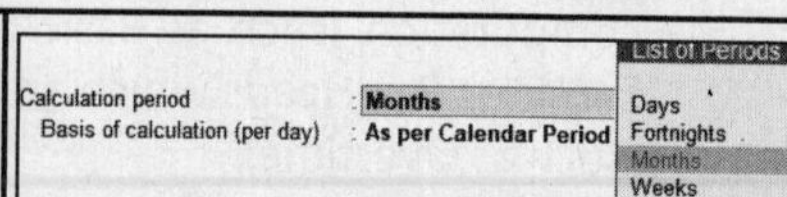

F-3C: Period Selection

05 Employee Master Creation

Select *GoT>Create>Employee.* At Employee Master creation (F-4B), click F12:- Configure and set the options (F-4A). At Employee Master Creation / Alteration screen (F-4B), enter the respective personal details of the Employee.

Configuration	
Provide aliases for Name	: No
Provide language aliases for Name	: No
Provide display name for Employee	: Yes
Provide Notes for Employees	: No
Provide Statutory Details	: No
Provide Passport and Visa Details	: No
Provide Contract Details	: No

F-4A: Employee Master Configuration

Salary Details: To enter Pay Head details manually in Pay Voucher, as explained later, set No at *Define Salary Details*. To get Pay computed from Attendance & Pay Details in Employee master, set *Yes* at *Define Salary Details* and enter the Salary Structure & Rates in respect of the Employee, as explained at *Employee Pay Structure* in next chapter (§03/04-02).

Other Details: Enter other details of the Employee. Save the Employee master. This way, enter the details in respect of each employee.

Employee Alteration

Name	: Lal Prasad Dubey
Display name in reports as	: Lal Prasad Dubey
Under	: General Office (Primary)
Date of joining	: 1-Apr-2020
Define salary details	: No
Date of resignation/retirement	:

General Information		
Employee Number	: 1234	Provide bank details : No
Designation	: Data Entry Operator	
Function	:	
Location	:	
Gender	: Male	
Date of birth	: 1-Apr-1990	
Blood group	:	
Father's/mother's name	: Late B P Yadav	
Spouse's name	:	
Address	:	
Phone no.	:	
E-Mail	:	

F-4B: Employee Master creation

GoT>Create से *Payroll Masters* section में Employee (F-2A) select कर Configuration set कर (F-4A) Employee Master create करे।

06 Payroll Masters - Key Points

- F11 से Company Features में Maintain Payroll में Yes set Company में Payroll option activate करे।
- *GoT>Create* से *Employee Group* Select कर Employee Group Master create करे।
- GoT>Create से Attendance / Production Type select कर Attendance / Production head create करे।
- *GoT>Create* से Pay Heads select कर Pay Heads create करे।
- *GoT>Create* से Employee (F-2A) select कर Employee Master create करे।
- Employee master की complete details की कोई list नहीं मिलती। Chart of Accounts से सिर्फ Employee Name और Alias के अलावा और कोई भी details show नहीं होता।

Payroll Voucher 04-02

01 Payroll Voucher creation

After creation of required Masters, create Attendance / Production Vouchers and set up Employee Pay Structure (Pay & Deduction Rates and computation rules) to compute Pay & Deduction for printing Pay Slip and related Reports.

There are 2 methods of Payroll Voucher creation:

- **Manual Pay Voucher entry**: In this method, enter the computed values of each Pay & Deduction head to Maintain Employee Pay accounts and generate related Reports. This is like simple Accounts Voucher entry. Select Employee name and then enter the values of each pay & deduction head.
- **Pay Computation from Attendance / Production Voucher**: In this method, Employee Pay & Deduction Rates and computation rules are entered in Employee Master, and the periodic Attendance / Production data is entered in Voucher. The Pay & Deduction for each Employee is computed using the Attendance / Production Voucher Data and Pay Structure from Employee Master.

Payroll Voucher में calculated data entry करे, या Employee Pay Rates और Attendance entry कर Tally से Payroll computation करे।

02 Payroll Voucher Manual Entry

Here we explain the manual pay voucher entry. Accounts Voucher Entry has been explained at Accounts section. Here we explain additional info in respect of Payroll Voucher entry, for payment of Net Pay to the Employee. At Voucher Entry (GoT>Voucher) screen, click *Ctrl+F4* to get Payroll Voucher entry screen (F-1A).

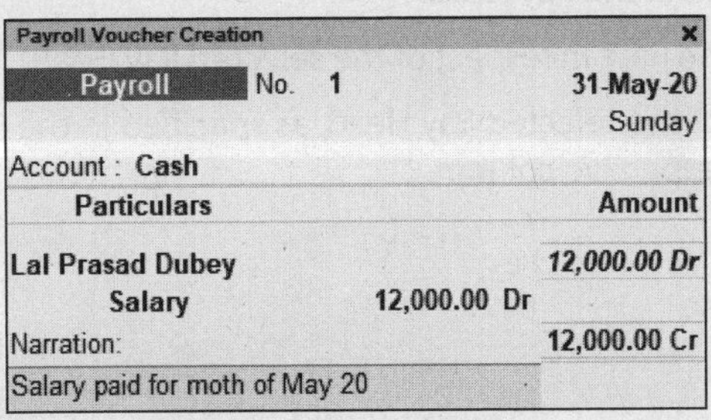

F-1A: Payroll Voucher Entry

At Payroll Voucher entry screen, like Payment Voucher entry in single mode, enter as follows (F-1A):

Cash / Bank Account: At the Header, select Cash / Bank A/c by which payment is made to the Employee

Under details section, enter the Employee name and Pay Head details as follows:

- **Employee Name**: First select the Employee from the list
- **Pay / Deduction Head**: After selection of Employee, select the Pay Head and enter the amount & Dr (for Pay Heads) / Cr (for Deduction Heads) sign. This way, select Pay Head and enter amount in respect of each Pay / Deduction head for the selected employee. Select *End of List* to terminate entry for the Employee

This way, enter the details of each Pay Head in respect of each Employee. Enter Narration. Save the Voucher.

GoT>Voucher से Ctrl+F4 से *Payroll* Voucher में *Employee Head* select कर *Pay Head* में amount entry करें। Voucher Narration entry कर Voucher save करें (F-1A). इस तरह Multiple Employee के Salary एक Voucher में ही entry कर सकते हैं।

03 Employee Pay Structure Set Up

Employee Master creation has been explained earlier (§05/04-01). To get the Pay computed from Computation Rules and Rates, at Employee Master Creation (GoT>Create> Employee) / Alteration (GoT>Alter> Employee), screen (F-2A), at *Define Salary Details*, set Yes to get *Employee Salary Details* screen (F-2B).

At *Employee Salary Details* (Pay Structure), in respective column, enter as follows (F-2B)

- **Effective Date**: At Effective Date, Enter the Date from which Rate of the Pay Head is applicable.
- **Pay Head**: Select the Pay Head.
- **Rate**: Enter the Rate in respect of the selected Pay Head.

All other details of the selected Pay Head, as specified in the Pay Head Master are displayed in respective column.

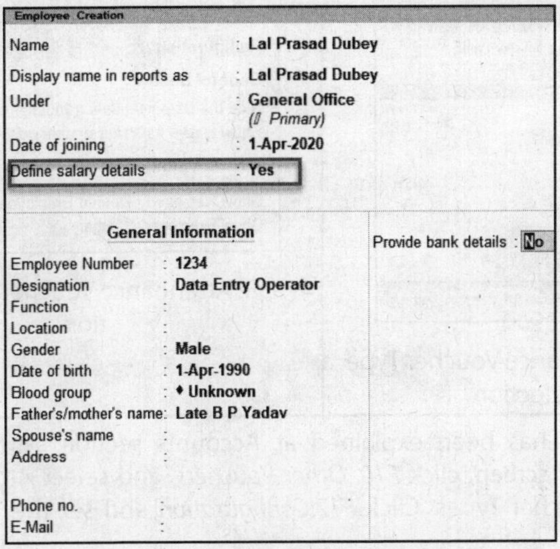

F-2A: Employee Master Creation / Alteration

GoT>Create>Employee या GoT>Alter>Employee से Employee Master में Default Salary Details पर Yes set कर (F-2A) Employee की Salary Details (Pay Structure) entry करे (F-2B)।

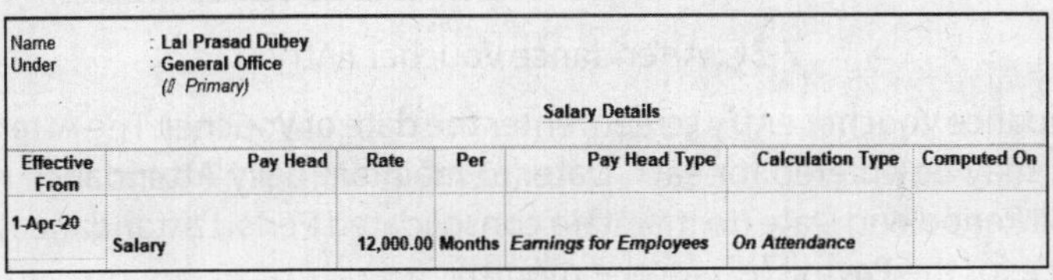

Name : Lal Prasad Dubey
Under : General Office
(Primary)

Salary Details

Effective From	Pay Head	Rate	Per	Pay Head Type	Calculation Type	Computed On
1-Apr-20	Salary	12,000.00	Months	*Earnings for Employees*	*On Attendance*	

F-2B: Employee Salary Details (Pay Structure)

04 Attendance Voucher Entry

To compute Pay, Attendance / Production Voucher data is to be entered for each Employee for each Head. The Pay head values would be computed by Tally from the Voucher Data using the Pay Details specified in Employee Master, as explained above.

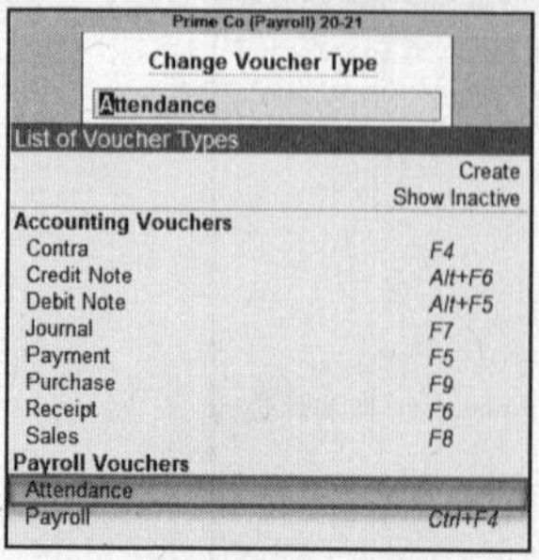

F-3A: Attendance Voucher Type selection

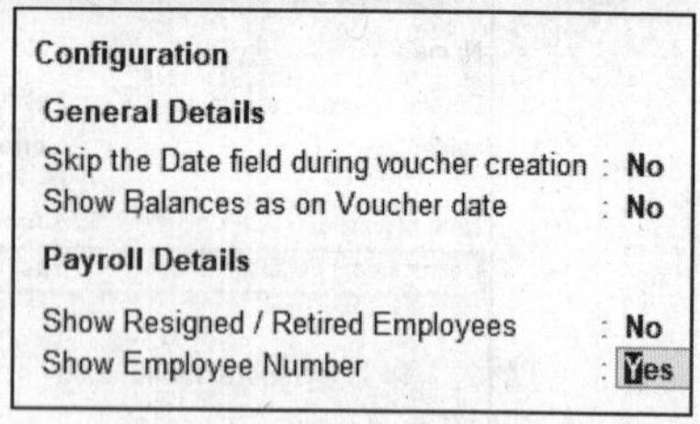

F-3B: Attendance Voucher Configuration

Voucher Entry has been explained at Accounts section. At *Voucher Entry* (GoT>Voucher) screen, click *F10: Other Vouchers*, and select *Attendance* from the list of Voucher Types. Click *F12:Configuration* and set the Configuration options.

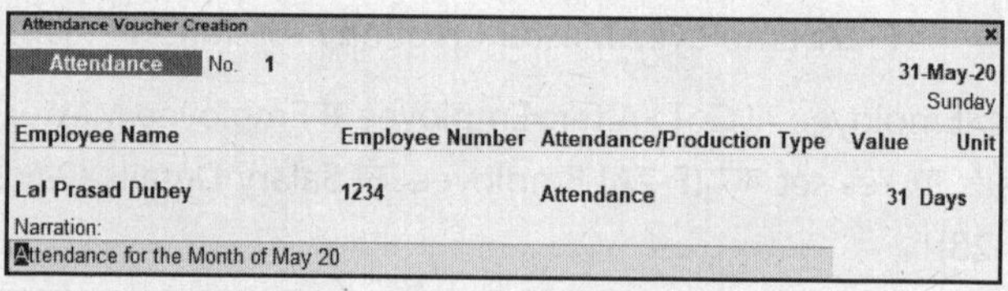

F-3C: Attendance Voucher Entry

At Attendance Voucher entry screen, enter the date of Voucher. The Attendance Voucher may be entered for each Date (to maintain daily Attendance record), or Payroll Period end Date (to maintain consolidated Period Attendance / Leave / Absence for the Payroll (e.g for the month).

Select the Attendance Head and enter the value. This way, enter value for each Attendance Head, for each Employee.

GoT>Voucher में F10 click कर *Voucher Type* list से *Attendance* (F-3A), select करे। F12 से Attendance Voucher Configuration set करे (F-3B)। Attendance / Production Voucher में Employee Name और Attendance entry करे (F-3C)।

05 Payroll Voucher Auto Fill

To get the Payroll Auto computed from the Pay Heads and Rates specified in Employee Pay Structure in Employee Master, and the Attendance Production data, at Payroll Voucher Entry screen, after entry of Voucher Date, click *F:Auto Fill* button.

	Autofill
Type of transaction	: **Payroll Autofill**
Process for	: **Salary**
From (blank for beginning)	: **1-7-2020**
To (blank for end)	: **31-7-2020**
Employee/Group	: **♦ All Items**
Sort by	: **Employee Name**
Payroll/Bank/Cash Ledger	: **Cash**
Include Employee having 'For Banking' details:	**Yes**

F-4A: Payroll Auto Fill

At Auto Fill screen, enter as follows:

- **Salary Process**: At *Process For*, select *Salary* from the Process List to Process Salary.
- **Pay Period**: At *From* & *To*, enter the Start & End Date of Pay Period.
- **Employee/ Group**: Select *All* (to compute for All Employees in one shot) / Employee Group (to compute for Employees of a selected Employee Group) / Employee (to compute for a selected Employee only).
- **Sort By**: Select Employee Name / Employee Code, from the list.
- **Payroll Cash /Bank Ledger**: Select Cash / Bank / Salary payable Account.
- **Include Employees having 'For Banking Details'**: Set Yes to process payroll who have Bank Account details in Employee Master.

After entry of All details, you will get the Voucher filled up with values for Pay Heads for the specified Employees for the specified period, as if all data have been entered manually in the Payroll Voucher.

Payroll Computation के लिए GoT>Voucher में Ctrl+F4 press कर Payroll Voucher में F:AutoFill button click करे। Auto Fill screen में processing के details entry करने से (F-4A) Computed Payroll data fill up हो जाएगा। अब उस period के Payroll reports Display / Print कर सकते हैं।

06 Payroll Voucher - Key Points

- GoT>Alter> Employee से Employee Master में Salary Details entry करे।

- Payroll Voucher में Calculated Pay Data entry के लिए GoT> Voucher में Ctrl+F4 से Payroll Voucher में F:Autofill से computed Payroll Voucher create करे।
- Employee master की complete details (pay Structure और बाकी सभी details) की कोई list नहीं मिलती। Chart of Accounts से सिर्फ Employee Name और Alias के अलावा और कोई भी details show नहीं होता।
- GoT>Vouchers से Attendance/Production select कर Attendance / Production Voucher में entry करे। Attendance voucher के लिए कोई shortcut key नहीं हैं।

Payroll Reports 04-03

Display / Print Payroll Reports after manual Payroll Voucher entry or Payroll Voucher creation through Auto fill.

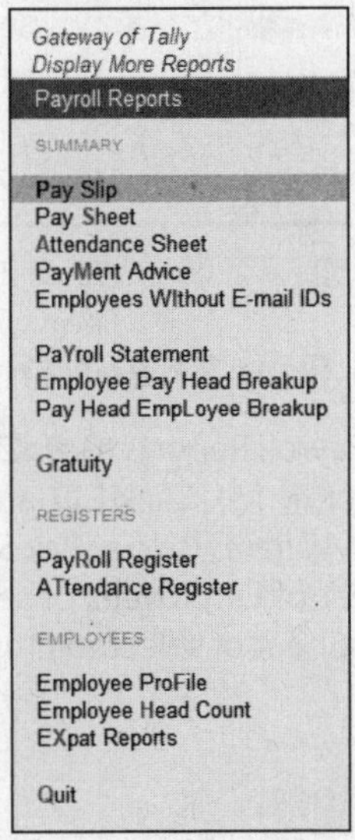

F-1A: Payroll Reports Menu

01 Payroll Reports Menu

Select *GoT>Display More Reports> Payroll Reports* to get *Payroll Reports* Menu (F-1A).

Payroll Reports के लिए *GoT>Display More Reports> Payroll Reports* select कर Payroll Reports Menu (F-1A) में Payroll Report select करे। GoTo tab में Payroll related report नहीं है।

02 Pay Slip Display & Printing

At Payroll Reports *(GoT>Display More Reports> Payroll Reports)* menu, select *Pay Slip* (F-1A). Click F12 and set the Payslip Configuration options (F-2A). Select *All Items* (to get Pay Report of all Employees), or *Employee Group* (to get Pay Report of Employees of selected Employee Group) or specific Employee (to get Pay Slip of selected Employee : F-2B).

More Reports> Payroll Reports>Payslip select कर, F12 से Configuration set करे (F-2A)। List of Employees / Group से *All Items/ Employee / Employee Group* select कर Payslip Display / print करे (F-2A)।

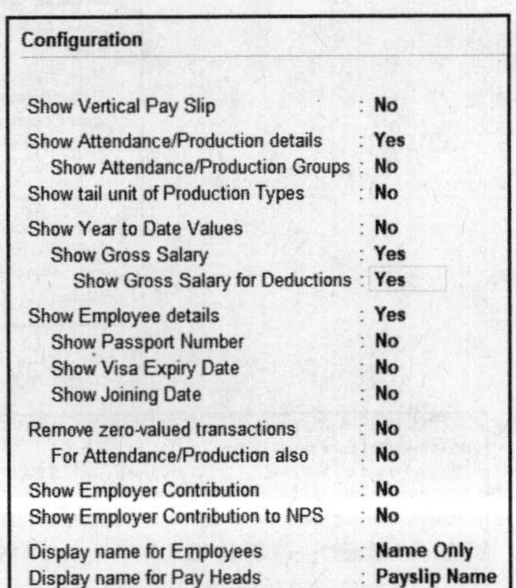

F-2A: Pay Slip Configuration

Pay Slip for May-2020

Lal Prasad Dubey

Employee Number : 1234
Function :
Designation : Data Entry Operator
Location :
Bank Details :

Attendance Details		Value			
Attendance		31 Days			
Earnings	**Amount**	**Gross Salary**	**Deductions**	**Amount**	**Gross Salary**
B.Sal	12,000.00	12,000.00			
Total Earnings	**12,000.00**	**12,000.00**	**Total Deductions**		
			Net Amount	**₹ 12,000.00**	**₹ 12,000.00**

F-2B: Pay Slip of specific Employee

03 Pay Sheet Display & Printing

At Payroll Reports (*GoT>Display More Reports> Payroll Reports)* menu, select *Pay Sheet* (F-1A). Click F12 and set the Paysheet Configuration options (F-3A). Select *All Items* (to get Pay Sheet of all Employees), or *Employee Group* (to get Pay Sheet of Employees of selected Employee Group) or specific *Employee* (to get Pay Sheet of selected Employee : F-3B)

Configuration

Show Gross Salary	Yes
Show column subtotal	Yes
Show Attendance details	Yes
Show tail unit of Production Types	No
Show Employees by Categories & Groups	No
Show Category / Group Total	No
Show Category / Group in Column	No
Show Serial Number	No
Show Grand Total	Yes
Format of Report	Detailed
Expand all levels in Detailed format	Yes
Show Employee Number	Yes
Show Employee Bank details	No
Show Employee Designation	No
Show Employee Function	No
Show Date of Joining & Resignation	No
Remove zero-valued transactions	Yes
Display name for Employee Groups	Name Only
Display name for Employees	Name Only
Display name for Pay Heads	Payslip Name
Sorting Method	Default

F-3A: Pay Sheet Configuration

Pay Sheet — Prime Co (Payroll) 20-21

For employee: Lal Prasad Dubey — 1-May-20 to 31-May-20

Employee Name	Employee Number	*B.Sal*	Total Gross Salary	*Attendance*	B.Sal	Total Earnings	Total Deductions	Net Amount
Lal Prasad Dubey	1234	12,000.00	**12,000.00**	31 Days	12,000.00	**12,000.00**		**12,000.00**
Grand Total		**12,000.00**	**12,000.00**	**31 Days**	**12,000.00**	**12,000.00**		**12,000.00**

F-3B: Pay Sheet of specific Employee

GoT>Display More Reports> Payroll Reports>Pay Sheet select कर, F12 से Configuration set करे (F-3A)। List of Employees / Group से *All Items/ Employee / Employee Group* select कर Paysheet display / print करे (F-3B)।

04 Payment Advice Printing

Payment Advice is a letter to Bank to credit the Net Amount payable to respective Employees personal Bank Account. At *Payroll Reports* (*GoT>Display More Reports> Payroll Reports)* menu, select *Payment Advice* (F-1A) to get the Payment Advice Print screen(F-4A). Click F12 and set the Pay Advice Configuration options (F-4B). At Employees/ Employee Group, select *All Items* (to get Payment Advice for all Employees), or Employee Group (to get Payment Advice for Employees of selected Employee Group) or specific Employee (to get Payment Advice of selected Employee). The Payment Advice would be printed only for Employees for whom Bank Details are entered in the Employee Master and the specified Bank has been selected in Payroll Voucher entry / Auto Fill (F-4C). The Payment Advice Date will be current system date irrespective of the Date of Advice specified at Configuration / Printing screen.

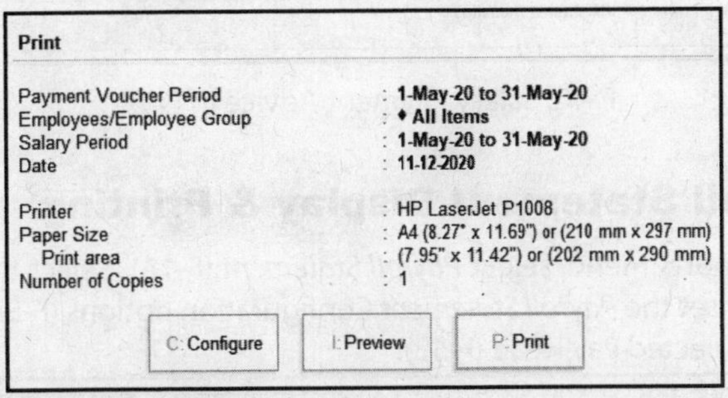

F-4A: Salary Payment Advice Printing

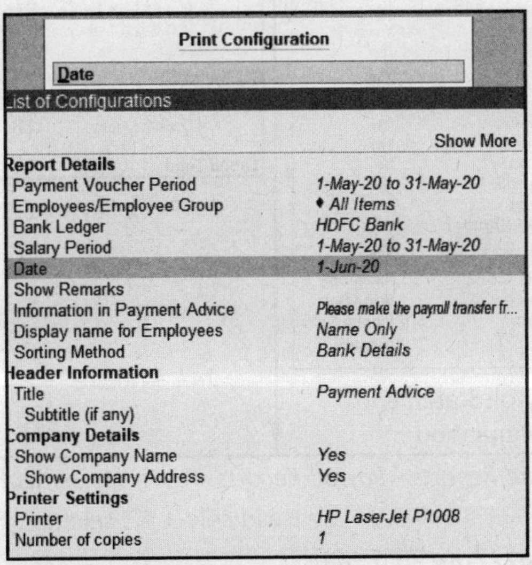

F-4B: Salary Payment Advice Configuration

GoT>Display More Reports> Payroll Reports>Payment Advice select कर, F12 से Configuration set करे (F-4A / F-4B)। List of Employees / Group से *All Items/ Employee / Employee Group* select कर Paysheet display / print करे (F-4B)।

Prime Co

Payment Advice

11-Dec-20

The Manager
HDFC Bank
Dear Sir,

Payment Advice from Prime Co A/c No. 0123456789 for period 1-May-20 to 31-May-20

Please make the payroll transfer from above account number to the below mentioned account numbers towards employee salaries:

Sl. No.	Name of the Employee	Account No.	Amount
1.	Lal Prasad Dubey	0012345678	12,000.00
	Total		**12,000.00**

Amount (in words) : INR Twelve Thousand

F-4C: Salary Payment Advice in Print

05 Payroll Statement Display & Printing

At Payroll Reports menu, select *Payroll Statement* (F-1A). Select the Pay Head. Click F12 and set the *Payroll Statement* Configuration options (F-5A), to get Report for the selected Pay Head (F-5B).

Configuration

Show Employees by Categories & Groups	: Yes
Show Category / Group Total	: Yes
Show Category / Group in Column	: No
Show Grand Total	: Yes
Format of Report	: Detailed
Expand all levels in Detailed format	: Yes
Show Employee Number	: Yes
Show Employee Bank details	: No
Show Employee Designation	: No
Show Employee Function	: No
Show Date of Joining & Resignation	: No
Remove zero-valued transactions	: Yes
Display name for Employee Groups	: Name Only
Display name for Employees	: Name Only
Display name for Pay Heads	: Payslip Name
Sorting Method	: Default

F-5A: Payroll Statement Configuration

Payroll Statement

For all employees — **1-May-20 to 31-May-20**

Particulars	Employee Number	*B.Sal*
Primary Cost Category		12,000.00
General Office		12,000.00
Lal Prasad Dubey	1234	12,000.00
Grand Total		**12,000.00**

F-5B: Payroll Statement

GoT>Display More Reports> Payroll Reports>Payroll Statement select कर, F12 से Configuration set करे (F-5A)। Pay Head select कर selected Head का Payroll Statement Display / Print करे (F-5B)।

06 Payroll Register Display & Printing

At Payroll Reports (*GoT>Display More Reports> Payroll Reports)* menu, select *Payroll Register* (F-1A) to get the monthly statistics of Payroll Vouchers. Click F12 and set the *Payroll Register* Configuration options(F-6A), to get Report showing the list of Vouchers for the selected Pay Period (F-6B).

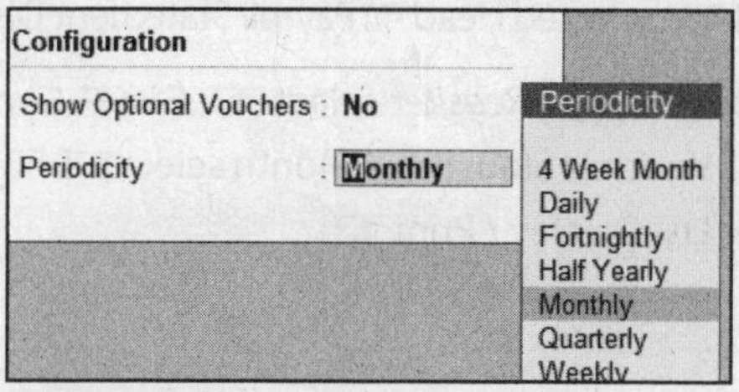

F-6A: Payroll Register Configuration

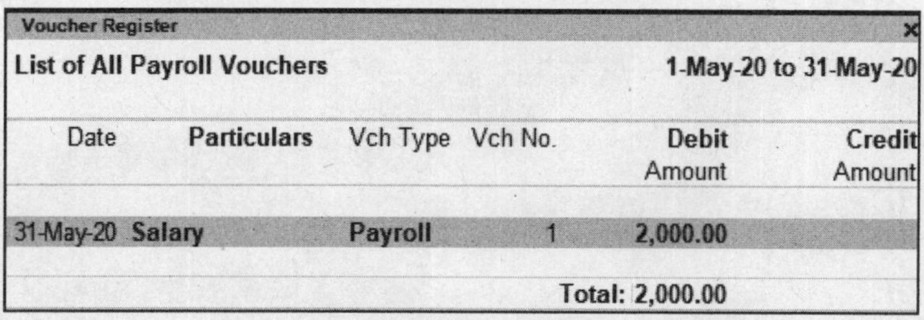

F-6B: Payroll Register

GoT>Display More Reports> Payroll Reports>PayRoll Register select कर, F12 से Configuration set करे (F-6A)। Monthly Payroll Voucher Statistics से Month select करे. F2 से Period select कर Payroll Voucher List Display / Print करे (F-3B)।

07 Payroll Reports - Key Points

- Payroll Reports के लिए GoT>Display More Reports> Payroll Reports select कर Payroll Reports Menu में Payroll Report select करे।
- **Pay Slip**: *Payslip* select कर, F12 से Configuration set कर List of Employees / Group से *All Items/ Employee / Employee Group* select कर Payslip display / print करे।
- **Paysheet**: *Paysheet select* कर, F12 से Configuration set कर। List of Employees / Group से All Items/ Employee / Employee Group select कर Paysheet display / print करे।

- **Payment Advice**: *Payment Advice* select कर, F12 से Configuration set कर List of Employees / Group से *All Items/ Employee / Employee Group* select कर Payment Advice display / print करें।
- **Payroll Statement**: *Payroll Statement* select कर, F12 से Configuration set कर Pay Head select कर selected Head का Payroll Statement Display / Print करें।
- **Payroll Register**: *PayRoll Regsiter* select कर, F12 से Configuration set कर. Monthly Payroll Voucher Statistics से Month select करे. F2 से Period select कर Payroll Voucher List Display / Print करें।

PART 5
Practical Assignments

After completing each Chapter, carry out the assignments of the respective chapter, one by one.

Visit the website **www.dvidya.com/tallyprime**, for operational details and videos of the Practical Assignments, and all resources of FREE Tally Prime Training Course.

Financial Accounting – Practical Assignments 05-01

01-01 Company Creation

- **Load Educational version of Tally installed in the Computer**

  [To work with Tally Educational Version, click Tally icon at desktop. Select *T:Continue in Educational Mode]*.

- **Create a Company of your Name**

  Create Company of your Name & Financial Year 01-4-2021 to 31-3-2022. (e.g AK Sinha – B Accnts 21-22), at folder c:\tpdata, for Accounts Only. Change the Mailing Name, removing 21-22 (e.g AK Sinha – B Accts). Save the Company.

  [Select *K:Company>Create* to get to get Company Creation screen. Press Shift+Tab (at *Company Name* field) to move up to Company Data Path field and change the Directory Name to C:\TPdata. At Name, enter your Roll Number, Name- Accts (e.g 014 AK Sinha – Accts). At *Mailing Name*, remove the Roll Number but keep the Name (e.g AK Sinha- B Accts). At *Financial Year From*, enter 01-4-2021. Press Ctrl+A to save the Company]

- **Shut the currently selected Company**

  [Hints : Select *K:Company*>Shut (or type Ctrl+F3) and select the Company to shut, from the list]

- **Exit Tally shutting all selected Companies**

  [Select *GoT>Quit* (or press <Esc>) or click Cross (x) at rightmost upper corner, and select Y (Yes) to Exit from Tally Prime shutting all the selected Companies.

- **Enter Company Address and other unfilled info**

  [Load Tally Prime (Click the Tally Prime icon at desktop. Click *T:Continue to work in Educational Mode.* Select *K:Company>select* and select the Company. Select *K:Company>Alter* to get *Company Alteration*. Fill up Company Address and other data in blank fields. Save (Ctrl+A) the changed Company Data.

01-02 Gateway of Tally

- **Set the Current Period as 01-4-2021 to 31-8-21**

  [At *GoT, Press Alt+F2.* At Change Period, at *From*, enter 01-4-2021, at To, enter 31-8-2021. The changed *Current Period* would be shown at Gateway of Tally at Upper left side.]

- **Activate Accounting Features**

  [*Press F11.* At Company Features set *Yes* at *Maintain Accounts*, No at other options]

- **Load the Help screen**

  Press Ctrl+F1 to load *Tally Prime Help*

- **Compute the value of {12 x (36+45)÷ 20)}+30 in Tally Prime**

  [At any place, press Ctrl+N to get Calculator panel at the bottom. Type the arithmetic expression (12*(36+45)/ 20)+30 to get the result (=78.60). Click the (x) button of the Calculator panel or type Ctrl+N to close Calculator.

01-03 Account Masters

- **Create following Ledger Accounts under existing Reserved Groups**

  – A K Sinha (under Capital), Opening Balance 1,00,000 Cr
  – HDFC Bank (under Bank Accounts) Opening Balance 10,000 Dr
  – SBI C/C A/c (under Bank OCC Accounts) Opening Balance 20,000 Cr
  – A K Enterprises (under Sundry Debtors), Opening Balance 30,000 Dr
  – B K Suppliers (under Sundry Creditors), Opening Balance 25,000 Cr
  – Furniture (under Fixed Assets), Opening Balance 60,000 Dr
  – Stock (under Stock-in-Hand), Opening Balance 35,000 Dr

  [Select *GoT>Create>Ledger* At *Ledger* creation screen, at *Name*, enter the Ledger Name, at *Under*, select the Parent Account Group, at *Opening Balance*, enter the Opening Balance Amount with Dr / Cr sign].

- **Enter Cash Account Opening Balance 10000 Dr**

  [Cash Account is auto created. Select *GoT>Accounts Info>Ledgers>Alter* and then select *Cash* Account, At Opening Balance, enter 10000 Dr].

- **Enter Address at *A K Enterprises & B K Suppliers* Ledger Accounts and enter the Mailing Details & Contact Details as per your own assumed data**

  [Select *GoT>Accounts Info>Ledgers>Alter*, Select the Ledger Accounts. *At Ledger Alteration*, under *Mailing Details* section, enter data in all fields. Set *Yes* at *Provide Contact details*. At Contact Details sub screen, enter data at

Contact Person, Phone Number and *e-mail* fields, for both the Party Ledger Accounts.

- **Create Account Group - Freight Inwards (under *Direct Expenses*)**

  [Select *GoT>Create>Ledgers.* At *Ledger Creation*, at name, enter *Freight Inwards.* At *Under, select Direct Expenses*].

- **Create Ledger Account *Salary*, simultaneously creating new parent Group *Employee Expenses* (Under *Indirect Expenses*)**

  [Select *GoT>Create>Ledgers.* At *Ledger Creation* screen, at Name, enter *Salary.* At Under, press *Alt+C* to create *Account Group creation* (*secondary*) screen. At *Name*, enter Employee Expenses. At *Under*, select *Indirect Expenses.* Press Ctrl+A to save the created Account Group. The New created Group *Employee Expenses* would appear at *Under* field of Ledger Account *Salary.* Press Ctrl+A to save the Ledger Account created.].

- **Display Chart of Accounts**

  [Select GoT>Chart of Accounts to Display Chart of Accounts].

- **Display Ledger Accounts with Opening Balance**

  [Select *GoT>Display More Reports>Trial Balance.* Click *F5:Ledgewise.* Click F12:*Configure and set Yes at Opening Balance and set No at other options*]

01-04 Account Vouchers

- **On 1-5-21, A K Sinha (Proprietor) withdraws Rs 500 for personal expenses. From SBI C/C A/c, by cheque # 123321). Create as Double Entry Voucher. Create Drawing Account (under Capital) during Voucher entry**

  [This entry should be made through *Payment* Voucher as money is paid out. Select *GoT>Vouchers.* Click *F5:Payment* Voucher. Click *H:Change Mode* button (or press Crtl+H) and select *Double Entry* from the option list. Enter Voucher Date (1-5-21). At first ledger (Dr) entry, press Alt+C to get Ledger Creation screen. Create *Drawing* Account, select Capital Accounts at *Under* field and press *Ctrl A* to save the newly created *Drawing* Ledger Account and get back to the voucher entry screen. At Particulars column, select *Drawing* A/c from list of ledger accounts and enter 500 at Debit column].

  Next select Cr. At Particulars column, select SBI C/C A/c and enter 500 at Credit column.

  As the Debit & Credit columns are now equal, cursor will go to Narration field. Enter Ch No 123321 and enter the Narration in short (like Withdrawn by A K Sinha, proprietor). Press Ctrl+A and save the voucher].

- **On 2-5-21, Conveyance expenses of Rs 400 is paid in Cash to A K Sinha for attending a client. Create Single Entry Mode voucher**

  [Create a Payment Voucher (Select GoT>Voucher. Click *F5:Payment* button). Select *Single Entry* Mode (Ctrl+H) as explained. Enter Voucher Date 2-5-21. At the header, select Cash A/c. To create Conveyance Expenses ledger, at *Particulars* column, at first line, press *Alt+C* to get Ledger Creation (secondary) screen. Create the Conveyance Expenses ledger account (under *Indirect Expenses*) and select it. Enter 400 at *Amount* column. In next line, At Narration, field, write proper Voucher Narration. Save the Voucher].

- **On 1-7-21 A K Sinha receives Rs 1000 in cash from a client as consultancy Fees. Create Voucher in Double entry mode**

  [Select GoT>Voucher. Click *F6:Receipt* button. Select *Double Entry* Mode (Ctrl+H) as explained. At *Particulars* column, at first line, press *Alt+C* and create a Ledger Account *Consultancy Fees* (under Direct Income) and enter Rs 1000 at Credit Column. At next line, select Dr, select Cash Account and enter Rs 1000 at Debit Column. Enter the Narration. Save the Voucher (Ctrl+A)].

- **On 1-10-21 State Bank of India, charges Interest of Rs 650 on the C/C Account**

  [Select *GoT>Voucher*. Click F7:Journal. Enter Voucher Date. At *Particulars* column, at first line, press *Alt+C* and create Interest Ledger Account under *Indirect Expenses* and enter Rs 650 at Debit column. At next line, select Cr, select SBI C/C Account and enter Rs 650 at Credit column. Enter Voucher Narration (e.g Interest Debited by SBI on CC A/c for 1-4-16 to 30-09-16) Save the Voucher (Ctrl+A)].

- **On 1-12-21, A K Enterprises remitted 12000 against outstanding dues, into the HDFC Account by electronic transfer**

  [Select GoT>Voucher. Click F6:*Receipt* button to create a Receipt Voucher. Select *Double Entry Mode* (Ctrl+H) as explained. Enter Voucher Date. At Particulars column, at first line, select A K Enterprises. Enter Rs 12000 at Credit column. At next line, select Dr, select HDFC Bank, enter Rs 12000 at Debit column. Enter the Narration (e.g Amount received from A K Enterprises through Electronic transfer)]

- **On 1-1-22, cheque # 123322 was issued in favour of B K suppliers for Rs 10000, from HDFC bank, for outstanding dues payable to them**

  [Select GoT>Voucher. Click F5:Payment button to create a Payment Voucher. Select *Double Entry* Mode (Ctrl+H). At Particulars column, at first line, select B K suppliers, enter Rs 10000 at Debit column. At next line, select Cr, select HDFC Bank, enter Rs 10000 at Credit column. Enter Voucher Narration. Save Voucher (Ctrl+A)]

- **On 1-3-22, Stock Costing Rs. 12000 was sold in Cash for Rs. 15000**

  [Select GoT>Voucher. Click F8:Sales button to create a Sales Voucher. At *Particulars* column, at first line, select Cash Account. Enter Rs 15000 at Debit column. At next line, select Cr, Press Alt+C and Create Sales Ledger Account under Sales Group. Enter Rs 15000 at Credit column. Enter Voucher Narration. Save Voucher (Ctrl+A)]

- **On 2-3-22, Rs 14000 Cash was deposited into SBI C/C Account**

  Select GoT>Voucher. Click F4:Contra to create Contra Voucher. At *Particulars* column, at first line, select SBI C/C Account. Enter Rs 14000 at Credit column. At next line, type Dr. Select Cash A/c. Enter Rs 14000 at Debit column.

- **Interest on SBI C/C Account Rs 560 for 1-10-21 to 31-3-22 was debited by SBI on 4-4-22**

  [Select GoT>Voucher. Click F7:Journal to get Journal Voucher. Enter Voucher Date 31-3-22. At *Particulars* column, at first line, select Interest A/c. Enter Rs 560 at Debit column. At next line, type Cr, select SBI C/C Account. Enter Rs 560 at Credit Column. Enter Voucher Narration (e.g Interest for the period 1.10.21 to 31.3.22)

01-05 Reports

- **Preview Cash Book for the entire Financial Year 1-4-2021 to 31-3-2022 on screen. Print Cash Book on Printer from the Preview**

  [Select *GoT>Display More Report>Account Books> Cash / Bank Books. Select Cash Account*. At Monthly Cash Summary, Drill Down through any Month. Click F2:Period button (or F2) and Enter the Period from 1-4-2021 to 31-3-2022. Click *Ctrl+P* Button. At print screen, click *I:With preview* toggle button to preview the Report. At Preview screen, Click Zoom to view full screen. Click on Print to *print* the report on printer.

01-06 Cash Bank Book

- **Display and Print Cash Bank Book for the period 1-4-2021 to 31-7-2021**

  Show Detailed format, Opening & Closing balance, Narration, Voucher Numbers.

  [Select *GoT>Display More Reports>Account Books>Cash/Bank Books*. Select *Cash* Account to get Monthly Break up of Cash Book Summary. Drill Down through any month. Click *F2:Period* and set the Period 1-4-2021 to 31-7-2021. Click C:Configure Button. Set *Yes* at *Show Narration*, At *Format of the Report*, select *Detailed*. At Cash / Bank Book Display, Click Ctrl+P. At Printing screen, click C:Configure button (or type C). Set Yes at Show *Voucher Number*. Click P:Print button to print Cash / Bank Book].

01-07 Journal Register

- **Display and Print Journal Registers for the period 1-3-21 to 31-3-22**

  [Select *GoT>Display More Reports >Account Books>Journal Register* to get Statistics of Monthly Number of Journal Vouchers. Select any month, click *F2:Period* and enter period from 1-3-21 to 31-3-22, Click F12:Configure. At *Format of Report*, select *Detailed*. Set *Yes* at *Show Narrations*, to *Display* the Journal Book. At Journal Book Display, Click Ctrl+P. At Printing screen, Click C:Configure button (or type C). Set Yes at Show Voucher No. click *P:Print* Button (or type P) to print the Cash / Bank Book on Printer].

- **Print Sales Register for the period 1-4-17 to 31-8-21**

  [Select *GoT>Display More Reports >Account Books>Sales Register* to get Monthly Summary of Sales Accounts. Select any Month, click F2:Period and enter period from 1-4-21 to 31-8-21. Click F12:Configure. At *Format of Report*, select *Detailed*. Set *Yes* at *Show Narrations*, to *Display* the Sales Register.

  At *Sales Register* display, type Ctrl+P. Click C:Configure Button. Set *Yes* at *Show Voucher Numbers*. Click *P:Print* button (or type P) to *Print* the Sales Register at printer].

01-08 Ledger Book

- **Print Confirmation of Accounts for A K Enterprises for 1-4-21 to 31-3-22**

  [Select *GoT>Display More Reports >Account Books>Ledger*, select *A K Enterprises*. Click *F2:Period*, set Period as 1-4-21 to 31-3-22. At Ctrl+P. At Ledger Printing, click *C:Configure* button (or type C). At *Report Type*, select *Confirmation of Accounts*. At *Format of Report*, select *Detailed*, At *Show Narrations*, Set *Yes*. Click P:Print button (or type P) to Print Confirmation of Accounts on Printer].

01-09 Trial Balance

- **Display and Print Extended Trial Balance**

  Showing Opening Balance, Debit & Credit Transaction Totals and Closing Balance of all Ledger Accounts, in Alphabetical Order of Ledger Name.

[Select *GoT>Display Display More Reports>Trial Balance*. Click F12:Configure. Set Yes at Show *Opening Balance*, set *Yes* at *Show Transactions*, and then set *No* at *Net Transactions* only, set Yes at *Show Closing Balance*. Select *Ledgerwise* at *Type of Grouping*. At *Format of Report*, select *Detailed*., and then set Yes at *Expand All Levels in Detailed Format*. At Trial Balance Display, press Ctrl+P. At Print, Click P: Print to *Print* the Trial Balance at Printer].

- **Print List of Ledger Accounts with Opening Balance with Account Group/ Ledger Account in hierarchical order**

  [Select *GoT> Display Display More Reports>Trial Balance*. Click F2:Period and enter 1-4-21 to 31-3-22. Press *Ctrl+P* to get *Print*. Click *C:Configure* button (or type C). Set *Yes* at *Show Opening Balance*, set No at Show Transactions, set No at *Show Closing Balance*. at *Type of Grouping*, select *Groupwise*, at At *Format of Report*, select *Detailed*., and then set *Yes* at *Expand All Levels in Detailed Format*. Click P:Print button (or Type P) to Print Trial Balance].

01-10 P L Statement

- **Enter Closing Stock Value as on 31.3.22 Rs 23,000**

  [Select *GoT>Accounts Info>Ledgers>Alter* and then select Stock Account (under Stock In Hand Group) from the list of Ledgers. At Ledger Alteration, at Closing Balance, at first column, enter Date 31-3-22. In next column, enter Rs 23,000) . The sign Dr appears alongside. Press Ctrl+A to save.]

- **Print P L Statement for the period 1-4-21 to 31-3-22**

  [Select *GoT>Profit & Loss A/c*. Click *F2:Period* and set the Dates 1-4-21 to 31-3-22. Click F12:Configure. At *Format of Report*, select *Detailed*. At *Profit & Loss A/c Display*, press *Ctrl+P*. Click P:Print Button (or type P) to print the Profit & Loss Statement on Printer].

  Print P L Statement for the period 1-4-21 to 31-3-22 with Cost of Sales figures

  Cost of Sales figure is shown in Vertical Format of Profit & Loss A/c.

  [Select *GoT>Profit & Loss A/c*. Click *F2:Period* and set the Dates 1-4-21 to 31-3-22. Press Ctrl+P to get Print screen. Click C:Configure. At *Format of Report*, select *Detailed*, Set Yes at *Show Vertical Profit & Loss*. Click P:Print Button (or type P) to print the Profit & Loss Statement (in Vertical Format) on Printer].

01-11 Balance Sheet

- **Print Balance Sheet as on 31-3-22**

  Select *GoT>Balance Sheet*. Click *F2:Period* and set the Dates 1-4-21 to 31-3-22. Press *Ctl+P* to get Print screen. Click C: Configure button (or type C). At

Format, select *Detailed*, Set No at *Show Vertical Balance Sheet*. Type Y (for Yes) to print the Balance Sheet on Printer.

- **Print Balance Sheet as on 31-3-22 in Vertical Format, with Working Capital figures**

  Select *GoT>Profit & Loss A/c*. Click *F2:Period* and set the Dates 1-4-21 to 31-3-22. Click P:Print button to get Profit & Loss A/c printing screen. At *Format of Report*, select *Detailed*, Set *Yes* at *Show Vertical Balance Sheet*, set Yes at Include Working Capital. Click P:Print Button (or type P) to print Balance Sheet on Printer.

01-12 Accounts Receivables / Payables

- **Activate AR/AP Features for the Company**

  Select *K:Company* tab. Select *Features* (or *press F11*). Set Yes at *Enable Billwise Entry*

- **Create Customer Ledger Account - ABC Traders, activating Bill by Bill Feature**

  [Select GoT>Create>Ledger. At ledger creation, at *Name*, enter ABC Traders. At *Under*, select *Sundry Debtors*. Click F12:Configure. Set Yes at *Maintain Balances Bill by Bill*]

- **Create Supplier Ledger Account - PQR Traders, and set Bill By Feature**

  [Select GoT>Create>Ledger. At ledger creation, at *Name*, enter PQR Traders. At *Under*, select *Sundry Creditors*. Set *Yes* at *Maintain Balances Bill* by *Bill*]

- **On 1-6-2021, Goods purchased from PQR Traders for Rs 15000 by Bill No 125 dt 31-5-2021.**

  Enter Purchase Voucher in Single Entry Mode

  [Select *GoT>Vouchers*. Click *F9:Puchase* button to get Purchase Voucher entry screen. Click H:*Change Voucher* (or press Ctl+H) and select Accounting Invoice. Enter Voucher Date 1-6-2021. at Supplier Invoice No., enter 125, and 31-5-2021 as Supplier Invoice Date. At *Party Account Name*, select *PQR Traders*. At *Particulars* column, select Purchase Account, and enter 15000 at Amount column. At Bill Details screen, At Type of Ref column, select New Ref from the list of Method of Adj. At Name column, the Party Bill Ref Number (i.e 125) as entered earlier is carried (press <enter> to accept it). At Amount column, the amount 15000 as entered earlier is carried (press <enter> to accept it). Press Ctrl+A to save the Voucher].

- **On 1-7 -2021, Goods sold to ABC Traders Rs 12000 in Voucher mode**

  [Select *GoT>Vouchers*. Click F8: Sales to get Sales Voucher entry screen. Click *H:Change Voucher* (or press Ctl+H) and select *As Voucher*. The Voucher No 1 is shown. Enter 1-7-2021 at Voucher Date. At Particulars column, select ABC Traders and enter 12000 at Debit Column. At Billwise Details, At Type of Ref column, select New Ref. At Name column, the Voucher No 1 is carried (press <enter> to accept it). At Amount column, the amount 12000 as entered earlier is carried (press <enter> to accept it). In second line of Particulars Column, Type Cr and select Sales Account from List of Ledger Accounts and enter 12000 at Credit Column. Enter Voucher Narration (Goods sold to ABC Traders Bill No 1 dt 1-7-2016). Press Alt+A to save the Voucher].

- **On 1-8-2021 Rs 4000 received from *ABC Traders***

  By cheque No 456789 on Canara Bank, Ballygunge Br., dt 31-7-21,against Bill Number 1. The cheque was deposited in SBI CC Account. Enter in Single Entry Mode

  [Select GoT>Vouchers. Click F6: Receipt to get Receipt Voucher entry screen. Enter 1-8-2021 at Voucher Date. Click H:Change Voucher (or press Ctl+H) and select Single Entry from Change Voucher Mode. Click F12:Configure and set Yes at Show List of Bills. At Header, at Account, select SBI CC Account (the Bank in which Cheque is deposited). At Particulars, select ABC Traders and enter 4000 at Credit column. At Bill Allocation screen for allocation of Rs 4000. At Type of Ref select Agst Ref. At Name, select the Bill against which the payment is received (i.e Bill Number 1). At Amount, Rs 4000 (as entered in voucher) is carried. Press <enter>. You get back to main voucher entry screen. Press Ctrl+A to save the voucher].

- **On 2-8-2021, Rs 6000 was paid to *PQR Traders***

  By cheque No 123123 on HDFC Bank, against Bill Number 125. Enter voucher in Double Entry Mode

  [Select GoT>Accounting Voucher. Click F5: Payment to get Payment Voucher entry screen. Enter 2-8-2021 at Voucher Date. Click H:Change Voucher (or press Ctl+H) and select Double Entry. Click F12:Configure and set Yes at Show List of Bills. At Particulars, select PQR Traders and enter 6000 at Debit column. At Bill Allocation screen for allocation of Rs 6000. At Type of Ref select Agst Ref. At Name, select the Bill against which the payment is received (i.e Bill Number 125). At Amount, Rs 6000 (as entered in voucher) is carried. Press <enter>. You get back to main voucher entry screen. In next line, type C (for Cr). Select the Bank Account from which the Cheque is issued (i.e HDFC Bank). At Amount column, Rs 6000 is carried. Press <enter>. At Voucher Narration, enter Cheque details (i.e 123123). Press Ctrl+A to save the voucher].

- **Print Outstanding Bills Payables Statement, Age Analysis**

  [Select GoT>Display More Reports >Statement of Accounts>Outstandings>Payables. Press Alt+F1 to display Billwise details of all Outstanding Bills Payables. Click F8:Billwise toggle button (or press F8) to display Billwise details of all Outstanding Bills Payable. Click F6:Aging Method button and select Ageing by Bill Date. Set the Ageing slab (30, 60, 90+ days) to view the Age Analysis Report. Click Ctrl+P to get Print screen. Click P:Print button (or type P) to print the report on Printer]

- **Print Outstanding Bills Receivables Statement, Age Analysis**

  [Select GoT>Display More Reports >Statement of Accounts>Outstandings>Receivables. Press Alt+F1 to display Billwise details of all Outstanding Bills Payables. Click F8:Billwise toggle button (or press F8) to display Billwise details of all Outstanding Bills Receivables. Click F6:Aging Method button and select Ageing by Bill Date. Set the Ageing slab (30, 60, 90+ days) to view the Age Analysis Report. Click Ctrl+P to get Print screen. Click P:Print button (or type P) to print the report on Printer]

  Print Reminder Letter to ABC Traders for Payment of Due Bills Receivables

  Print Reminder Letter with Standard text, with Age Analysis

  [Select GoT>Display More Reports >Statement of Accounts>Outstandings>Ledger and select ABC Traders. Press Alt+F1 for Billwise Detailed figures. Press Ctrl+P to get Print screen. Click C:Configure (or type C). Select Reminder Letter at Report Type and set Age Analysis slab. Click P:Print button (or Type P) to print the Reminder Letter in Printer]

01-13 Banking

- **Set up Banking features for Bank Ledger Account**

  [Select GoT>Alter>Ledger and select the Bank Account (e.g HDFC Bank). Click F12:Configure and set Yes at Provide Cheque Book and Cheque Printing detail to set up Cheque Books details, set Yes at Provide Banking Details for Bank Ledgers to enable Banking Operations (like Cheque Issue / Deposit, Bank Reconciliation etc). At Ledger Alteration, under Banking details section, enter the relevant details of the Bank Account.

- **Payment made to Supplier by Cheque**

  Paid to PQR Traders against Bill No 123 by Ch No 123125 on HDFC Bank, on 1-10-2021 for Rs 2000. Create voucher in Double entry mode.

  [Select GoT>Vouchers. Click F5: Payment. At Payment Voucher entry screen click Ctl+H and select Double Entry from Change Voucher Mode. Enter 1-10-2021 at Voucher Date. At Particulars, select PQR Traders and

Invoicing & Inventory – Practical Assignments 05-02

Now maintain Inventory System also in the same Company in which Accounts system data was entered.

02-01 : Inventory Masters

- **Activate Inventory system for the Company**

  [At K:Company tab, Click F11:Features. At Company Features, under section Inventory, set Yes at Maintain Inventory].

- **Create Unit of Measure (UoM)**

  Create UoM Kg(Kilogram)

  [Select GoT>Create>Unit. At Unit creation, at *Type* Simple is displayed. At *Symbol* select *Kg.* At *Formal Name*, Enter *Kilogram*. At *Number of Decimal Places*, enter 3].

- **Create Stock Item Group**

  Create Stock Group Food Grains under *Primary*

  [Select *GoT>Create>Stock Group.* At *Name*, enter *Food Grains*. At *Under*, select *Primary*. At *Should Quantities of Items be Added*, set *Yes*]

- **Create Stock Item**

  Create Stock Item Wheat under Food Grains, UoM Kg, Opening Stock 100 kg @ 16/- per Kg

  [Select *GoT> Create>Stock Item.* At *Name*, enter *Wheat*. At *Under*, select *Food Grains*. At *Units*, select *Kg.* At *Opening Balance*, at *Quantity*, enter 100.000 kg. At *Rate*, enter 16.00. At *Value*, the Computed Amount 1600 is displayed. Press *Ctrl+A* to save].

- **Print Chart of Stock Groups / Stock Items**

  [Select *GoT>Chart of Accounts*. Select Stock Items to display Stock Groups / Stock Items in hierarchical order. Press Ctrl+*P*. At Print screen, Click P:*Print* button (or type P) to print on printer].

- **Print Opening Stock Statement Check List in order of Stock Item Name**

  [Select *GoT> Stock Summary.* Click *F5:Stock Itemwise* button. Click

enter 2000 at Debit column. At Bill Allocation, at Type of Ref, select Agst Ref. At Name, select the Bill against which the payment is received (i.e Bill Number 123). At Amount Rs 2000 (as entered in voucher) is carried. In main voucher screen, in next line, type Cr for Credit. At Particulars column, select HDFC Bank. At Amount column, Rs 2000 is carried. At Bank Details entry screen, At Favouring Name column, PQR Traders is carried. At Transaction Type, select Cheque from the list. At Instrument Number, enter the Cheque Number (i.e 123125), At Inst.Date, the Voucher Date is carried. At Main Voucher screen, enter Voucher Narration. Press Ctrl+A to save the voucher]

01-14 Tally Prime Data Management

- **Back Up Company data**

  Back up current data from C:\tpdata (working Directory) to c:\Bkup (Back up Directory)

  Select Back Up from Y:Data tab. At Back Up screen. Click Specify Path and type c:\tpdata. At Back Up Destination Path, enter C:\BkUp. Select the Company to be Backed up. Select End of List. Type Y to start back Up. The Back Up file (named TBK 900_10000.001) would be created at the folder C:\BkUp.

- **Restore Company data**

  Restore Data from c:\Bkup (Back up Directory) to C:\tpdata (working Directory)

  Select Restore from Y:Data tab. At left side, Restore Data Path, enter the current directory Path c:\tpdata (it is shown). At right side, specify path and enter c:\Bkup. Now select the company from the Back Up Data path c:\Bkup, showing the Company Name, Company Number and Date/Time of Back Up. Select End of List and Click Yes to start Restore process. The Backed data (i.e c:\Bkup) would be overwritten over the working data of the same company number in current data path (C:\tpdata).

F12:Configure. At *Configuration, set Yes at Show Quantity, set Yes at Show Rate, set Yes at Show Value.* Set Yes at *Show Opening Balance,* Set *No* at *Show Goods Inwards,* Set *No* at *Goods Outwards,* Set *No* at *Show Closing Balance.* Press *Ctrl+P* to get Print screen. Click *P:Print* button to print the report on Printer, useful to check Opening Stock details of Stock Item Masters].

02-02 Inventory Voucher

- **Cash Purchase entry**

  On 2-4-2021, Purchased 50 kg of Wheat @ 18.00 / kg by Cash by Cash Memo Number 35 dt 2.4.2021 (from Sundar Singh). Enter as Item Invoice.

  [Select *GoT> Vouchers.* Click *F9:Purchase.* Press Ctrl+H and select *Item Invoice.* At *Purchase Voucher entry* screen, Enter 2-4-2021 as Voucher Date. Click *F12:Configure.* Set *Yes* at *Provide Supplier Invoice Number.* At Voucher Entry screen, At *Supplier Invoice Number,* enter *35.* At *Date* enter 2.4.2021. At *Party Name,* select *Cash* Account. At *Purchase Ledger Account,* select *Purchase.*

  At *Name of Item* column, select *Wheat,* At *Quantity,* enter 50.000 kg, At *Rate,* enter 18.00. At *Amount,* the computed value (i.e 900.00) is shown. Enter Voucher Narration (purchased in Cash from Sundar Singh). Press Crl+A to save the Voucher].

- **On 1-5-2021, 10 Kg of Wheat was spoiled as the Wheat Bag was torn.**

  [Select *GoT>Vouchers.* Press *Alt+F7.* At Stock Journal entry screen, enter Date 1-5-2021. At *Source (Consumption)* at left part, at *Name of Item* column, select *Wheat.* At *Quantity,* enter 10.000, At *Rate* enter zero. and at Value, leave zero (loss). Press *Ctrl+A* to save the voucher].

02-03 : Invoicing

- **Sales Invoice creation**

  On 2-4-2021, sold 40 kg of Wheat @ 20.00 / kg to A K Traders.

  [Select *GoT> Voucher.* Click *F8:Sales.* Press Crtl+H and select *Item Invoice. At* Sales Invoice entry screen, enter 2-4-2021 at Voucher *Date.* At *Party A/c Name,* select A K Traders. At *Sales* Ledger, select Sales. At *Name of Item,* select *Wheat,* At *Quantity,* enter 40.000. The UoM *Kg* is displayed. Enter 20.00 at *Rate.* At *Amount* column, Rs 800.00 is displayed. Press <enter> at next line at *Particulars* column to terminate Items entry. Press *Ctrl+A* to save the Invoice.

02-04 : Invoice Printing

- Print Sales Invoice # 1 dt 2.4.2021 on A K Traders

  Select *GoT>Day Book*, press Alt+*F2* and enter the period 2.4.2021 to 2.4.2021 (or select *GoT>Display More Reports>Account Books>Sales Register* and drill down through April). Select the Sales Invoice (#1) and press <Enter>. At *Accounting Voucher Alteration*, press *Ctrl+P*. At Print screen, click *P:Print* Button (or type P) to Print the Invoice.

02-05 : Inventory Reports

- **Print Customer Ledger with Inventory Details**

  Print Ledger Account of A K Traders with Inventory Details, Voucher Narration,

  Select *GoT>Display More Reports>Account Books>Ledger* and select A K Traders. At Ledger Voucher of A K Traders, Click F12:Configure. Set Yes at Show Narration, Set Yes at *Show Inventory Details*. At Ledger, press CTrl+*P*. At print screen, type P*:Print* Button to print Ledger Account with Inventory details of the respective vouchers (like Sales, Purchase, Debit Note, Credit Note etc).

- **Display and Print Sales Register**

  Detailed sales Register for 1-5-21 to 31-7-21

  [Select *GoT>Display more Reports>Account Books>Sales Register*. Drill down through any month. Type Alt+F2 and enter Dates 1-5-2021 to 31-7-2021. Click *F1* to *Display* detailed Sales Register. Press Ctrl+P. At Print screen Click P:Print button (or type P) to Print the Sales Register in Printer].

- **Print Stock Summary for 1-4-21 to 31-7-21**

  With Opening Balance, In & Out Transaction totals and Closing Stock figures, with Quantity, Rate & Value with Stock Groupwise / Itemwise details

  [Select *GoT>Stock Summary*. Click *F2:Period* and enter period 1-4-21 to 31-7-21. Click *F5:Stock Groupwise* toggle button. Click *F1:Detailed* toggle button. Click *F12:Configure*. Set *Yes* at *Show Quantity, Show Rate, Show Value, Show Opening Balance, Show Goods Inwards, Show Goods Outwards, Show Closing balance*. Press *Ctrl+P* to get Print screen. Click *P:Print* button (or type) to print Stock Summary].

02-06 Point of Sales

- **Create Point of Sales (PoS) Voucher Type**

  [Select *GoT>Create>Voucher Types* to get *Voucher Type* creation screen. At *Name*, enter *Point of Sales*. At *Type of Voucher*, select *Sales*. At *Abbr* , enter

PoS. At *Method of Numbering* field, select *Automatic.* At *Use Advance Configuration,* set *No.* At *Use Common Narration*, set *No.* At *Narration for each entry*, set *No.* at *Print after Saving*, set *Yes*; at *Use for PoS Invoicing*, set *Yes*. At *Print Message 1 & Print Message 2* , enter the messages texts to be printed at the bottom of Invoice. At *Default Print Title*, enter 'Cash Sales Memo'. At *Declaration*, enter the text that would be printed at the end of the Invoice. Press Ctrl+A to save the PoS Voucher Type].

- **Create PoS Sales Voucher and Print**

  On 1-5-2021, 5 kg of wheat sold @ 19 /kg in Cash.

  [Select *GoT>Vouchers*. Click *F8:Sales* and then select *Point of Sales* from list of Sales Voucher Types. Enter 1-5-2021 at Voucher Date. Click *F12:Configure*. At *PoS Configuration* screen, set *No* at *Skip the Quantity field during entry*. At Voucher entry screen, at Party A/c Ledger, select *Not Applicable;* at *Sales Ledger*, select *Sales*; at *Name of Item*, select *Wheat*; at *Quantity*, enter 5. The UoM Kg is displayed. At *Rate*, enter 19. At Amount, 95 is displayed. At next line, at *Name of Item*, press <enter> to terminate Sock Item entry. At the bottom line, at *Cash*, select Cash Account. At *Amount Tendered*, enter 100. At *Balance*, 5 is displayed. Type *Y* to Save the PoS. Next, at Print screen, Click P:Print to Print the PoS Invoice].

Tax Accounting - Practical Assignments 05-03

Continue in same Company after previous assignments

03-01 GST Masters

- **Set GST Features and Company Details**

  [Click F11. At Company Features, under section Taxation, set Yes at Enable Goods & Services Tax (GST). At GST Details screen, under GST Registration Details section, enter the relevant details]

- **Create SGST Ledger Account**

  [Select GoT>Create>Ledger. At Ledger Account creation, at Name, enter SGST; at Under, select Duties & Taxes; at Type of Duty/ Tax, select GST; at Tax Type, select State Tax; At % of Calculation, enter 0%; At Rounding Method, select Normal Rounding; At Rounding Limit, enter .01]

- **Create CGST Ledger Account**

  [Select GoT>Create>Ledger. At Ledger Account creation, at Name, enter CGST; at Under, select Duties & Taxes; at Type of Duty/ Tax, select GST; at Tax Type, select Central Tax; At % of Calculation, enter 0%; At Rounding Method, select Normal Rounding; At Rounding Limit, enter .01]

- **Create IGST Ledger Account**

  [Select GoT>Create>Ledger. At Ledger Account creation, at Name, enter IGST; at Under, select Duties & Taxes; at Type of Duty/ Tax, select GST; at Tax Type, select Integrated Tax; At % of Calculation, enter 0%; At Rounding Method, select Normal Rounding; At Rounding Limit, enter .01]

- **UQC set up in UoM Master**

  Set UQC in UoM - Kilograms

  [Select GoT>Alter>Unit. Select Kilogram. At Unit Alteration, at Unit Quantity Code (UQC), select KGS-Kilograms from the UQC list. Press Ctrl+A to save].

- **GST details set up in Stock Item Master**

  Set GST details in Stock Item Wheat, HSN Description – Food grains, HSN Code- 1234, GST Rate 5% on Value

[Select GoT>Alter>Stock Item. Select Wheat. At Stock Item Alteration, at Statutory Details, at GST Applicable, select Applicable. Set Yes at Set Alter GST. At GST details for Stock Item, At Description, enter Food Grains, At HSN/ SAC, enter 1234, At Calculation Type, select On Value, at Taxability, select Taxable. At Integrated Tax, enter 5%. At Cess, enter 0%. Press Ctrl+A to save.

- **Set GST details in Supplier Master**

  At Supplier Ledger Account, enter Tax related details

  For ABC & Co, enter Registration Type- Regular, GSTIN 19AAAC1234K1Z, state – West Bengal, PAN ABCPN1234K.

  [Select GoT>Alter>Ledger, select ABC & Co. At Ledger Alteration, click F12:Configure.

  At Configuration screen, under Party Tax Registration details, set Yes at Provide GST Registration details. At Ledger Alteration screen, Under the section, Tax Registration details, at Registration Type, select Regular. at GSTIN/ UIN, enter 19AAAC1234K1Z . At Set Alter GST details, set Yes and enter the relevant details at GST Details screen. At Ledger Alteration screen, press Ctl+A to save the changes.]

03-02 GST Invoicing

- **Create GST Sales Invoice.**

  10 kg of Wheat @25 per kg sold to ABC & Co on 1-5-21.

  [Select GoT>Vouchers. Click F8:Sales (or press F8). Select Sales Voucher type from List. Click Ctrl+H and select Item Invoice. Enter Voucher Date 1-5-21. At Party A/c Name, select ABC & Co. At Sales Ledger, select Sales. At Name of Item, select Wheat, At Quantity, enter 10 kg. at Rate, enter 25/kg. The amount 250 would be shown. In next line, select End of List. Next select SGST, the SGST amount (15.00) would be auto calculated. Next select CGST. the CGST amount (15.00) would be auto calculated. The total Invoice amount (250.00+15.00+15.00 = 280.00) is displayed. Press Ctrl+A to save the Voucher].

- **Print the Sales Voucher**

  Voucher dated 1-5-21 on ABC Co

  [Select GoT>Day Book. At Day Book display, press F2 and Date 1-5-21. Select the Sales Voucher from the list to get the Voucher Alteration. Press Ctrl+P to get the Print screen. Click P Button to print the Voucher]

03-03 GST Reports

Display GSTR-1 for 1-4-21 to 31-7-21

[Select GoT>Display more reports>GST Reports>GSTR-1. Click F2:Period (or press F2) and enter Period from 1-4-21 to 31-7-21 to display GSTR-1 Report

03-02 TDS

- **Set TDS Features and Company Details**

  [Click F11. At Enable Tax Deducted at Source, set Yes. At Company TDS Deductor Details, at TAN Registration Number, enter PQRS12345S. At Tax Deduction and collection Account Number TAN, enter ABCX12345A. At Deductor Type, select Individual / HUF. At Deductor Branch / Division, enter Kolkata, At STD Code, enter 033, At Phone Number, enter 12345878, at e-mail, enter mail@nomail.com, at Set / Alter TDS Details of Person responsible, set Yes and enter Person responsible Details. At Rate and Exemption details section, set No in all the options.

- **Create TDS Ledger Account**

  Create TDS Ledger Account for Deduction on Interest Paid other than Interest on securities.

  [Select GoT>create>Ledger. At Ledger Account creation screen. At Name, enter TDS on Interest. At Under, select Duties & Taxes. At Type of Duty /Tax, select TDS from the list. At Nature of Payment, select Interest other than Interest on Securities].

- **Set TDS related info at Deductee Ledger Account**

  Set TDS details at Ledger of A B C Finance Co.

  [Select GoT>Account Info>Ledger>Alter and then select A B C Finance Co. At Ledger Alteration, under Statutory Details section, set Yes at Is TDS Deductible ?. Set No at Is TDS treated as Expenses.

  [At Deductee Type, select Individual / HUF - Resident. At Deduct TDS in same Voucher, set Yes. At right part, at PAN, enter PAN].

- **Set TDS related info at TDS Deductible Expenses Ledger**

  Set TDS details in Interest Paid Leger Account.

  [Select GoT>Account Info>Ledger>Alter. Select Interest Paid Ledger Account. At Statutory Information section, At Is TDS Applicable, set Yes. At Default Nature of Payment, select Interest other than Interest on Securities from the list of TDS Nature of Payment].

- **Interest TDS Adjustment Voucher entry**

  On 31-12-2022, Adjust TDS on Interest payable on Rs 5000 to A B C Finance Co., on 1,00,000 @ 10% for July 21 to Dec 21.

  [Select GoT>Vouchers. Click F7:Journal button. At Journal Voucher creation, enter voucher date 31-12-2021. Voucher No is displayed. At Particulars, select Interest Paid Ledger Account. Enter 5000 at Debit column. At TDS Nature of Payment Details. select Interest other than Interest on Securities from the list of TDS Nature of Payment. At 2nd entry, at Main Voucher screen, type C for Cr. select TDS Ledger Account. At Amount, enter 500 at Credit column. At 3rd entry, type Cr and select A B C Finance. Enter 4500 at Credit Column].

- **TDS Deposit to Government and Challan Print**

  On 1-1-2022, the amount of TDS (500) is deposited with Government by Ch# 123456 on HDFC bank for the period 1-12-21 to 31-12-21, and the Challan is printed.

  [Select GoT>Vouchers. Click F5:Payment button. Click F:Auto Fill button (or type Ctrl+F). At Autofill Screen, at Type of Transaction, Stat Payment. select At Tax Type, select TDS. At Period, enter 1-12-21 to 31-12-21. At Deducted Till Date, enter 31-12-2021. At Section, enter 194A. At Nature of Payment, select Interest other than Interest on Securities. At Deductee Status, select Non Company. At Residential Status, select Resident, At Cash / Bank, select HDFC Bank Account. Back at Main voucher screen, enter Voucher Narration. Press Ctrl+P to get Print screen. Click C:Configure button (or press C). At Print screen, Click P:Print button (or type P) to print the Challan on Printer].

Payroll - Practical Assignments

05-04

Continue in same Company after the previous assignments

04-01 Payroll Masters

- **Activate Payroll Features for the Company**

  At K:Company Tab, click F11. At Company Features, at the top left, set Yes at Show More features and set Yes at Show All Features. At right part, under Payroll section, set Yes at Maintain Payroll, to activate Basic Payroll Features for the Company

- **Create Attendance Master**

  Select GoT>Create> Attendance / Production Types. At Attendance / Production Type creation, at Name, enter Attendance. At Under, select Primary. At Attendance Type, select Attendance / Leave with Pay. At Period Type, select Days.

- **Create Basic Salary Pay Head**

  Create Pay Head Basic Salary (in Payslip shown as Basic as short), as Earnings Head, computed on Attendance, and is subject to Gratuity computation.

  [Select GoT>Create> Pay Heads. At Pay Head creation, at Name, enter Basic Pay. At Pay Head Type, select Earnings for Employees. At Income Type, select Fixed. At Under, select Indirect Expenses. At Affect Net Salary, set Yes. At Name to Appear in Payslip, enter Basic. At Use for Gratuity set Yes. At Calculation Type, select On Attendance. At Attendance / Leave with Pay type, select Attendance. At Calculation Period, select Months. At Basis of Calculation (per Day), select As per Calendar Period. At Rounding Method, select Normal Rounding, at Limit, enter .01. Press Ctrl+A to save.

- **Create Employee Master**

  [Select GoT> Create> Employee>. At Employee creation, at Name, enter Asok Kumar Das. At Display Name in Reports, enter A K Das. At Under, select Primary. At Date of Joining, enter 1-4-2020. Enter other details of the Employee as per record. At Define Salary Details, set Yes. At Salary Details, at Effective From column, enter 1-4-2020. At Pay Head column, select Basic Pay. At Rate column, enter 12000. Other info are displayed from the respective Pay Head master]. Back at Employee creation screen, under the Head General Information, enter other relevant details. press Ctrl+A to save.

04-02 Pay Voucher

- **Enter Attendance Voucher**

  [Select GoT>Vouchers. Click F10:Other Vouchers and select Attendance. At Attendance Entry screen. Enter 31-07-2021 at Voucher Date. At Employee Name, select Asok Kumar Das. At Attendance / Production Head Type column, select Attendance. At Value column, enter 28].

- **Create Payroll Voucher**

  [Select GoT>Vouchers. Type Ctrl+F4. At Payroll Voucher creation, enter 31-07-2021 at Voucher Date. At Account, select Cash. Click F:Auto Fill button. At Autofill screen, at Type of Transaction, select Payroll Autofill. At Process For, select Salary. At From & To, enter 1-07-2021 to 31-07-2021. At Employee Group, select All Items. At Sort by, select Employee Name. At Payroll / Cash / Bank, select Cash. At Include Employees having banking Details, set No. The computed Pay, Basic Salary Rs 10838.71 {(12000/31)x28} is shown].

04-03 Payroll Reports

- **Print Payslip**

  [Print Payslip for A K Das for July 21]

  Select GoT>Display more Reports>Payroll Reports>Payslip. Select A K Das from list. Click F2:Period and enter 1-7-21 to 31-7-21. The Payslip is displayed. Press Ctrl+P. At Printing screen, click P:Print Button to print the Payslip on Printer].

- **Print Pay Sheet**

  Print Payslip for all employees for July 21.

  [Select GoT>Display more Reports> Payroll Reports> Paysheet and then select All Items. Click F2:Period and enter 1-7-21 to 31-7-21. to display Pay Sheet for all employees. Press Alt+P to get Print screen. Click P:Print button (or type P) to print the Paysheet on Printer].